TRAINING AND REFERENCE MANUAL FOR TRAFFIC ACCIDENT INVESTIGATION

2nd edition, 1995
(revised)

R. W. Rivers

First edition published in 1988 under the title
Traffic Accident Investigation
A Training and Reference Manual

Published by the Institute of Police
 Technology and Management
University of North Florida
4567 St. Johns Bluff Road, S.
Jacksonville, Florida 32224-2645
(904) 620-IPTM

DISCLAIMER

The information contained in this manual is based to the best of IPTM's knowledge on the current practices and formula applications in traffic accident investigation. However, neither IPTM nor the author assumes any liability in connection with the use of this material. Every acceptable procedure may not have been presented and some circumstances may require additional or substitute procedures. Also, statutes, ordinances and organizational policies differ widely and wherever these are in conflict with the information contained herein, the former should govern.

COPYRIGHT

ACKNOWLEDGEMENTS

The author wishes to thank IPTM staff members Ralph Ebert, Jody Hicks, Mike Matuszak, Richard Parkos, and Neil Robar for their extensive input in the revising and updating of this manual as it appears in the 1995 edition.

IPTM wishes to thank Charles C. Thomas, Publisher, for granting permission to include in this manual various passages, diagrams and photos from textbooks authored by R.W. Rivers and published by Charles C. Thomas. IPTM recommends these textbooks (see last page of this manual) for additional reading, study and reference.

EDITOR'S NOTE

At present, English does not have a third-person singular personal pronoun that can be used to refer to someone of either gender.

While several methods purporting to overcome this deficiency are in vogue, they tend to be either cumbersome or restrictive and are often grammatically annoying to readers of both genders, particularly when applied in a lengthy text covering many diverse topics.

This edition therefore retains use of the third-person singular masculine pronoun forms *he, his, him* to refer to a person of either gender. However, use of the masculine pronoun is in no way intended to suggest that accident investigation is the exclusive preserve of men or that women are less adept than men in this field.

It is anticipated that an increasing number of women will become accident investigators in the coming years. The author and publisher welcome them as readers and ask their understanding in regard to the grammatical usage in the text.

TABLE OF CONTENTS

INTRODUCTION

Lesson 1

SUBJECT: Introduction to Traffic Accident Investigation

Police personnel, including traffic accident investigators, receive reports of, respond to and investigate traffic accidents.

This lesson will provide an overview of the traffic accident investigation process by outlining for the student the procedures for taking and recording a report of a traffic accident, proceeding to the scene, protecting the scene, taking action under the many circumstances which may be encountered at the scene, and conducting the investigation.

The investigator needs certain basic equipment in order to perform his duties. An inventory of required items is appended to this lesson.

The investigator must be familiar with the terms used in accident investigation and their meanings. A guide to these terms is provided at the end of this lesson immediately before the Accident Investigator's Inventory.

Lesson Contents

This lesson will cover the following topics:

a.   Definition of *accident*
b.   Definition of *accident investigation*
c.   Definition of *highway, traffic unit, trafficway*

d. Objectives of a traffic accident investigation

e. Elements of the at-scene investigation

f. The at-scene investigator

g. Receiving the report of an accident

h. Proceeding to the scene of an accident

i. Procedures and duties upon arrival at the scene

j. Setting of priorities

k. Aid to the injured

l. Assistance that may be required by the investigator

m. Traffic control at the scene

n. Protection of personal property

o. Use of highway flares

p. Accidents involving fires and materials

q. Investigation procedures

r. Hit and run accidents

s. Vehicle inspections

t. Accident causes

u. Enforcement procedures

v. Duties before leaving the scene

w. Follow-up investigation procedures

x. Traffic Accident Definitions, Types and Classifications

y. Accident Investigator's Inventory

Lesson Objectives

1. Upon completion of this lesson, the student will be able to define:

   a. *Accident*

   b. *Highway*

2

c. *Traffic accident investigation*

d. *Traffic unit*

e. *Trafficway*

2. Upon completion of this lesson, the student will be able to state to the instructor's satisfaction:

a. The objectives of a traffic accident investigation

b. The initial information required when the report of a traffic accident is received

c. The criteria for determining the speed or urgency with which a trip to an accident scene should be made

d. The immediate duties relating to scene protection that must be carried out upon arrival at the accident scene

e. The steps that must be taken to ensure completeness of an investigation

f. The additional steps that must be taken in a hit-and-run accident investigation

g. The steps that should be taken when interviewing drivers and witnesses

And will be able to state at least:

h. Three highway engineering problems that can contribute to accident causes

i. Three atmospheric conditions that can contribute to accident causes

j. Three sources of information that will identify hazardous materials

k. Three recognized agencies or departments that should be notified of materials spill

Lesson 1

INTRODUCTION TO TRAFFIC ACCIDENT INVESTIGATION

The Accident

C1.001 To effectively carry out his duties, it is essential that the investigator understand what the problem is (*the accident*), what he is responsible for (*the investigation*), and what he must strive to accomplish in discharging his responsibilities (*the objectives of the investigation*).

Accident Defined

> The U.S. National Safety Council defines an accident as "That occurrence in a sequence of events which usually produces unintended injury, death or property damage."

Accident Investigation Defined

> The Highway Safety Division of the International Association of Chiefs of Police, in a report prepared for the United States Department of Transportation, National Highway Traffic Administration, defines a traffic accident investigation as "the thorough examination of all elements contributing to the accident, resulting in a well-founded explanation of the series of events which occurred based upon the factual data."

Objectives of a Traffic Accident Investigation

> The objectives of a traffic accident investigation are to determine:

4

a.   WHAT happened, i.e., the type of accident

b.   WHERE the accident occurred

c.   WHEN the accident occurred

d.   WHY the accident occurred, e.g., violation of law, highway or mechanical engineering defects, etc.

e.   WHO was involved

At-Scene Investigation

C1.002 The at-scene investigator must:

a.   Care for the injured.

b.   Protect persons and property from further injury, damage or loss.

c.   Gather evidence at the scene that will

    i   assist in determining the cause of the accident, and

    ii   provide information that will assist in accident prevention, including information for *engineering, enforcement* and *education programs*.

Figure C1-1

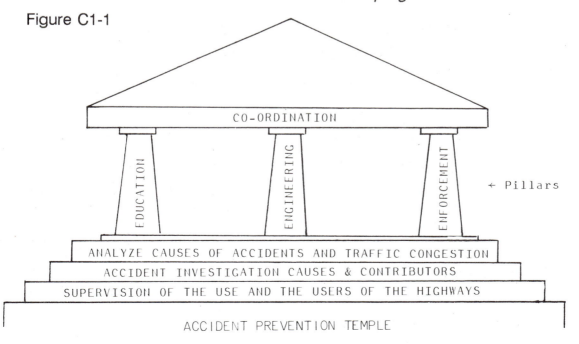

d. Gather evidence that will support those who are involved in an accident in exercising legitimate claims under civil proceedings.

e. Interview drivers, victims and other witnesses.

f. Verify identity of drivers and occupants through proper identification, e.g., driver's license, passport, military identification, etc.

g. Verify vehicle information through vehicle registration and/or title.

h. Verify vehicle insurance through proper documents, e.g., insurance cards.

i. Conduct mechanical inspection of vehicles.

j. Record facts by making notes, taking statements, scene measurements and photos.

At-Scene Investigator

C1.003 An at-scene traffic accident investigator should:

a. Have a particular aptitude for this type of investigative work.

b. Have a good basic knowledge of accident causes and investigative methods and techniques, and have at least a general knowledge of accident reconstruction principles.

c. Further his expertise and competency by taking training in advanced traffic accident investigation techniques and undertaking self-study through various courses and literature available to him.

Receiving Report of Accident

C1.004 When the report of an accident is received, obtain:

a. Precise location

b. Information pertaining to the nature and severity of any injuries

c. Information pertaining to the disruption to traffic, e.g., blocked roadway

d. Emergency equipment required, e.g.,

    i   ambulance

    ii   fire-fighting equipment

    iii   rescue squads

    iv   tow-trucks

    v   HAZMAT (hazardous materials) unit of the fire department

C1.005 Obtain the name of the person calling and, if possible, the names of all witnesses and the address and telephone number at which each person can be contacted. If a false alarm or report is suspected, call the person back. If more than one call is received on apparently the same accident, check to ensure that there is not yet another accident being reported that is near the same location.

Proceeding to the Scene

C1.006 When a call is received to respond to an accident, it should be borne in mind that the accident has already happened. While it is essential that there be no unnecessary delay in responding, driving at high speed and in a manner that causes risk to other highway users must be avoided. An accident that has already occurred is not grounds to cause yet another accident. The investigator must not endanger his own life nor the lives and safety of others. He must use reasonable care and comply with local legislation and policies respecting the use of emergency vehicles at all times. SAFETY FIRST!

C1.007 When proceeding to the scene:

a.   Proceed quickly, but SAFELY.

b.   Do not depend on emergency equipment, such as siren and flashing red/blue light, to get you to the scene safely. Drive with proper care.

c.   Consider the apparent urgency of the trip from the standpoint of:
   i   Seriousness of the accident
   ii   Aid required to injured persons
   iii   Need to protect the scene from further damage and from alteration to or loss of evidence and to prevent the scene from posing a danger to passing traffic
   iv   Consequences of delays allowing drivers and witnesses to leave the scene before your arrival
   v   Danger from hazardous materials, if applicable

d.   Consider the traffic problems that may be encountered enroute and possible solutions:
   i   Congestion
   ii   Detours that will enable quicker response time

e.   Select the route that will allow the quickest and safest arrival at the scene.

f.   The accident may have been a hit-and-run accident, or there may be witnesses who will leave the scene prior to the investigator's arrival:

8

i   Look for damaged vehicles leaving the scene area.

ii   Look for suspicious vehicles and those which might be carrying witnesses.

Note descriptions and license numbers of these vehicles for follow-up investigation purposes.

g.   When possible, place warning devices, e.g., signs and/or flares, on the approach to the accident scene.

Arrival at the Scene

C1.008 Upon arrival at the accident scene, an investigator should:

a.   Park his vehicle in a highly visible location and in such a way as to protect the scene.

b.   Avoid parking the vehicle in such a way that it will obstruct the safe movement of other vehicles and/or pedestrians that are free to proceed past the scene. Consider an approach driver's ability to see the accident scene.

c.   Consider the convenience of the parking location. The vehicle may have to be used, and safety or emergency equipment carried by the vehicle must be readily available.

d.   Avoid parking the vehicle in such a way that it may be blocked in or obstructed by other traffic.

e.   Ensure that his vehicle will be safe from theft, other loss, or damage.

f.   Use emergency lights, as required, to protect the scene. This is very important during hours of darkness.

g.   During darkness, park the vehicle in such a way that the headlamps will illuminate the accident scene. This will assist an oncoming driver to recognize the situation, and will also assist the investigator in seeing details.

h.   Place sufficient and adequate warning devices, e.g., signs, reflectors, flares or fusees, and/or traffic cones on approaches to the scene as well as appropriate directional signs within the scene area, to give proper warning to drivers and other highway users.

i.   Examine the scene for downed or damaged electrical wires and hazardous goods spills or cargo damage.

j.   Check the general area for possible witnesses.

C1.009 Whenever passage by vehicles or pedestrians past the scene is dangerous or impossible, it may be necessary to block the road. When this step is necessary:

a.   Consider entrance and exit requirements of emergency vehicles.
b.   Provide detours past the scene, if possible.

C1.010 Always be clear and concise in giving directions to motorists and pedestrians. There should be no doubt in their minds as to what they are required to do or how they are to proceed.

Priority Setting

C1.011 An investigator must carry out certain duties immediately upon his arrival at an accident scene. Priorities will vary depending upon the seriousness of a particular aspect of the accident in relation to all other aspects, and the assistance that is available. Priority setting will generally require that the following be taken into consideration:

   a. Type of injuries sustained, i.e., serious or minor
   b. Hazardous cargoes or down electrical wires which are likely to cause damage or injury
   c. Blocked or obstructed roadway requiring immediate attention
   d. Protection or gathering of evidence
   e. Protection of scene, e.g., flags, flares, signs
   f. General traffic-control duties

Injured Persons

C1.012 Injured persons must be properly and adequately cared for.

   a. Determine extent and nature of injuries suffered. Examine a victim for *Medic-Alert* tags or cards. Give information gained to medical and ambulance attendants and to hospital officials.

   b. Arrange for attendance of professional medical assistance and/or ambulance services, who will remove seriously injured persons to proper medical facilities as quickly as possible.

   c. When it is necessary to move an injured person, consider the type and nature of the injury.

d.   Arrange for the *coroner* and other officials or persons, e.g., next-of-kin, to be notified of fatalities and/or serious injuries in accordance with legislation and departmental or other policies.

e.   When possible, mark and photograph the location of a victim on the highway before his removal.

f.   Ensure that all vehicle occupants and pedestrians involved in an accident are accounted for in the event a victim was thrown or dragged away from the immediate scene area.

Assistance

C1.013   After the circumstances have been reviewed, request additional help to assist at the scene, if necessary, from:

a.   The fire department
b.   Rescue equipment personnel
c.   Tow-truck operators
d.   The police department
e.   The HAZMAT unit

C1.014   Request the assistance of regular police members when:

a.   There is a heavy traffic volume.
b.   Vehicles are situated in positions that obstruct or impede the free flow of traffic so that major traffic control is required.
c.   There is a large number of onlookers or pedestrians.

C1.015 When crowds gather, it may be necessary to have additional police assistance to remove intoxicated or disorderly persons or others who interfere with the investigation. Assistance may also be required to remove impaired drivers.

C1.016 Provide for the safe passage of vehicles and pedestrians and the resumption of normal traffic flow as quickly as possible.

    a.   A single investigator at the scene must review the scene, establish top priorities and carry these out.

    b.   When two investigators are present, one should immediately take charge of traffic control and establish the desired flow pattern.

    c.   Police officers should be positioned at strategic locations to facilitate safe and orderly movement of traffic at and near the scene.

C1.017 Civilian *volunteers* may be used in emergencies, such as when there is an emergent need for assistance and professionally trained persons are not available.

    a.   Select only those who appear to be responsible, competent and capable of carrying out the tasks involved.

    b.   Do not ask civilians to perform potentially dangerous tasks.

    c.   Volunteers must be given specific instructions on how their tasks are to be performed.

    d.   Make sure volunteers and officers are wearing reflective vests for their protection.

C1.018 In some investigations, particularly hit-and-run cases, it may be necessary to block off the collision area in order to carry out a minute search for all possible forms of physical evidence.

Traffic Control

C1.019 Traffic congestion should not be allowed to occur. Delays in free traffic flow will often hinder the investigation.

    a.   Minor traffic obstructions, such as partially damaged or stalled vehicles and spilled cargoes, should be removed as soon as possible.

    b.   Major traffic obstructions such as fallen trees and broken power lines, which may block traffic for a considerable period of time, require re-routing of traffic.

C1.020 In selecting a detour route, consider:

    a.   Where most of the traffic is going and what route will allow it to get there with the least delay.

    b.   Whether the suggested alternate route can handle the traffic volume. If not, consider using other alternate routes.

    c.   Whether alternate routes are adequately marked so that motorists will have no difficulty in reaching their destination.

C1.021 Pedestrians and bystanders should not be allowed to obstruct the scene or the investigation.

a. Keep spectators away. Protect them from possible injury and ensure that they in no way obstruct the investigators' ability to satisfactorily carry out their duties.

b. The manner in which pedestrians, bystanders and motorists are handled and given directions is very important. Always be courteous and have a positive, commanding approach.

Personal Property

C1.022 Protect personal property and other items, e.g., vehicle parts at the scene, from theft or pilferage. Inventories of valuable items should be made as soon as possible. When an item is released that is in the possession or under the control of the investigator, a receipt should be obtained.

Highway Flares

C1.023 Highway flares are used as a temporary measure to control traffic for a relatively short period of time during which the situation can be corrected or barricades, directional signals, flashers and/or officers can be put into place.

Precaution in Use of Flares

C1.024 Some danger is associated with flare use, particularly during the lighting process. Injuries to the eyes, face and hands and damage to the clothing can occur unless certain care is taken.

a. Follow closely the directions for use of the particular type of flare.

b. Point the burn end away from the body, and turn head and eyes away when igniting the flare. This is done because some flares have a tendency to pop when ignited, causing molten particles to fly through the air and possibly injure the face and eyes.

c. After ignition, hold the burning end of the flare away from the body, face and clothing.

d. Hold the burning flare with an extended arm and hold it no higher than the hand with which it is held, because some flares have a tendency to allow molten materials to drip from the burning end.

e. Do not allow a flare to be positioned or held in such a way that its toxic fumes will be breathed in by yourself or any other person.

f. Do not use a burning flare as a traffic wand unless it is specially designed for this purpose.

g. Walk towards traffic when placing flares, if at all possible. The investigator should not have his back to oncoming traffic.

h. Examine the area for conditions that could make the use of a flare dangerous:

   i   Leaking gasoline, butane and other flammable liquids. Some liquids are heavy and will run into drains or ditches. Many liquids will give off fumes that will ignite and cause explosions and fires.

ii   Wind conditions. Sparks may fly and ignite dry grass or other materials in the area.

i.   Do not place a burning flare on highway markings such as plastic-type strips, guard rails, painted areas or lane lines, because not only will these be damaged by this practice but also fires can be caused.

j.   Do not allow a flare to roll or get out of place because of weather conditions, such as wind. If placed in a lay-down position, put the flare cap or small rocks or other objects in a position alongside or under the flare to prevent it from rolling.

k.   When picking up a burning flare, remember that the flare becomes molten for a considerable distance back from the actual burning end. Grasp the flare by the end away from the burning end, being extremely careful that there is no molten material where it is grasped. Tap the burning end on the roadway surface to remove any molten particles. Then snuff out the flame by sticking the burning end into soft dirt, gravel, snow or water, for example.

l.   Do not attempt to snuff out a burning flare by stepping on it. Flare materials can burn through the sole of a shoe.

Flare Pattern

C1.025 There are many things to consider before establishing a flare pattern. Every accident is different; therefore, no standard pattern can be established to meet the requirements of every accident scene. Traffic volumes, speed, stopping distances, view obstructions, type of roadway, weather conditions and the general environment must all be taken into consideration.

a. Flare patterns should limit the necessity for decision making by motorists as to where and how they must proceed.

b. A motorist should normally not be given more than one lane in which to travel past the scene.

c. Too many flares can cause confusion to an approaching motorist. Flares placed close together tend to blend in with each other, often failing to delineate a specific path to be followed. Generally, flares that are set in a straight line near the actual accident site should be 20 to 25 ft (7 to 8 m) apart. Gradual increases in spacing can be introduced away from the actual site, with as much as 50 to 100 ft (15 to 30 m) between flares at the furthest point.

d. Patterns should be developed that will direct traffic to only one side of an obstruction, whenever possible.

e. When it is necessary to have traffic change lanes, set a gradual angle of alignment in accordance with the speed of passing traffic.

Other devices can be used instead of traffic flares or fusees to control traffic. These devices include but are not limited to:

a. Traffic cones

b. Traffic barrels

c. Standards

d. Barricades

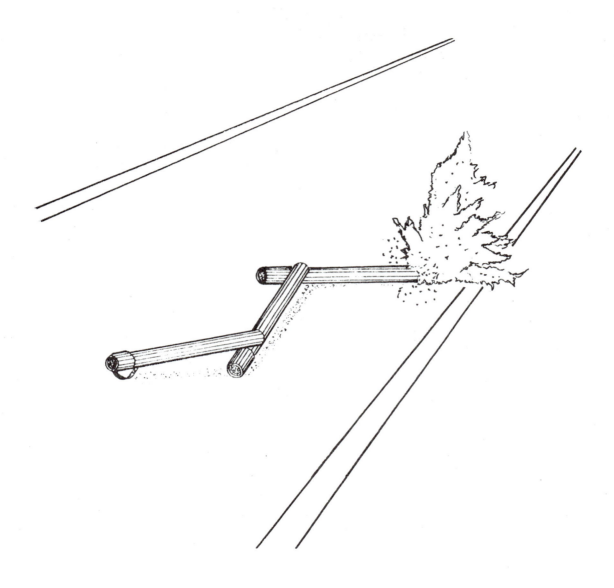

Figure C1-2 When an investigator is alone at the scene of an accident, certain time savers can be used. Place the flares in a *criss-cross* pattern or stacking, so that when the first flare has nearly burned out, it will light the next flare, and so on. Remove the caps from the flares prior to stacking.

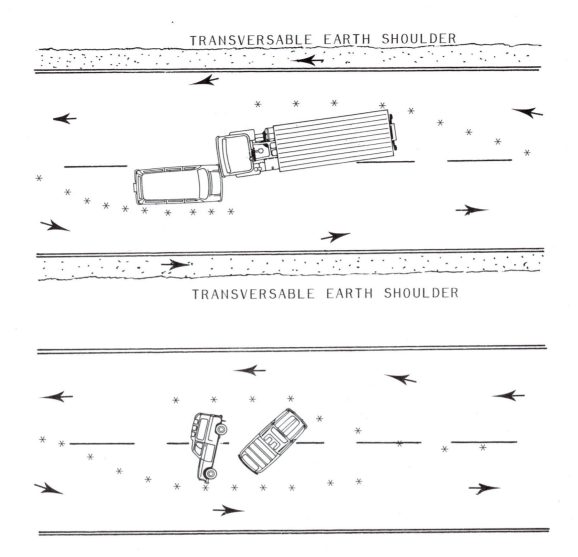

Figure C1-3 Possible patterns for placing flares or other devices to route traffic past an accident scene.

HILLCREST

Figure C1-4 Ensure that the first flares are placed far enough from the crest of a hill so that approaching traffic will have time to decrease speed sufficiently.

FREEWAY OVERPASS

Traffic
Control

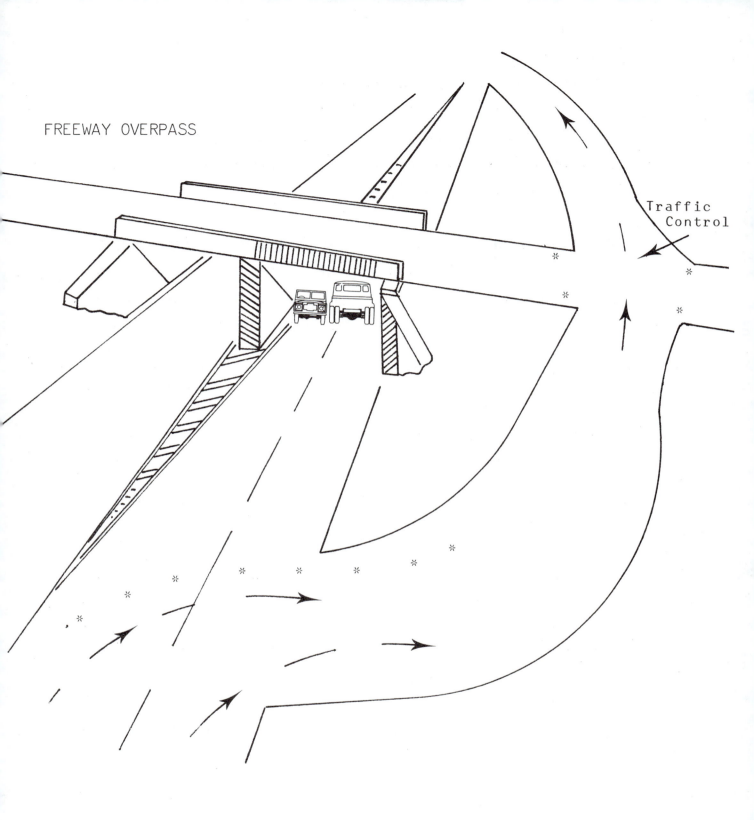

Figure C1-5 Placement of traffic control devices for routing vehicles around
a freeway overpass.

21

Fires and Hazardous Materials (General)

C1.026 *Examine the scene from a safe distance for the possibility of fire, spilled or damaged hazardous cargo (e.g., chemicals, explosives,* liquid fuels such as gasoline) or radioactive materials.

C1.027 Where a danger of the above is believed to exist, request additional police units, take immediate action to prevent traffic from entering the area and to otherwise safeguard the scene, and notify the appropriate authorities. (See the Hazardous Materials Notification Chart below.) *Such action should be consistent with jurisdictional instructions, policies and procedures.*

C1.028 Fires and hazardous materials pose a danger not only to persons involved in the accident but also to persons entering the area to rescue the victims.

    a.   Larger fire departments usually have a specially trained HAZMAT unit in additional to fire-fighting and fire-rescue personnel.

    b.   Assuming timely arrival of the fire department at the scene, the fire department should be the agency to conduct rescue operations, combat fires, and handle materials spills.

    c.   If the situation demands immediate rescue efforts by the police prior to the arrival of the fire department, officers should approach the collision site from upwind.

    d.   Police officers will normally concentrate on:

i   Securing the area

ii   Directing traffic

iii   Setting up alternate routes

iv   Evacuating a greater area, if necessary

v   Locating all drivers and witnesses and moving them to a safe location, e.g., patrol cars

vi   Recording descriptions of the drivers and witnesses

vii   Checking the drivers and witnesses for physical evidence

viii As soon as safety considerations permit, measuring the scene and recording and preserving evidence as would be done for any accident

e.   After the hazardous situation has been contained, police officers will prepare for resumption of regular traffic flow by:

i   Checking the roadway

ii   Disposing of flares

iii   Checking the general safety of the area

iv   Reopening the road

Hazardous Materials (See DOT Labels)

C1.029 The investigator should be able to recognize dangerous and hazardous cargoes.

a.   The law requires that vehicles and containers be properly marked.

b.   The investigator should be familiar with all hazardous materials warning labels and placards.

U.S. Department of Transportation

Research and Special Programs Administration

DOT CHART 9
Hazardous Materials Marking, Labeling & Placarding Guide

This Marking, Labeling and Placarding Guide will assist shippers, carriers, fire departments, police, emergency response personnel, and others in complying with, and enforcing the regulations governing the safe transport of hazardous materials by highway, rail, water and air.

The information and illustrations presented in this Guide are intended to serve as an introduction to regulations governing hazardous materials transportation. The Guide should be read in conjunction with the Hazardous Materials Regulations (HMR; 49 CFR 100-199). Published annually, and amended periodically, the HMR are the key to compliance and contain the information needed to comply with the requirements for the safe transport of hazardous materials.

Hazardous materials markings, labels, placards, and shipping papers serve to communicate the hazards posed by materials in transportation. Hazard communication is the key to effective emergency response, and is also used to alert transportation workers and the general public of the presence of hazardous materials, insure that non-compatible materials are not loaded together in the same transport vehicle, and provide the necessary information for reporting hazardous materials incidents. The purpose of this Guide is to explain and identify the markings, labels and placards which appear on packages, freight containers and transport vehicles containing hazardous materials.

Marking regulations (Section 172.300) require information, specific to the hazardous material, to be "marked" on the outside of the package. Examples of the information required to be marked on the package are the proper shipping name, identification number and consignor's or consignee's name. For how markings required by the HMR are to be applied to a package, see Section 172.304. For exceptions to the marking requirements and additional marking requirements, see Section 172.300. This chart does not attempt to cover all the marking requirements. In particular this chart does not contain any information related to specification packaging markings addressed in the Parts 178 and 179 of 49 CFR. For further details on required markings, consult the appropriate sections in the HMR.

The Labeling of a package of hazardous material is specific to the hazard class of the material. The Hazardous Material Tables, Section 172.101 and 172.102, identify the proper label(s) for the hazardous material listed. In some cases, a hazardous material will meet the definition of two or more hazard classes. In these instances, the additional labeling requirements of Section 172.402 must be met. Labels, when required, must be placed next to the marked proper shipping name (Section 172.406). The requirements for labels can be found in Section 172.400–172.450.

Placards represent the hazard class(es) of the material(s) contained within the freight container, motor vehicle or rail car. The requirements for placarding are contained in Section 172.500–172.558. **NOTE: This document is for general guidance only and is not a substitute for the requirements of 49 CFR 100-199.**

Response begins with identification.

A transport vehicle carrying 1 package of Radioactive Material labeled Yellow III, 500 pounds of Flammable Liquid and 600 pounds of Corrosive Materials would be placarded with both RADIOACTIVE and DANGEROUS placards.

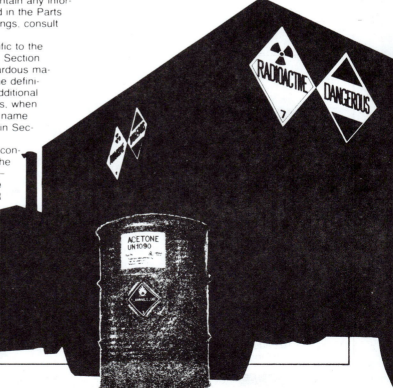

Hazardous Materials Warning Labels

DOMESTIC LABELING

General Guidelines on Use of Labels
(CFR, Title 49, Transportation, Parts 100-177)

- Labels illustrated above are normally for *domestic shipments*. However, some air carriers *may* require the use of International Civil Aviation Organization (ICAO) labels.
- Domestic Warning Labels *may* display UN Class Number, Division Number (and Compatibility Group for Explosives only) [Sec. 172.407(g)].
- Any person who offers a hazardous material for transportation MUST label the package, if required [Sec. 172.400(a)].
- The Hazardous Materials Tables, Sec. 172.101 and 172.102, identify the proper label(s) for the hazardous materials listed.

- Label(s), when required, must be printed on or affixed to the surface of the package near the proper shipping name [Sec. 172.406(a)].
- When two or more different labels are required, display them next to each other [Sec. 172.406(c)].
- Labels may be affixed to packages (even when not required by regulations) provided each label represents a hazard of the material in the package [Sec. 172.401].

Check the Appropriate Regulations
Domestic or International Shipment

Additional Markings and Labels

HANDLING LABELS

Cargo Aircraft Only
172.402(b)

Bung Label
172.402(e)

ORM-E
172.316

INNER PACKAGES
COMPLY WITH
PRESCRIBED
SPECIFICATIONS
173.25(a)(4)

Package
Orientation
Markings
172.312(a)(c)

Fumigation
173.9

173.427

Here are a few additional markings and labels pertaining to the transport of hazardous materials. The section number shown with each item refers to the appropriate section in the HMR. The Hazardous Materials Tables, Section 172.101 and 172.102, identify the proper shipping name, hazard class, identification number, required label(s) and packaging sections.

Poisonous Materials

172.505   172.301

Materials which meet the inhalation toxicity criteria specified in Section 173.3a(b)(2), have additional "communication standards" prescribed by the HMR. First, the words "Poison-Inhalation Hazard" must be entered on the shipping paper, as required by Section 172.203(k)(4), for any primary capacity units with a capacity greater than one liter. Second, packages of 110 gallons or less capacity must be marked "Inhalation Hazard" in accordance with Section 172.301(a). Lastly, transport vehicles, freight containers and portable tanks subject to the shipping paper requirements contained in Section 172.203(k)(4) must be placarded with POISON placards in addition to the placards required by Section 172.504. For additional information and exceptions to these communication requirements, see the referenced sections in the HMR.

Keep a copy of the DOT Emergency Response Guidebook handy!

Hazardous Materials Warning Placards

DOMESTIC PLACARDING
Illustration numbers in each square refer to Tables 1 and 2 below.

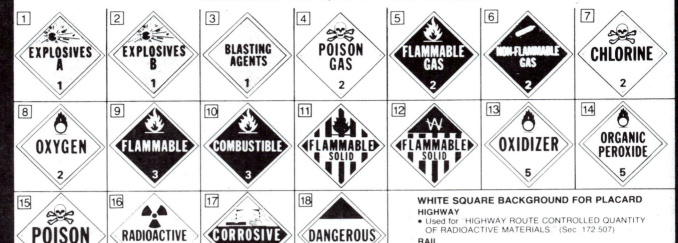

1 EXPLOSIVES A — 1	2 EXPLOSIVES B — 1	3 BLASTING AGENTS — 1	4 POISON GAS — 2	5 FLAMMABLE GAS — 2	6 NON-FLAMMABLE GAS — 2	7 CHLORINE — 2
8 OXYGEN — 2	9 FLAMMABLE — 3	10 COMBUSTIBLE — 3	11 FLAMMABLE SOLID	12 FLAMMABLE SOLID (W)	13 OXIDIZER — 5	14 ORGANIC PEROXIDE — 5
15 POISON — 6	16 RADIOACTIVE — 7	17 CORROSIVE — 8	18 DANGEROUS			

WHITE SQUARE BACKGROUND FOR PLACARD
HIGHWAY
- Used for "HIGHWAY ROUTE CONTROLLED QUANTITY OF RADIOACTIVE MATERIALS." (Sec. 172.507)

RAIL
- Used for RAIL SHIPMENTS "EXPLOSIVE A." "POISON GAS" and "POISON GAS RESIDUE" placards. (Sec. 172.510(a))

Guidelines
(CFR, Title 49, Transportation, Parts 100-177)

- Placard any transport vehicle, freight container, or rail car containing any quantity of material listed in Table 1.
- Materials which are shipped in portable tanks, cargo tanks, or tank cars must be placarded when they contain any quantity of Table 1 and/or Table 2 material.
- Motor vehicles or freight containers containing packages which are subject to the "Poison-Inhalation Hazard" shipping paper description of Section 172.203(k)(4), must be placarded POISON in addition to the placards required by Section 172.504 (see Section 172.505).
- When the gross weight of all hazardous material covered in TABLE 2 is less than 1000 pounds, no placard is required on a transport vehicle or freight container.
- Placard freight containers 640 cubic feet or more containing any quantity of hazardous material classes listed in TABLES 1 and/or 2 when offered for transportation by air or water (see Section 172.512(a)). Under 640 cubic feet see Section 172.512(b).

TABLE 1

Hazard Classes	No.
Class A explosives	1
Class B explosives	2
Poison A	4
Flammable solid (DANGEROUS WHEN WET label only)	12
Radioactive material (YELLOW III label)	16
Radioactive material:	
Uranium hexafluoride fissile (Containing more than 1.0% U235)	16 & 17
Uranium hexafluoride, low-specific activity (Containing 1.0% or less U235)	16 & 17

Note: For details on the use of Tables 1 and 2, see Sec. 172.504 (see footnotes at bottom of tables.)

TABLE 2

Hazard Classes	No.
Class C explosives	18
Blasting agent	3
Nonflammable gas	6
Nonflammable gas (Chlorine)	7
Nonflammable gas (Fluorine)	15
Nonflammable gas (Oxygen, cryogenic liquid)	8
Flammable gas	5
Combustible liquid	10
Flammable liquid	9
Flammable solid	11
Oxidizer	13
Organic peroxide	14
Poison B	15
Corrosive material	17
Irritating material	18

UN or NA Identification Numbers

MUST BE DISPLAYED ON TANK CARS, CARGO TANKS, PORTABLE TANKS AND BULK PACKAGINGS

PLACARDS OR ORANGE PANELS

1090 and

FLAMMABLE 3 · 1090 3 · 1017 2 · 1993 3

Appropriate Placard must be used

- When hazardous materials are transported in Tank Cars (Section 172.330), Cargo Tanks (Section 172.328), Portable Tanks (Section 172.326) or Bulk Packagings (Section 172.331), UN or NA numbers must be displayed on placards, orange panels or, when authorized, plain white square-on-point configuration.
- UN (United Nations) or NA (North American) numbers are found in the Hazardous Materials Tables Sections 172.101 and 172.102.
- Identification numbers may not be displayed on "POISON GAS," "RADIOACTIVE," or "EXPLOSIVE A," "EXPLOSIVE B," "BLASTING AGENTS," or "DANGEROUS" placards. (See Section 172.334.)
- In lieu of the orange panel, identification numbers may be placed on plain white square-on-point configuration when there is no placard specified for the hazard class (e.g., ORM-A, B, C, D, or E) or where the identification number may not be displayed on the placard. See Section 172.336(b) for additional provisions and specifications.
- When the identification number is displayed on a placard the UN hazard class number must be displayed in the lower corner of each placard (see Section 172.332 (c)(3)).
- Specifications of size and color of the Orange Panel can be found in Section 172.332(b).
- NA numbers are used only in the USA and Canada.

Additional Placarding Guidelines

DANGEROUS

A transport vehicle or freight container containing two or more classes of material requiring different placards specified in Table 2 may be placarded DANGEROUS in place of the separate placards specified for each of those classes of material specified in Table 2. However, when 5000 pounds or more of one class of material is loaded therein at one loading facility, the placard specified for that class must be applied. This exception, provided in Section 172.504(b), does not apply to portable tanks, tank cars, or cargo tanks.

CAUTION: Check each shipment for compliance with the appropriate hazardous materials regulations — Proper Classification, Packaging, Marking, Labeling, Placarding, Documentation — prior to offering for shipment.

In an emergency, call Chemtrec, 1-800-424-9300

Examples of Canadian and International Placards and Labels

The shipment of hazardous materials internationally is governed by one or more regulatory bodies with regulations that may be similar to domestic regulations or radically different. Canada, for example, has adopted wordless placards and labels because their country is bilingual. Canada also requires cargo and rail tanks to use retro-reflective placarding. However, Canada and the United States have reciprocity regarding the use of wordless and worded placards and labels.

Several international organizations govern the transportation of hazardous materials according to the mode of transportation. If a shipment is going by water, the International Maritime Organization (IMO) has authority. The International Civil Aviation Organization (ICAO) is concerned about the safe shipment of dangerous goods

(*i.e.*, hazardous materials) by air. Transport Canada (TC) is the Canadian counterpart to the U.S. Department of Transportation (DOT).

The United Nations publishes "Recommendations for the Transport of Dangerous Goods," a publication that is used by many nations of the world when promulgating regulations. Since the safe transport of hazardous materials is of concern to people everywhere, the work done by the United Nations is of critical importance world-wide. Labels and placards used in the Canadian, IMO, and ICAO regulations are generally based on the U.N. Recomendations, although Canada has some labels and placard designs that vary from the U.N. White borders are optional on International Placards.

Examples of Wordless Placards and Labels

Pictured here are typical wordless placards and labels required for use in Canada and many other countries around the world.

Examples of International and Canadian Placards and Labels

Spontaneously Combustible and Keep Away From Food placards and labels are used internationally and in Canada. The Corrosive Gas placard and label are used exclusively in Canada. Most placards and labels used internationally are similar (color and symbols) to those required by DOT regulations.

UN Class Numbers

Class 1: Explosives
Class 2: Gases (compressed, liquified or dissolved under pressure
Class 3: Flammable liquids
Class 4: Flammable solids or substances
Class 5: Oxidizing substances. Division 5 1, Oxidizing substances or agents Division 5 2. Organic peroxides
Class 6: Poisonous and infectious substances
Class 7: Radioactive substances
Class 8: Corrosives
Class 9: Misc. dangerous substances

Flammable Solid   Oxidizer   Non-flammable Gas

Spontaneously Combustible   Keep Away From Food   Corrosive Gas

Flammable Gas   Flammable Liquid   Dangerous When Wet

Poison   Miscellaneous Dangerous Substances   Infectious Substance

Examples of Explosive Labels

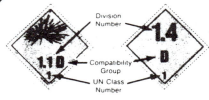

Division Number — Compatibility Group — UN Class Number

The Numerical Designation represents the Class or Division. Alphabetical Designation represents the Compatibility Group (for Explosives only). Division Numbers and Compatibility Group combinations can result in over 30 different "Explosives" labels (see IMDG Code/ICAO).

For complete details, refer to one or more of the following:
- Code of Federal Regulations, Title 49. Transportation. Parts 100-199. [All modes]
- International Civil Aviation Organization (ICAO) Technical Instructions for the Safe Transport of Dangerous Goods by Air [Air]
- International Maritime Organization (IMO) Dangerous Goods Code [Water]
- "Transportation of Dangerous Goods Regulations" of Transport Canada. [All Modes]

U.S. Department of Transportation
Research and Special Programs Administration

Copies of this Chart can be obtained by writing OHMT/DHM-51, Washington. D.C. 20590.

CHART 9
REV. NOVEMBER 1988

Hazardous Materials Notification Chart

Agency	Jurisdiction/Branch
Air Resources Board	- Regional
Army	- U.S., EOD
	Control Center
	Decontamination,
	Explosives
County Agricultural Agent	
County Disaster Services	- Civil Defense
Coast Guard	
Department of Defense	- Nuclear Accident Center
Department of Water Resources	
Energy Research & Development Administration, Oakridge, TN	- Nuclear Incidents
Environmental Protection Agency	- Health Division
	- Water Pollution
	- Radiological Officer
Fire Department	- City
	- County
Fish & Game (Wildlife)	
Health Department	- State
Highways Department	- City
	- County
	- State
O.E.S.	
News Media	
Nuclear Regulatory Commission	
Police Departments	- Local, County,
	State, Federal

28

Sheriff's Office

Sanitation District — Local

NOTE: This is a partial list of agencies to be notified. Each department should prepare a complete list of all agencies, together with emergency telephone numbers, to meet local requirements.

Vehicle Fire Investigation

C1.030 When there is a vehicle fire, all the information needed to complete an investigation may not be available at the time of the at-scene investigation. Much information will probably have to be obtained from a follow-up investigation. Over the course of the entire investigation you should ascertain the following:

1. Determine the cause of the fire.
   a. Ascertain the condition of the vehicle before the fire.
   b. Determine if the fire was accidental, resulting from
      i Smoking
      ii A short circuit
      iii Gas leakage, e.g., from a broken fuel line
      iv Other cause
   c. Determine if the fire was deliberate, started by
      i Someone looking to file an insurance claim to obtain money for such purposes as to pay off loans, satisfy liens or cover gambling debts.
      ii Someone wanting to destroy a vehicle in poor mechanical condition in order to collect insurance money.

iii   Someone seeking revenge. The vehicle was destroyed in anger because of a domestic problem, for example.

iv   An employee in order to cover up some form of negligence on his part, e.g., failure to properly maintain the vehicle.

v   A mentally deranged person.

d.   Determine if the fire was started to cover up some form of crime, such as murder. Examine for bullet holes, traces of clothing, etc.

2.   Check for it being a stolen vehicle.

3.   Question the driver, passengers and any other witnesses.

4.   Be aware that there can be danger in towing a damaged vehicle away from the scene.

a.   Evacuate the area if sufficient danger is present.

b.   Keep bystanders away.

5.   Confirm the isolation of the fire (normally done by the fire department).

6.   Be cautious around escaped fuel.

7.   If there is fire under the hood, do not raise the hood unless necessary to spray fire containments on the source (normally done by the fire department).

8.   Confirm that the following actions are taken by the fire department after the fire is believed to be out:

a.   Ensure that the fire does not start up again.

b.   Remove all hazards before the vehicle is moved.

c.   Move burned parts away from the immediate scene.

d.   Do not allow smoking in the immediate area.

The Investigation

C1.031 An at-scene traffic accident investigation must be carried out in a professional manner. This type of investigation is just as important as other investigations carried out by police departments, special fraud squads, insurance investigators and others.

a. Set up an investigatorial plan. Conduct the investigation methodically and thoroughly.

b. Make sound judgments. Keep an open mind and re-evaluate facts as the investigation progresses. Place emphasis on gathering and recording facts. Do not depend upon inference and possibilities in regard to how or why the accident occurred.

c. Keep in mind that the accident may have in fact been staged with the intent to defraud an insurance company, or to cover up some other crime.

d. Keep in mind that the accident may in fact have been a *suicide* or a *homicide*.

e. Avoid forming biased opinions either prior to or during the investigation. Biased opinions may hamper the completion of an accurate investigation.

C1.032 Examine the scene to determine what evidence is available.

a. Ensure that sensitive or short-lived evidence is not removed, moved, lost, destroyed or mutilated.

b. Locate, collect or preserve short-lived evidence, and also mark the precise location of evidence with chalk or in some other suitable manner so that proper measurements may be made later.

C1.033 Do not interfere with traffic by standing or walking in places that are not essential to carrying out a particular aspect of the investigation. For example:

a. Do not make notes while standing in a lane open to traffic movement.

b. Do not endanger the safety of a witness or driver by having him stand in such places while a statement is taken.

C1.034 Be methodical. Use the same procedures that would usually be followed in any serious type of investigation at the crime scene.

a. Examine the
    i   vehicle,
    ii immediate collision area, and the
    iii general scene for an overview of the entire area.
b. Take measurements of the scene and prepare a preliminary field sketch showing, particularly, all short-lived evidence.
c. Take photographs, if necessary.
d. Collect and preserve evidence.
e. Make sufficient, adequately detailed, well prepared notes.
f. Visualize the scene as the involved drivers and witnesses could have seen it.

Witnesses and Drivers

C1.035   Locate and identify drivers and witnesses (any persons having information relating to the accident) for the purpose of aiding in the investigation, particularly with their verbal and written statements, and for follow-up investigation purposes.

   a.   Check the scene for actual or potential witnesses.

   b.   Make notes on vehicles near persons who are discussing how the accident occurred.

   c.   Make notes on all other vehicles, including their license numbers, at or near the scene.

   d.   When contacting bystanders to inquire whether they are drivers or witnesses, be courteous and tactful. Although laws generally require drivers to identify themselves, most people are reluctant to identify themselves as witnesses.

   e.   Use caution in accepting witnesses' information. A witness may be:
   - i   Prejudiced or biased
   - ii   A friend or relative of one of the persons involved
   - iii   A person who is trying to gain the attention of or to gain favor with the investigator

   f.   Be careful not to guide witnesses in answering your questions. However, you should require witnesses to give precise answers as to:

     i   Where they were when the accident occurred

     ii   What they saw or heard

g.   Make drivers and witnesses feel at ease. The accident could have had an extreme emotional impact on them.

h.   Make intentional mistakes when discussing the accident events to see if they will correct you.

C1.036 In many cases, the drivers hold the key to the accident cause; therefore, they must be examined thoroughly.

a.   Check all information contained on a driver's license.

b.   Question drivers separately at first, if possible. Allow them to tell their story freely, with the minimum of interruptions.

c.   If you feel it is necessary and safe to do so, bring both drivers together later and allow their stories to be compared, clarifying any issue that might seem to be contradictory.

d.   Gather factual information from drivers for report information.

e.   Check the physical condition of each driver, including any indication of impairment due to the use of alcohol or drugs.

f.   Obtain a preliminary statement. A detailed statement can be obtained later, if necessary. If there is any question as to there being a violation on the part of a driver, read the person his rights under Miranda.

34

C1.037 Once the scene has been secured in terms of protection and aid to the injured and protection of property, an in-depth investigation may be conducted.

Hit and Run

C1.038 A *hit-and-run* accident is a motor vehicle accident in which an involved driver fails to comply with the legal requirement to stop, give aid and/or information (depending upon the jurisdiction) and reveal his identity following the accident.

C1.039 The same accident investigation procedures followed in a usual traffic accident should be followed in a hit-and-run accident -- except that the investigation must be enlarged to include locating the driver and in many cases the vehicle as well.

Hit-and-Run Driver

C1.040 Attempt to locate all drivers involved in the accident.

    a.   Determine whether the missing driver left the scene on foot or by vehicle.

    b.   Consider the fact that the missing driver might have been injured in the accident and that he might have been taken for medical treatment by a passing motorist. In this case, the accident might not be a hit-and-run.

c.   If there is an indication that the driver and/or passenger was injured and neither is at the scene, have doctors' offices, hospitals and other medical facilities checked. Sometimes an uninjured driver will accompany an injured passenger to a treatment facility.

d.   Notify the dispatch office that the accident involves a hit-and-run driver.

e.   Advise, or arrange for advice to, all patrol units, both in the local area and in the surrounding areas. Provide as much information as possible.

f.   Accept information from a willing bystander with some caution. A hit-and-run driver or one of his passengers or some conspirator may return to the scene and provide false information with the intention to mislead the investigator.

C1.041 Obtain as much information as possible relating to the description of the offending driver and his passengers. The following information should be sent out immediately (along with information on the driver's vehicle -- see C1.046):

a.   Sex and age of the driver
b.   Clothing: color, etc.
c.   Complexion
d.   Length and color of hair
e.   Moustache?
f.   Sideburns?
g.   Eyeglasses?

h. Stature, e.g., heavyset, slim, approximate standing height, estimated while the driver was seated in the vehicle, 6 ft (183 cm)

i. Total number of passengers in the vehicle, including identification particulars of each and the seating arrangement

C1.042 Some of the reasons why a driver will flee the scene of an accident are:

a. Driving while under the influence of alcohol or a drug

b. Driving without a valid driver's license

c. Driving without adequate insurance coverage

d. Being a married person accompanied by someone other than his or her spouse

e. Having stolen goods in the vehicle

f. Fleeing a previous accident

g. Fleeing from a recently committed crime, such as armed robbery

h. Being wanted for a crime, e.g., there is an outstanding warrant for his arrest

i. Being panic-struck. When a suspected driver is located and the only reason he can give for leaving the scene is that he was panic-struck, his background, associates and activities just prior to the accident should be closely investigated.

j. Being injured, e.g., suffering from concussion and leaving the scene without any criminal or civil intent, leaving the scene to obtain medical assistance or treatment

C1.043 Attempt to relate the locale where the accident occurred to what the driver might have been doing in the area.

a. Go back through the pre-scene and pre-trip events in an attempt to determine where the driver might have been.

    i   The driver might have been traveling to or from work.

    ii   The driver might have been attending a house party, meeting, or some other function in the neighborhood.

b. Carry out an investigation to determine whether there was a party or some other function in the neighborhood; check factories, conference centers, liquor outlets and other places of business on the chance someone might recognize the type of vehicle that was involved and be able to give information as to its driver or owner.

C1.044   Beer bottles, stolen property and other items may have been thrown from the vehicle after the accident.   These articles might have fingerprints on them which, in turn, might lead to the hit-and-run driver's identity.   Additionally, if the driver stopped at the scene momentarily, he might have left fingerprints on the victim's vehicle or some other item that he touched.

C1.045   The offending driver or his passengers may have dropped such things as envelopes, litter, business cards, etc., which may have the business or residence address of the owner, driver or passenger, or some other person or business that will lead to the driver's identity.

Hit-and-Run Vehicle

C1.046 Obtain as much information as possible relating to the description of the hit-and-run vehicle. Determine and send out the following information immediately, if available:

a. The license plate number, including the jurisdiction.

    i   The series of letters or numerals sometimes indicates a particular town or city, or part of a jurisdiction.

    ii   When the issuing jurisdiction is determined, patrol units should pay particular attention to traffic routes leading to that area.

    iii   If all numbers or letters of a license plate are not available, those that are available will be of value in eliminating other vehicles that would otherwise fit the description of the hit-and-run vehicle.

    iv   Bear in mind that the driver may have switched plates on his vehicle immediately after the accident.

b. Include the make, year, model, type and color of the vehicle in its description.

c. Determine the location and extent of damage to the vehicle body, windshield or other part.

d. Determine the direction of travel.

e. Include other details that will help identify the vehicle:

    i   Grille features

    ii   Burned out or broken headlamps, taillamps, and other lamps

    iii   Hood, fender and tail-pipe ornaments

    iv   Type and location of mirrors

    v   Type and location of radio aerial

    vi   Description of tires, e.g., black walls, wide tread

    vii   Clean or dirty body

    viii   New or faded paint job

    ix   Window and windshield stickers or decals

    x   Noise level of muffler

    xi   Noisy body parts, e.g., loose doors, fenders, tail pipe, muffler

C1.047 Note and collect evidence at the scene which might be matched up to a suspect vehicle.

    a.   Broken glass from windows, windshield, headlamps or other lamps, and mirrors.

    b.   Broken body parts or items which might have fallen off or been thrown from the vehicle during the collision:

        i   Headlamp parts, e.g., headlamp rim

        ii   Hubcaps; door handles; chrome pieces from the grille, fenders or side panels; bumper or bumper guards; tail-pipe extension; and such

        iii   Paint chips or scrapings

        iv   Parts of the load or cargo

        v   Soil or other debris which could have been knocked off or fallen from the hit-and-run vehicle, e.g., dirt from the underside of fenders or body

        vi   Tire prints

        vii   Fluids, e.g., radiator fluid. It is often possible to make an assumption as to how far a vehicle will be able to travel after the collision based on the amount of fluid lost. Fluid trails also allow for the direction of travel and vehicle movements to be traced.

C1.048 Check surrounding areas where vehicle could have been abandoned, hidden or otherwise removed from immediate sight, such as garages, auto body repair shops, parking lots and other places where the vehicle could have been placed among other vehicles and not be readily seen.

C1.049 When a suspect vehicle is located soon after the accident has occurred, check the motor, radiator, exhaust system, brake discs/drums and tires for warmth, which would indicate recent travel. If the vehicle is located some time after the accident has occurred, examine it for any indication of recent repairs to the body and any repairs or replacement of other parts. A hit-and-run driver will often replace old tires with new tires, or vice-versa, and replace matched tires with mismatched tires with the intent to mislead the investigator.

C1.050 Obtain assistance from garages, vehicle dealers, body repair shops and vehicle supply outlets in identifying the make and model of a vehicle from a broken part left at the scene. Request them to advise you if a replacement part is ordered or purchased.

C1.051 Examine the undercarriage, grille, all protruding parts (e.g., mirrors, fender and hood ornaments) and damaged areas for blood, hair, clothing fabrics, paint chips or scrapings, tire marks and other similar evidence that might be matched to the object which was struck.

C1.052 Record the time a vehicle theft is reported. If the report is received before the time established for a hit-and-run accident to have occurred, the thief could have been the driver. If the report is received sometime after a hit-and-run accident has occurred, consider the possibility that the owner, or someone known by him, might have been driving at the time of the accident and that the stolen car report is intended to mislead the investigator. Similarly, a vehicle that is reported to have been destroyed by fire, to have run away over a cliff or embankment, or to have met some similar end should be examined for evidence that might relate it to a hit-and-run accident.

C1.053 When a report is received involving a parked vehicle, check the motor, tires and exhaust system for warmth. Also check the immediate vicinity for the presence or absence of debris that might indicate that the accident did in fact occur at that location or did not occur there, respectively. The driver may have been involved in an accident at another location and driven the vehicle to the parked location in an attempt to cover up his involvement in the accident.

Hit-and-Run Victim

C1.054 Examine and record the exact place and type of damage suffered by the victim's vehicle or injury suffered by a pedestrian, or other person not in a vehicle, in a hit-and-run accident. When the victim is a pedestrian who is killed, it may be necessary to have hair samples taken before burial in order to match such samples against hair which might be found on a suspect's vehicle at a later time. When a pedestrian is struck, record and, if possible, photograph the location of the injury so that the height of that portion of the vehicle which struck the person can be properly related. In all cases, a victim's articles of clothing should be held as exhibits and for follow-up investigation, if at all possible.

C1.055 Examine and collect evidence from a victim's vehicle in the same meticulous way as was done in respect to the offending vehicle. This is just as essential, because matching of evidence must take place once a suspect vehicle is located.

Hit-and-Run Follow-Up Investigation

C1.056 Have the investigation extended to the pre-scene and post-scene areas while action is taken at the scene.

a. Check to see if anyone saw unsafe or erratic driving by a driver of a vehicle sometime prior to the hit-and-run accident, generally in close proximity to the accident scene and shortly before the accident.

b. If the accident occurred during darkness, did anyone see a vehicle with a broken headlamp or with some other damage in the vicinity? Check garages and service stations to determine whether such a vehicle was observed and whether or not parts were purchased, such as a replacement headlamp.

C1.057 Seek the assistance of the news media. Radio and television can be of immediate assistance. Newspapers can be of assistance later.

a. Radio news or special broadcasts normally cover a great area, giving considerable coverage to the description of a suspect vehicle.

b. Considerable help can be expected from the motoring public when broadcasts are made over radio and television.

c. Have broadcasts made over civilian-band radio systems to truck operators, taxis, and others who monitor those frequencies.

C1.058 Visit the accident scene on subsequent days, particularly on the same day of the week and at the same time of day as the accident occurred. Observe the vehicles, particularly those traveling in the same direction as the hit-and-run vehicle was traveling, and note those vehicles that have damaged areas or that appear to have been recently repaired and/or newly painted. Investigate all suspicious vehicles and drivers.

Accident Investigation

Vehicle Inspection

C1.059 Inspect and test a vehicle that has been involved in an accident for any form of mechanical defect or device that could have caused or contributed to the accident.

a. Determine the location, nature, and extent of damage to the vehicle.

b. Note prior vehicle damage. Do not confuse any prior damage with damage resulting from the accident under investigation.

c. Examine the vehicle for evidence of violations or defects:

i Stuck speedometer needle that might indicate speed at the time of collision

ii Brake systems

iii Steering and suspension systems

iv Equipment such as windshield wipers, turn signals, turn signal indicator lights, brake lights, headlamps, horn, etc.

v Vehicle safety inspection sticker

d. Look for unusual gadgets that might have contributed to the accident:

i Knob on the steering wheel

ii Shrunken heads or dice dangling from the rear-view mirror or some other object that could have obstructed the driver's view

iii Stickers or decals on the windshield or windows that could have obstructed the driver's view

Accident Causes

C1.060 The true causes of accidents can be said to be:

    a.   A driver's failure to adjust to conditions prevalent at the time

    b.   Mechanical failure of the vehicle, such as brake failure

Drivers will often list other factors, such as:

    a.   Weather

    b.   Road conditions

    c.   Age of the other driver

    d.   Driver of the opposite sex

    e.   Use of alcohol or drugs

    f.   Acts of God

Notwithstanding whatever might be perceived as a cause, the actual cause is usually that a driver failed to adjust his driving in accordance with conditions at the time.

C1.061 Accident prevention starts with the elimination of unsafe driving practices, such as traveling at excessive speed, unsafe passing, following too close, failing to signal. Educating drivers as to the rationale for observing traffic regulations helps to reduce such unsafe driving practices.

Enforcement

C1.062 Proper enforcement action is one of the most important aspects of promoting traffic safety. Enforcement helps to prevent traffic accidents, whether such action is taken in connection with an actual accident investigation or as a result of encountering a violation that could be a cause or a contributing factor in an accident.

C1.063 An investigator should look for violations that contribute to accidents. He must be alert to discover hazardous type violations or, for that matter, violations that are non-hazardous at the time but could be a contributing factor under other conditions. For example, during daylight hours he may see a vehicle that is without proper lighting equipment. Enforcement under these circumstances will reduce the likelihood that the driver will operate his vehicle in that condition during hours of darkness.

C1.064 During the normal process of investigation, look for traffic violations that may have contributed to an accident. This is done through:

    a.   Observations

    b.   Questioning drivers and witnesses

    c.   Performing test skids to determine a vehicle's approximate minimum speed

    d.   Attempting to find a witness who can testify to the violation or some element of it

C1.065 Some violations are indicated by physical evidence found at the accident scene, such as:

    a.   Skid marks on which a minimum speed can be based

    b.   Skid marks that begin on one side and end on the other side of a sign or signal, indicating a sign or signal violation

    c.   Skid marks on the wrong side of the roadway, indicating that the vehicle was, in fact, on the wrong side

C1.066 Offenses other than those connected with the actual accident may come to the attention of the investigator during the accident investigation. For example, a car theft may come to his attention through a vehicle registration check.

C1.067 Nonmoving violations may come to the investigator's attention, such as double parking. Although double parking is usually not considered a serious violation per se, such a practice can be a contributing factor in an accident.

C1-068 A police officer investigator who, as a result of his investigation, has specific information and corroboration that a person has committed an offense, should initiate some kind of enforcement action, according to jurisdictional guidelines.

Leaving the Scene

C1.069 Before leaving the scene, ensure that drivers are made aware of their responsibilities as drivers, that injured persons and personal property are properly cared for, and that the scene is left in a safe condition.

a. Advise drivers which forms must be completed according to law.

b. Assist drivers in completing exchange of information forms, or ensure that they are aware of what information they require from each other.

c.   When a vehicle cannot be removed from the scene by its driver, assist the driver by arranging for a tow vehicle or by making other arrangements if he wishes.

d.   Restore normal traffic flow.

e.   Clear the scene of all debris and indications that an accident has occurred.

f.   Ensure that each driver and others involved in the accident leave the scene safely. Offer any additional assistance that is required.

Follow-Up Investigation

C1.070   In many cases, the investigation of an accident cannot be completed at the scene.

a.   Follow up on the nature of injuries at the hospital, doctor's office, or -- in the event of a fatality -- at the morgue.

b.   Take additional statements as required.

c.   Take necessary action to complete the investigation in a professionally thorough manner.

A Guide to Traffic Accident
Definitions, Types and Classifications

Primary Source (with Permission): National Safety Council, *Manual on Classification of Motor Vehicle Traffic Accidents* (3rd ed), Chicago, Illinois, 1989.

The following is a guide to traffic accident definitions and classifications for the purposes of this course. Usage that governs drivers and police is generally established by state law or city ordinance. Usage for investigation and department reporting is usually specified in administrative policies or regulations of the department. However, the following definitions provide a means to promote uniformity in the terminology used by traffic accident investigators and others involved in traffic accident investigations.

DEFINITIONS

ACCIDENTS

Accident

An accident is best described as: *That occurrence in a sequence of events which usually produces unintended injury, death or property damage.*

An accident is an unstabilized situation which includes at least one harmful event not directly resulting from a cataclysm (see below).

A *traffic accident* is a road vehicle accident in which (1) the unstabilized situation originates on a trafficway or (2) a harmful event occurs on a trafficway.

A *motor vehicle accident* is a transport accident that (1) involves a motor vehicle in transport, (2) is not an aircraft or watercraft accident, and (3) does not include any harmful event involving a railroad train in transport prior to the involvement of a motor vehicle in transport.

Harmful event

A *harmful event* is an occurrence of *injury* or *damage*.

Cataclysm

A *cataclysm* is a cloudburst, cyclone, earthquake, flood, tornado, or volcanic eruption.

Unstabilized situation

An *unstabilized situation* is a set of events not under human control. It originates when control is lost and terminates when control is regained or, in the absence of persons who are able to regain control, when all *persons* and *property* are at rest.

> Exclusions:

> > *Deliberate intent* -- Suicide, homicide, and other harmful events under human control do not imply the existence of an unstabilized situation. A set of unintended consequences of such acts might be an unstabilized situation, however.

> > *Legal intervention* -- Legal intervention is a type of deliberate intent involving intentional acts by a law-enforcing agent or other official.

Stabilized situation

A *stabilized situation* is the condition prevailing after motion and other action constituting the events of an accident have ceased and no further harm will ensue unless a new series of events is initiated by some means.

Accident collision

For the purposes of this course, *accident*, *crash* and *collision* have the same meaning.

PERSONS

Driver

A *driver* is an occupant who is in actual physical control of a transport vehicle or, in the case of an out-of-control vehicle, an occupant who was in control until control was lost.

Occupant

An *occupant* is any person who is part of a transport vehicle.

Passenger

A *passenger* is any occupant of a road vehicle other than its driver.

Pedestrian

A *pedestrian* is any person who is not an occupant.

Traffic unit

A *traffic unit* is a *road vehicle* or a *pedestrian*.

VEHICLES

Motor vehicle

A motor vehicle is any motorized (mechanically or electrically operated) road vehicle not operated on rails.

Motorcycle

A motorcycle is a two-wheeled or three-wheeled motor vehicle designed for carrying one or two persons. Motor scooters, minibikes, and mopeds are motorcycles.

Road vehicle

A *road vehicle* is any land vehicle other than a railroad vehicle.

Other road vehicle

An *other road vehicle* is any road vehicle other than a motor vehicle.

Inclusions:

Animal-drawn vehicle (any type)

Animal harnessed to a conveyance

Animal carrying a person

Street car

Pedalcycle

Land vehicle

A *land vehicle* is a transport vehicle which is neither an aircraft nor a watercraft.

TRAFFICWAY

Bikeway

A *bikeway* is that part of a trafficway specifically designated as being open for *pedalcycle* travel or, where various classes of pedalcycle travel are segregated, that part of a trafficway open for a particular class.

Bicycle lane

A *bicycle lane* is a bikeway that (1) is contiguous with a parallel roadway and (2) has been designated for preferential or exclusive use by *pedalcycles*.

Bicycle trail

A *bicycle trail* is a bikeway reserved exclusively for *pedalcycles* and separated from roadways by open space or barriers.

Channelized intersections

A *channelized intersection* is an *at-grade intersection* in which traffic is directed into definite paths by raised or painted traffic islands.

Collector-distributor road

A *collector-distributor road* is an *auxiliary roadway*, separated laterally from and parallel to a through roadway, which serves to collect traffic from or distribute traffic to access connections at selected points of egress from or ingress to the *through-traffic lanes*.

County road

A *county road* is a trafficway within a county trafficway system that is not an interstate highway, other U.S. route numbered highway, or other state route numbered highway.

Crosswalk

A *crosswalk* is (1) that part of a roadway at an intersection included with the connections of the lateral lines of the sidewalks on opposite sides of the roadway measured from the curbs or, in the absence of curbs, from the edges of the traversable roadway, or (2) any portion of a roadway at an intersection or elsewhere distinctly indicated for *pedestrian crossing* by lines or other markings on the surface of the roadway.

Curb return

A *curb return* is the curved section of curb used at intersections in joining straight sections of curb.

Driveway access

A *driveway access* is a roadway providing access to property adjacent to a trafficway.

> Inclusions:
>> Entrances to gas stations
> Exclusions:
>> Any area not within a trafficway

Frontage road

A *frontage road* is a roadway generally paralleling an expressway, freeway, parkway, or through street, which is designed to intercept, collect, and distribute traffic desiring to cross, leave, or enter such facility and to furnish access to property that otherwise would be isolated as a result of controlled access features. The frontage road may be within the same trafficway as the main roadway or in a separate trafficway.

Intersection

An *intersection* is an area that (1) contains a crossing or connection of two or more roadways not classified as driveway access and (2) is embraced within the prolongation of the lateral curb lines or, if none, the lateral boundary lines of the roadways. Where the distance along a roadway between two areas meeting these criteria is less than 10 meters or 33 feet (where there are two intersections close together), the two areas and the

54

roadway connecting them are considered to be parts of a single intersection.

Interstate highway

An *interstate highway* is a trafficway in the *Interstate System*.

Interstate System

The *Interstate System* is the National System of Interstate and Defense Highways as defined in Section 101, Title 23, United States Code.

Junction

A *junction* is either an intersection or the connection between a driveway access and a roadway other than a driveway access.

Fully controlled access highway

A *fully controlled access highway* is a trafficway on which preference is given to through traffic by permitting access only from other trafficways and by providing grade separations at all crossing trafficways.

Gore

A *gore* is a pointed area of land at the fork created by the convergence of two roads at a sharp angle and bounded by the edges of the roads.

Grade separation

A *grade separation* is a crossing of two trafficways or of a trafficway and a railway at different levels.

Highway

A *highway* is the entire width between the boundary lines of every publicly maintained way whereof any part is open to the use of the public for the purposes of vehicular travel. A highway can also be considered to be a *publicly maintained street* or trafficway.

Interchange

An *interchange* is a system of interconnecting roadways in conjunction with one or more *grade separations*, providing for the movement of traffic between two or more roadways on different levels.

Landway

A *landway* is the space within property lines or other boundary lines of any transport way that is neither an airway nor a waterway.

Local street

A *local street* is a trafficway within a city trafficway system that is not an interstate highway, other U.S. route numbered highway, other state route numbered highway, or county road.

Other U.S. route numbered highway

An *other U.S. route numbered highway* is a trafficway numbered by the American Association of State Highway and Transportation officials but not an interstate highway.

Other state route numbered highway

An *other state route numbered highway* is a trafficway within a state trafficway system but not an interstate highway or other U.S. route numbered highway.

Private way

A *private way* is any land way other than a trafficway. The space within a crossing of a private way and a trafficway shall be considered to be a trafficway.

Ramp

A *ramp* is an auxiliary roadway used for entering or leaving through-traffic lanes.

Road

A *road* is that part of a trafficway which includes both the roadway and any *shoulder* alongside the roadway.

Roadway

A *roadway* is that part of a trafficway designed, improved, and ordinarily used for motor vehicle travel or, where various classes of motor vehicle travel or motor vehicles are segregated, that part of a trafficway used by a particular class. Separate roadways may be provided for northbound and southbound traffic or for trucks and automobiles.

    Exclusions:

        Bridle paths, bicycle paths

Shared road

A *shared road* is any bikeway that is part of a roadway but not a bicycle path.

Shoulder

A *shoulder* is that part of a trafficway which is contiguous with the roadway and is for emergency use, for accommodation of stopped road vehicles, and for lateral support of the roadway structure.

Trafficway

A *trafficway* is any land way open to the public as a matter of right or custom for moving persons or property from one place to another.

Transport way

A *transport way* is any way or place reserved or commonly used for the operation of transport vehicles.

Exclusions:

Hiking trail, sidewalk, footpath

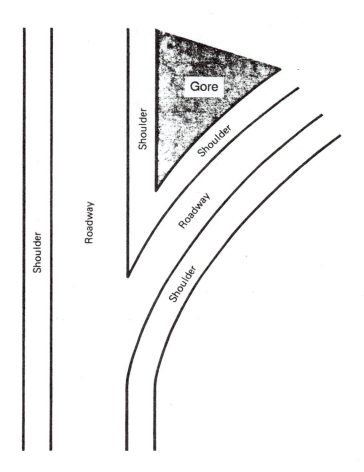

Figure C1-6 A diagram of a highway showing the roadway, shoulders and gore. Source: National Safety Council, *Manual on Classification of Motor Vehicle Traffic Accidents*, 3rd ed., D16.1, 1976, p. 16.

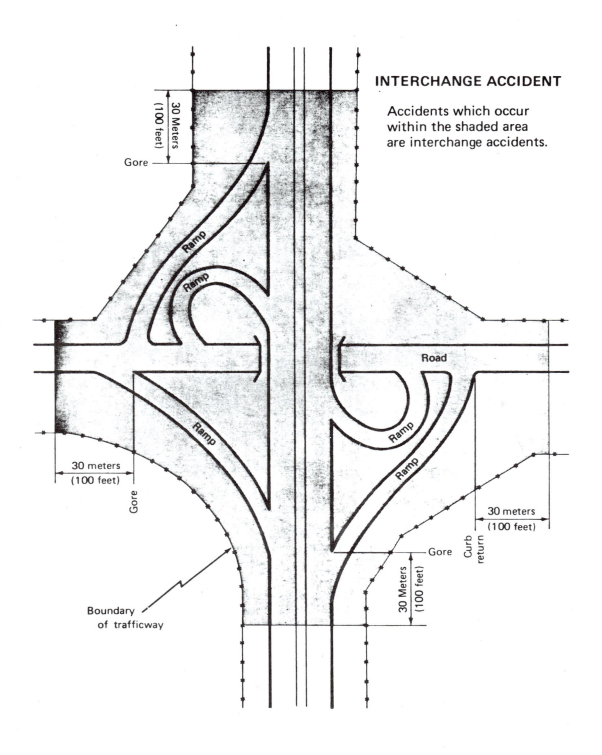

INTERCHANGE ACCIDENT

Accidents which occur within the shaded area are interchange accidents.

Figure C1-7   A diagram of an interchange.   Source: National Safety Council, *Manual on Classification of Motor Vehicle Traffic Accidents*, 3rd ed., D16-1, 1976, p. 19.

ACCIDENT TYPES AND CLASSIFICATIONS

First Harmful Event

The *first harmful event* in an accident is generally used to classify the accident.

The definition of a harmful event: *An occurrence of injury or damage.*

Categories

Including both noncollision and collision accidents, there are ten mutually exclusive categories for classification of *motor vehicle accidents* and nine mutually exclusive categories for classification of *other road vehicle accidents*.

Motor Vehicle Accident Categories

Noncollision Accident

Overturning accident

Other noncollision accident

Collision Accident involving:

Pedestrian

Motor vehicle in transport

Parked motor vehicle

Railroad vehicle

Pedalcycle

Animal

Fixed object

Other object

Other Road Vehicle Accident Categories

Noncollision Accident

Overturning accident

Other noncollision accident

Collision Accident involving:

Pedestrian

Other road vehicle in transport

Parked motor vehicle

Railroad vehicle

Animal

Fixed object

Other object

Types of Road Vehicle Accidents

There are three types of road vehicle accidents:

1. Overturning Accident

    An *overturning accident* is a road vehicle accident in which the first harmful event is the overturning of a road vehicle.

2. Collision Accident

    A *collision accident* is a road vehicle accident other than an overturning accident in which the first harmful event is a collision of a road vehicle in transport with another road vehicle, other property or pedestrians.

3. Noncollision Accident

    A *noncollision accident* is any road vehicle accident other than a collision accident.

Inclusions:

Overturning accident

Accidental poisoning from carbon monoxide generated by a road vehicle in transport

Breakage of any part of the road vehicle resulting in injury or in further property damage

Explosion of any part of the road vehicle

Fire starting in the road vehicle

Fall or jump from the road vehicle

Occupant being hit by an object in or thrown against some part of the road vehicle

Injury or damage from a moving part of the road vehicle

Object falling on the road vehicle

Toxic or corrosive chemicals leaking out of the road vehicle

Injury or damage that involves only the road vehicle and results from an event of a noncollision nature, such as the vehicle causing a bridge to give way under its weight, striking holes or bumps on the surface of the trafficway, or driving into water without overturning or collision

Exclusions:

Occupant being pushed from a road vehicle when this is an act of deliberate intent

Object being thrown towards, or in, or on the road vehicle by a person when this is an act of deliberate intent

Motor Vehicle Accident Classification by Type

There are eight mutually exclusive categories for classification of motor vehicles by type. These are:

Motorcycle

Automobile

Bus

Light truck

Single-unit truck

Truck tractor

Truck combination

Other motor vehicle

Accident Classification by Number of Vehicles

The categories for classification of road vehicle accidents by number of vehicles are:

Single-vehicle accident

Two-vehicle accident

Three-vehicle accident

(and so on)

Accident Classification by Severity

There are five categories of damage severity for classification of motor vehicle accidents or other road vehicle accidents.

Motor Vehicle Accidents

Accident categories in order of precedence are:

Disabling damage accident

Functional damage accident

Other motor vehicle damage accident

Other property damage accident

No-damage accident

Other Road Vehicle Accidents

Accident categories in order of precedence are:

Disabling damage accident

Functional damage accident

Other *other road vehicle* damage accident

Other property damage accident

No-damage accident

Definitions in Respect to Damage

Disabling damage is road vehicle damage which precludes departure of the vehicle from the scene of the accident in the usual operating manner by daylight after simple repairs.

Functional damage is any road vehicle damage, other than disabling damage, which affects operation of the road vehicle or its parts.

A *property damage only accident* is any noninjury accident.

Accident Classification by Land-Use Character

There are two mutually exclusive categories for classifying road vehicle accidents with respect to location by land use character. These categories are:

Urban area accident

Rural area accident

Accident Classification by Political Jurisdiction

Any city, county, state, or other political jurisdiction is a possible category for classification of a road vehicle accident by political jurisdiction. Such categories are not necessarily mutually exclusive.

A guide to the classification of road vehicle accidents by political jurisdiction is provided by the location of the first harmful event.

Accident Classification by Administrative Class of Trafficway

There are six mutually exclusive categories for classifying traffic accidents by administrative class of trafficway. In order of precedence these are:

Interstate highway accident

Other U.S. route numbered highway accident

Other state route numbered highway accident

County road accident

Local street accident

All other traffic accidents

Definitions in Respect to Injury

An *injury* is bodily harm to a *person*. Exclusions to this definition are the effects of diseases such as cerebral hemorrhage, heart attack, diabetic coma, epileptic seizure.

An *injury accident* is any road vehicle accident that results in one or more *injuries*.

A *fatal injury* is an injury that results in *death*. Injuries should be classified on the basis of conditions at the scene of the accident. The single exception to this rule applies to fatal injuries. If any injury results in death within 90 days of the road vehicle accident in which the injury occurred, the *injury classification* should be changed to that of fatal injury.

A *fatal accident* is any injury accident that results in one or more fatal injuries.

Classifications Based on Injury

There are five mutually exclusive categories for the classification of road vehicle accidents on the basis of injury severity. These may be reduced to three mutually exclusive categories by combining the nonfatal injury categories (the second with the third, the fourth with the fifth) below. The five categories are:

Fatal accident

Incapacitating injury accident

Nonincapacitating evident injury accident

Possible injury accident

Noninjury accident

Likewise, there are five mutually exclusive categories for the classification of persons with respect to injury. In order of precedence, these are:

Person with no injury

Person with possible injury

Person with nonincapacitating evident injury

Person with incapacitating injury

Person with fatal injury

Traffic Accident Investigator's Inventory*

An at-scene investigator's inventory should include the following items. It is important that an investigator be properly trained and totally familiar with the proper use of this equipment. Equipment should be examined frequently and be well maintained.

Axe

Single blade, head type

Blankets

Minimum of two, disposable type

Broom

Push type with heavy fibre bristles

Camera

Complete with necessary equipment, e.g., tripod, extra film, flash equipment

Carrying Case

For camera and camera supplies, measuring tapes, traffic cuffs and vests, flares, fusees, etc.

Clinometer

For measuring grades

*Source: R.W. Rivers, *Traffic Accident Investigators' Manual*, Charles C. Thomas, Publisher, Springfield, Illinois, 1995

Clipboard

Portable type complete with light and plastic cover for rain

Communications Systems

Radio communications system for vehicle and a public address system

Compass

Directional

Compass

For preparing scale diagrams

Coveralls

Suitable for conducting mechanical inspections

Crayons

Yellow color, lumberman's type -- for marking vehicle positions on roadway and other evidence

Dash Pad

For dash of vehicle, complete with light

Envelopes

For protecting evidence, e.g., paint chips

Eraser

Fire Extinguisher

Multi-purpose, dry chemical type

First Aid Kit

Type and supplies dependent upon availability of other emergency services, e.g., ambulance

Flashlights

At least two, equipped with traffic wands

Forms

As required by departmental policies and legislation, e.g., statements and note-taking, field investigations, accident reports, inventory

Jack

Axle type for lifting vehicles in emergencies when bumper jack is not adequate

Knife

Sharp knife for cutting seat belts, clothing, etc.

Lights, Vehicle

Emergency flashing lights; and roof side-mounted flood lights

Light, Spot

Permanent mounted or portable, pistol-grip spot light

Measuring Devices

    a.   Tapes

    b.   Wheel

    c.   Clinometer

Nails

Common type -- remove after use

Paint

Spray type, bright yellow or orange, for marking evidence on roadway

Paper

Plain bond and graphic for preparing field sketches

Pencils

Pins

Surveyor's type, to hook end of measuring tape

Pry Bar

Safety Vests

Shovel

Signs

Warning type

Straightedge (rule)

For preparing scale diagrams

Tow Cable

Tire Gauges

      a.   Pressure

      b.   Depth

Traffic Cones

Traffic (Arm) Cuffs

Traffic Template

Traffic Accidents (ANSI D16.1-1976) -- Primary source

INTRODUCTION

Lesson 2

SUBJECT: Traffic Accident Series of Events

Traffic accident investigators investigate and reconstruct traffic accidents by identifying and applying the *series of events*.

This lesson will provide the student with in-depth knowledge of the series of events that make up a traffic accident. The basis for *fact finding* will be developed by identifying and defining the various elements of a traffic accident. The student will learn to identify events that may require further investigation.

Lesson Contents

This lesson covers the following topics:

a.   The series of events that make up a traffic accident.

b.   The application of the series of events to traffic accident investigation and reconstruction.

c.   Methods of identifying the series of events in a hypothetical or real traffic accident situation.

73

Lesson Objectives

Upon completion of this lesson, the student will be able to:

1.   List and define, without error, the traffic accident series of events.

2.   Identify and apply the series of events to a given hypothetical or to a real traffic-accident situation.

Lesson 2

TRAFFIC ACCIDENT SERIES OF EVENTS

Series of Events

Traffic Accident Defined

C2.001 For purposes of traffic accident investigation and reconstruction, the term *traffic accident* is defined as *that occurrence in a series of events which usually produces injury, death or property damage*. (In this manual, the term *traffic accident* is synonymous with the terms *accident, collision, crash* and *incident* or any other similar, applicable term used in various jurisdictions and in many published works.)

Series of Events Defined

C2.002 An investigator should be familiar with the various *events* that make up a traffic accident and should ensure that the investigation covers all such events. These events are referred to as the *series of events* and for purposes of traffic accident investigation include not only actions that take place but also *situations* that are in place or that arise. Events may be divided into two distinct categories:

1.   *Pre-scene series of events* -- the events that lead up to the driver's point of possible perception of a hazard.

2.   *On-scene series of events* -- the events that occur within the *on-scene area*, which includes the point of possible perception.

C2.003 The pre-scene series of events can be further divided into:

1.   *Pre-trip events* -- the events that occur or the conditions that exist, relative to the driver and the vehicle, before the trip is started, e.g., driver inexperience, impairment by alcohol or drugs, vehicle defects, vehicle overload.

2.   *Trip events* -- the events that occur or conditions that arise after the trip starts and lead up to the point of possible perception, e.g., driver stopping for a meal or coffee, driver fatigue, illness, consumption of alcohol or drugs, erratic driving, vehicle mechanical failure, view obstructions, load falling from the vehicle, weather and roadway conditions.

On-Scene Series of Events

C2.004 On-scene series of events (see Figures C2-1 through C2-5 below) include:

a.   *Point of possible perception* -- the place and time at which a *normal* person could perceive a hazard.

b.   *Perception delay* -- the time involved from the point of possible perception to the point of actual perception. When perception is not immediate, perception delay is included with reaction time and a total of 1.6 seconds may be used. This combination is called *perception-reaction time*.

76

NOTE: Recommended perception-reaction time varies depending on the source cited. No known study has yielded results that indicate definitively what perception-reaction time should be used in every instance. Because each accident has its own set of events, human perception and reaction times may differ greatly from case to case. Whenever possible, the investigator or reconstructionist should base perception-reaction time on the following: driver's vision and hearing, driver's driving experience, driver's medical problems, roadway characteristics, nighttime vs daytime driving, weather conditions, visibility, and any other factor that could affect perception and/or reaction. Giving consideration to these factors, the investigator or reconstructionist should complete some kind of analysis to determine the perception-reaction time of the driver of the accident vehicle in the particular situation. If such an analysis cannot be done, the investigator or reconstructionist may use 1.5 or 1.6 seconds for daytime and 2.5 seconds for nighttime, noting that the selected time represents a reasonable average figure but may vary from one driver to another and from one situation to another.

c. *Perception distance* -- the distance traveled during perception delay.

d. *Point of perception or actual perception* -- the point where a situation is comprehended or perceived as being what it is, such as a hazard.

e. *Reaction* -- the voluntary or involuntary response to a hazard or other situation that has been perceived.

f. *Action point* -- the action point follows reaction and is the place where a person puts into action his decision, such as braking or steering, based on his perception of a hazard.

g. *Reaction Time* -- the length of time from when a person perceives a given situation as a hazard to when he reacts to his perception.

h. *Reaction distance* -- the distance traveled during reaction time.

i. *Evasive action* -- the action or combination of actions taken, e.g., steering, braking, to avoid a collision or other hazardous situation. Evasive action includes the results of an initial evasive action such as braking, e.g., skidding or slowing.

j. *Evasive action distance* -- the distance traveled after the action point to (1) the point where the traffic unit stops by itself or is stopped by some external means and avoids a collision or (2) the point of impact.

k. *Point of no escape* -- the place and time after or beyond which the accident cannot be prevented by a particular traffic unit.

l. *Encroachment* -- entering or intruding into the rightful path or area of another traffic unit.

m. *Point of impact* -- the place where a traffic unit (1) strikes another traffic unit or some other object or (2) overturns.

n. *Primary contact* -- the first contact between two traffic units or a traffic unit and another object, or a vehicle's first contact with a highway surface during an overturn.

78

o.   *Engagement* -- the initial penetration of one traffic unit into another traffic unit or object during primary, secondary or post-secondary contact.

p.   *Maximum engagement* -- the point of a traffic unit's maximum penetration into another traffic unit or object during collision.

q.   *Separation* -- the disengagement of traffic units or disengagement of a traffic unit and another object after maximum engagement.

r.   *Secondary contact* -- a contact occurring when a traffic unit disengages from a primary contact and strikes the opposing traffic unit a second time or strikes another traffic unit or object. (What may be the secondary contact for one traffic unit may be the first or primary contact for another traffic unit.)

s.   *Post-secondary contact* -- a contact occurring when a traffic unit disengages after a secondary contact and again strikes a same traffic unit or object or has a first or primary contact with a third traffic unit or another object.

t.   *Final rest position* -- the location where a traffic unit comes to rest after collision. In determining final rest position, it is important for the investigator to learn whether the vehicle stopped at the position at which he found it, or whether it was driven or moved to that position after the collision. The term *final rest position* does not apply to a position to which the vehicle may have been moved after coming to rest following disengagement.

u.   *Personal injury* -- for investigation purposes, bodily harm caused to a person during the on-scene series of events.

v.   *Fatal injury* -- an injury that causes death during the on-scene series of events, or a personal injury sustained during the on-scene series of events that thereafter directly results in death of the injured person.

C2.005   Another element that should be considered in an accident investigation is the *stabilized accident situation*. A stabilized accident situation is reached when vehicles and other objects involved in the collision have come to final rest and any other action belonging to the on-scene series of events of that collision has ended.

C2.006 Each traffic unit involved in an accident has its own series of events that must be investigated separately. The series of events for any given unit may not be the same as the series of events for any other unit; some events may not be present in the series for another unit, and vice versa. Even if the events are the same, they may not always follow the same sequence.

C2.007 Drivers and witnesses generally describe events forward, leading up to the result. The investigator must, however, start with the result and investigate back through the events as far as necessary to determine where, when, how and why the accident occurred.

C2.008   The five figures that appear on the next two pages are to be referred to when you undertake the Series of Events Projects at the end of the lesson.

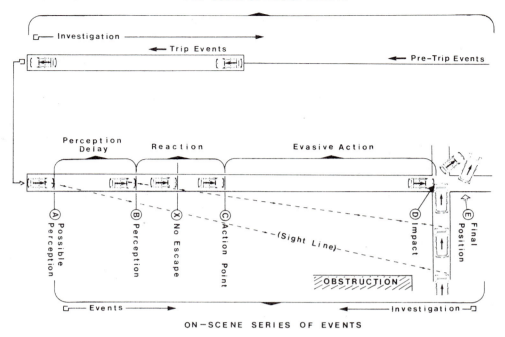

Figure C2-1

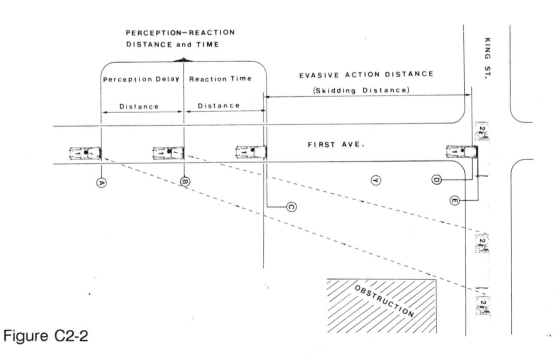

Figure C2-2

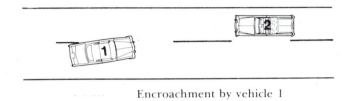

Encroachment by vehicle 1

Figure C2-3

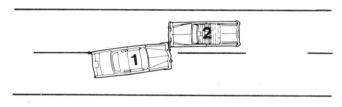

Primary or first contact

Figure C2-4

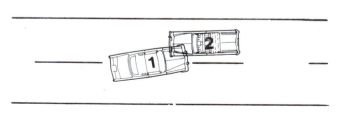

Maximum engagement

Figure C2-5

SERIES OF EVENTS

Projects

Instructions

Following are Series of Events Project Narratives which briefly describe traffic accident situations. As best you can with the amount of information supplied, determine, overline and label recognizable events in the Series of Events. Follow the instructions given below. (See the Series of Events Project Code Letters and Project Example that come after the instructions.)

1. Overline the words in each narrative which describe the events in a general way.

2. Use the designated Series of Events Project Code Letters to describe the separate events in the manner shown in the Project Example.

3. When there is more than one vehicle involved, attach a subscript number to each vehicle's Event Code Letter, e.g., Point of Possible Perception for Vehicle 1 would be shown as PP_1, Action Point for Vehicle 2 would be shown as AP_2. When an event such as road and weather conditions applies equally to all traffic units, a subscript number is not necessary.

4. Remember that an individual accident may not have all the events listed in the Series of Events. Remember also that all events do not necessarily fall in the same sequence in all accident situations, nor

do they necessarily fall in the same sequence for all vehicles in any one accident situation.

5. Whenever possible, the student should prepare on a separate sheet of paper a rough sketch of the Series of Events described in the project narrative and present it to the instructor with the project. A sketch is not necessary, nor indeed possible, with all project narratives.

6. Not all lines in a project narrative contain an event. Lines are numbered as a convenience for both the instructor and the student and are for reference purposes only.

7. Because of the limited information available in some of the project narratives, some events and consequently their respective Code Letters may occasionally be at the same place in the same line. For example, an Evasive Action may be described in a narrative at the same place where the Action Point would apply. Both these events should be covered by the same overline, but labeled separately, i.e., EA and AP.

SERIES OF EVENTS

Project Code Letters

PTE   Pre-trip Event

TE   Trip Event

PP   Point of Possible Perception

PDe   Perception Delay

PAP   Point of Actual Perception

PDi   Perception Distance

En   Encroachment

R   Reaction

RT   Reaction Time

RD   Reaction Distance

AP   Action Point

EA   Evasive Action

EAD   Evasive Action Distance

PNE	Point of No Escape
POI	Point of Impact
PC	Primary Contact
Eg	Engagement
ME	Maximum Engagement
S	Separation
SC	Secondary Contact
PSC	Post-secondary Contact
FP	Final Position
PI	Personal Injury
FI	Fatal Injury

SERIES OF EVENTS

Project Example

See Figure C2-2 preceding the Projects.

WHITE -- Vehicle 1

ADAMS -- Vehicle 2

1. $\overline{\hspace{2em}\text{PTE}_1\hspace{2em}}$ $\overline{\text{PTE}_1}$
    WHITE, who was 17 years old, had one year's

2. $\overline{\hspace{1.5em}}$ $\overline{\hspace{1em}\text{PTE}_1\hspace{1em}}$
    driving experience. He attended a party during

3. the evening at which he decided to leave early

4. next morning on a fishing trip. While at the

5. $\overline{\hspace{1em}\text{PTE}_1\hspace{1em}}$
    party, WHITE consumed 12 bottles of beer. He

6. stayed at the party until 6:00 a.m., and then

7. he drove to his home to obtain fishing gear.

8. $\overline{\hspace{1em}\text{PTE}_1\hspace{1em}}$
    Without taking time out to sleep, WHITE left

9. on his fishing trip. He $\overline{\text{felt dizzy and unsteady}}^{TE_1}$

10. while driving because of an overconsumption of

11. alcohol. While traveling north on First Avenue at

12. $\overline{\text{Point A}}^{PP_1}$, he saw the ADAMS vehicle on King Street

13. approaching an uncontrolled intersection from

14. his right. Because of a distraction caused by

15. a $\overline{\text{child playing alongside First Avenue}}^{TE}$ at Point Y,

16. WHITE did not recognize or perceive the ADAMS

17. vehicle as being a hazard. After traveling for

18. $\overline{\text{0.75 seconds}}^{PDe_1}$ over a distance of $\overline{\text{approximately}}^{PDi_1}$

19. $\overline{\text{50 ft (15 m)}}$, WHITE perceived at $\overline{\text{Point B}}^{PAP_1}$ that

20. ADAMS was not likely to stop at the intersection.

21. It took WHITE $\overline{\text{0.75 seconds}}^{RT_1}$ to make his decision

22. $\overline{\text{AP}_1}$
    and to react to that decision. At $\overline{\text{Point C}}$, WHITE

23. $\overline{\text{EA}_1}$ $\overline{\text{EAD}_1}$
    applied his brakes, but his vehicle skidded

24. $\overline{\text{En}_1}$ $\overline{\text{PC}_1\ \text{PC}_2}$
    $\overline{\text{100 ft (30 m)}}$ into the intersection and came into

25. $\overline{\text{ME}_1\ \text{ME}_2}$
    $\overline{\text{contact with}}$ and penetrated the ADAMS vehicle

26. $\overline{\text{POI}_1\ \text{POI}_2}$
    at $\overline{\text{Points D and E}}$. The collision or impact was

27. $\overline{\text{FP}_1\ \cdot\ \text{FP}_2}$
    minor. The vehicles did not move after impact.

28. Their positions remained relatively the same as at

29. the point of impact.

SERIES OF EVENTS

Overline using Code Letters.

Project A-1

1.   The driver did not sleep the night before

2.   the trip, which started early the following

3.   morning.

Project A-2

1.   The driver saw the child run in front of

2.   his car. However, he could not slow down

3.   or stop soon enough because he was too

4.   tired to react quickly.

Project A-3

1. As the driver drove around the corner, the

2. pedestrian was in clear view. The driver did

3. not immediately see the pedestrian, because

4. he was adjusting his car radio dial.

Project A-4

1. The driver was adjusting his radio dial.

2. He looked up and saw the pedestrian in front

3. of his car.

Project A-5

1. The driver swerved to miss the pedestrian.

2. The vehicle traveled 100 feet (30 m) into the

3. opposite lane in the face of oncoming traffic.

Project A-6

1.   The driver applied the brakes. The vehicle

      skidded 300 feet (100 m) to a stop.

Project A-7

1.   As the vehicle skidded in an attempt to

2.   avoid striking a pedestrian, it crossed

3.   over the center line into the lane of on-

4.   coming traffic. It struck an oncoming

5.   vehicle in that lane 3 feet (1 m) from the

6.   center line. Each vehicle embedded

7.   itself in the other vehicle to a depth of

8.   approximately 3 feet (1 m). The vehicles then

9.   rotated, pulled apart, and each then skidded to

10.   its opposite side, coming to rest in the ditch.

Project A-8

1. A heavily-loaded truck was traveling on a

2. highway when a front tire lost air pressure.

3. The driver braked quickly and slowed with the

4. intention of pulling off onto the shoulder.

5. The driver of a car following the truck

6. momentarily looked at a child passenger that

7. was misbehaving and did not notice the truck's

8. brake light and its rapid decrease in speed.

9. The car struck the rear of the truck and

10. stopped in the center of the roadway. The

11. truck continued moving forward and pulled off

12. the roadway and stopped.

Project A-9

1. A truck entered a right-hand curve at an

2. excessive rate of speed. The roadway was

3. wet and slippery. The curve was posted

4. "Curve Ahead, Slippery When Wet, Slow to

5. 30mph (50 km/h)" on the approach side.

6. When the truck entered the actual curve, it

7. began to sideslip toward the outer (left)

8. edge. The driver realized that he was

9. traveling too fast and that the vehicle was

10. going out of control. He applied his brakes

11. as he crossed over the center line. The

12. vehicle went into a straight skid for 300

13. feet (100 m) and skidded into the opposite

14. lane, across the roadway (left side) and

15. into a guard rail. The rail penetrated the

16. vehicle's front end to a depth of approxi-

17. mately 18 inches (46 cm). The truck pulled

18. away from the guard rail and went back out

19. onto the roadway into the left-hand lane

20. in front of an oncoming car. The car struck

21. the left-hand side of the truck at a point

22. near the center of the car's lane. The

23. manner of collision was basically a side-

24. swipe and damage was minor. The car spun

25. around, crossed over the center line to

26. its left-hand side, and stopped in the

27. center of the opposite lane. The truck

28. skidded to a stop in the ditch on its

29. right-hand (original) side.

1. Vehicle 1 was a logging truck which hauled logs

2. from a cutting site on a mountain to a sawmill at

3. the base of the mountain. The truck was driven

4. by Fred MARKS, an experienced motorcycle operator.

5. On a cool winter morning, MARKS left the cutting

6. area with a load. He had complained to the truck's

7. owner the day before that the air-brake system

8. was not functioning properly and that he had

9. difficulty in stopping the truck when it was

10. fully loaded. The owner told MARKS, who had

11. operated an air-equipped vehicle -- that being the

12. logging truck -- for only two days, to adjust the

13. brakes and they would then function properly.

14. MARKS had been at a party the night before, and

15.   had slept for only one hour before reporting for

16.   work. He was very tired and, although he did not

17.   know how to adjust the brakes, he was too tired

18.   to ask anyone how to make the adjustment. He

19.   did not feel the matter was important enough to

20.   worry about. He had never before felt concerned

21.   about such matters. Besides, he had a number

22.   of fingers amputated because of an earlier

23.   accident, and it was extremely difficult for

24.   him to carry out any form of mechanical work.

25.   MARKS started down the mountain highway with

26.   the load of logs.   After traveling for five

27.   miles (8 km), he stopped at a roadside res-

28.   taurant and had breakfast. He then left the

29.   restaurant and proceeded on his trip. About

30.   half-way down the mountain, it started to

31.   rain, causing the roadway to become slippery.

32.   The truck struck a pot-hole, and water and

33.   mud splashed onto the windshield, obstructing

34.   MARK's view. He tried to clear the windshield,

35.   but the windshield wiper broke when he attempted

36.   to turn it on. Because he had stopped for break-

37.   fast, MARKS was behind schedule for the

38.   delivery of his first load. To make up for lost

39.   time, he exceeded the speed limit by at least

40.   20 mph (30 km/h). As the truck approached a

41.   curve, a school bus, Vehicle 2, traveling in

42.   the same direction as MARKS one-half mile (0.8 km)

43.   ahead, stopped to load school children.

44.   The bus driver had the alternating red

45.	flashing lights activated. Vehicle 1 rounded

46.	the corner to a point from which the bus,

47.	500 ft (152 m) distant, could be easily

48.	seen but MARKS, because of the truck's dirty

49.	windshield, did not see the bus until

50.	he was within 150 ft (46 m). Because

51.	of its speed, Vehicle 1 would have required

52.	500 ft (152 m) to stop in time before arriving

53.	at the point where the bus was stopped. In

54.	order to avoid a collision, MARKS steered the

55.	truck to his left into the oncoming lane. The

56.	right-hand side of the truck struck the left

57.	rear corner of the school bus, penetrating the

58.	corner of the bus to a depth of approximately

59.	3 ft (1 m), but did not stop. During the time

60. the truck continued on, MARKS applied the

61. brakes, but this failed to slow the truck.

62. The bus remained stationary. At this time,

63. a car, Vehicle 3, approached from the opposite

64. direction. When the driver of Vehicle 3 was

65. 200 ft (60 m) from Vehicle 1, he saw the

66. truck proceeding directly at him in his car's

67. lane. He pulled his car onto the shoulder to

68. his right and stopped. The truck, out-of-control,

69. veered back to its right and overturned in

70. the ditch on the truck's right. Because of a

71. load shift, the chain bindings broke and the

72. logs were strewn across the highway.

INTRODUCTION

Lesson 3

SUBJECT: The Human Element

Investigators are required to relate the following to traffic accidents:

  a.   the general ability of a person to drive or walk safely,

  b.   human physiological and psychological factors, and

  c.   injuries

and to interview and take statements from drivers, pedestrians and witnesses.

This lesson will familiarize the student with the conditions that would lessen a person's ability to drive or walk safely, with the physiological and psychological factors that are related to driver and pedestrian behavior, with the effects of alcohol and drugs on human behavior, with the relationship of the injury sustained to the type of force/action and object that would have caused that type of injury, and with the knowledge necessary to enable him to interview and take statements in a correct and acceptable manner.

Lesson Contents

This lesson covers the following topics:

  a.   The general ability of a person to drive or walk safely

  b.   Driver and pedestrian characteristics related to traffic accidents

c. Perception and reaction

d. Impaired driving and tests for impairment

e. Interviews and statements

f. Injuries and their causes

g. Nomenclature of the human body

Lesson Objectives

Upon completion of this lesson, the student will be able to state to the satisfaction of the instructor:

1. The most common psychological and physiological factors which are related to unsafe driver and pedestrian behavior

2. The effect that blood-alcohol concentration levels have on a person's ability to drive a motor vehicle safely or to walk safely

3. The various indicators that assist in detecting impaired drivers

4. The most common types of traffic-related injuries and the types of force/action and objects collided with that would cause such injuries

5. The primary considerations in interviewing or taking a statement from a driver, pedestrian or witness

Lesson 3

THE HUMAN ELEMENT

Driver/Pedestrian

C3.001 Consider the ability of a person to control a vehicle on a highway. Observe a driver or pedestrian for any injury not caused by the accident and for any other condition that would lessen a person's ability to drive or walk safely. These conditions include:

a.   Injuries

b.   Fatigue

c.   Impairment by alcohol or drugs

d.   Carbon monoxide poisoning

e.   General health

   i   Vision

   ii   Hearing

   iii   Illnesses

   iv   Disease -- type and extent of any disease suffered by a driver that could adversely affect his ability to drive safely, e.g., advanced arthritis.

103

C3.002 Human factors that bear on the potential for a driver or pedestrian to become involved in an accident include the following:

1. Physical limitations

    Physical limitations seem to account for only a small percentage of accidents since drivers with deficiencies may compensate for their deficiencies by driving more slowly and/or carefully.

2. Handicap

    Look for evidence of handicap that could adversely affect a driver's ability to drive safely.

3. Reaction to external stimuli

    Reaction to external stimuli involves a series of events which are closely related to physical factors.

4. Vision

    Vision is important in perception and identification. Vision also provides the driver with information required for him to understand the relationship between perceived objects and events and enables him to receive traffic control messages.

5. Hearing

    Hearing is extremely important in the understanding of what is occurring in and around the area being driven. Can the driver hear horns sounding, tires squealing or other danger sounds? Are the windows closed so as to lessen the possibility of hearing?

6.   Total Driver Response

Total driver response time (perception, judgment and reaction) increases with the number of choices to be made.

7.   Temporary impairment

Drivers do not usually adjust driving habits to temporary impairments involving or caused by:

a.   Fatigue

b.   Illness and medicine

c.   Alcohol -- a major factor in accidents since its use affects judgment as well as coordination. It is not a stimulant.

d.   Attitude

e.   Knowledge and skill

f.   Judgment

g.   Attentiveness (e.g., *Sunday drivers*)

h.   Long trips

i.   Weather

8.   Heart ailments

Heart ailments of various kinds probably affect driving more than usually thought. Suspect a heart attack when the driver claims to have had a sudden blackout and is unable to explain it.

9.   Epilepsy

Look for signs that follow attacks of epilepsy such as bitten tongue, frothing at the mouth, and extreme weakness in the extremities.

10.   Diabetes

Diabetes is a deficiency of a gland which secretes insulin. Attacks are characterized by excessive thirst, loss of strength, and excessive appetite. Diabetic coma results when the disease is untreated.

11.   Attitudes and emotions

Attitudes and emotions are major factors in human behavior. A driver who has a poor attitude towards his driving responsibilities or a driver who is emotionally upset because of family or financial problems, for example, often exhibits driver behavior which causes traffic accidents.

12.   Personal desires and predispositions

a.   Inertia or velocitation

b.   Driver's reluctance to decelerate

c. Each driver's desire to select his own speed. This produces a spread or dispersion in speeds:

    i   Faster drivers are speed demons.

    ii   Slower drivers are road hogs, slow pokes, etc.

d. Straddling lanes

e. Shying away from obstacles such as bridge abutments and parked vehicles and as a result colliding with another vehicle

f. Impatience resulting in hazardous passing

13. Skills in making the vehicle behave

a. Manipulative skill

This skill can be tested for with driving problems such as parallel parking and starting on a steep grade without rolling back.

b. Recognizing road conditions

c. Sharing the roadway

d. Maintaining attentiveness

14. Natural abilities

Deficient natural abilities -- relatively permanent conditions, not diseases -- can contribute to accidents. A person may have been born with certain physical or mental deficiencies. Deficiencies in general fall into three areas:

a. Sensory conditions

Sensory conditions, especially those affecting sight and hearing, may keep the driver from becoming aware of road or traffic hazards.

b. Mind and nerves

Conditions of the mind and nerves may prevent the driver from understanding hazardous situations and making proper decisions with respect to them.

c. Bone and muscle conditions

Bone and muscle conditions may prevent the driver from operating the controls of a vehicle properly.

15. Knowledge of driving

a. Awareness of the need for care and maintenance of the vehicle

b. Knowledge of the vehicle's behavior under varying road conditions

108

c. Ability to avoid adverse traffic conditions

d. Understanding of traffic control devices and warnings. Is the driver able to read?

e. Practice of defensive driving

C3.003 *Psycho-physical tests* are of little value in identifying individual bad drivers. Tests normally identify differences on a *group basis*.

C3.004 Motor vehicle suicide

a. Very difficult, if not impossible, to prove.

b. Requires extensive background investigation.

c. Investigators tend to overlook and at times intentionally fail to report the probability of suicide in single vehicle accidents.

    i A suicide ruling may deprive a family of insurance benefits.

    ii A suicide ruling is usually an opinion of experts.

d. Medical examiners usually will rule suicide only with actual proof rather than probability.

Pedestrians

C3.005 Pedestrian characteristics are important because of the high incidence of pedestrian injury accidents and because of the difficulty in controlling the actions of pedestrians (no walking licenses).

1. Especially older people and college students sometimes feel that they have the right to cross highways at any location.

2. Many pedestrians do not appreciate driver and vehicle limitations.

3. Pedestrian walking speeds on sidewalks and ramps must be considered.

C3.006 The age of a pedestrian can be a contributing factor in vehicle-pedestrian accidents. As a group, elderly pedestrians are particularly vulnerable to being struck by vehicles because many have impaired ability to hear, see or otherwise sense the presence of vehicular traffic and consequently they fail to perceive a danger. Also, elderly pedestrians with lessened physical capabilities are often unable to react even to a perceived danger quickly enough to avoid being struck.

C3.007 Many accidents involving elderly pedestrians result from overconfidence regarding their own capabilities and particularly those of the driver. For example, during darkness or at other times of limited visibility, the pedestrian may assume that because he is able to see the headlights of an oncoming vehicle, the driver can also see him. Similarly, when stepping out in front of an oncoming vehicle, the pedestrian may assume that the driver has sufficient time to stop.

C3.008 Drunk or drugged pedestrians are another vulnerable group, having generally a slower reaction time, a loss of coordination to a greater or less degree, and, because of dulled sensory functions, a reduced awareness of their surroundings.

C3.009 Check the color of pedestrian clothing. During times of limited visibility, clothing colors may blend in with the surroundings or the shape or color of the roadway.

C3.010 Determine whether the pedestrian carried a flashlight. Examine the surrounding area in case the flashlight could have been thrown by the force of impact.

C3.011 Determine the pedestrian's condition and actions preceding the accident.

    a.   Did the pedestrian look before stepping onto the roadway?

    b.   Had he consumed an alcoholic beverage or taken a legal or illegal drug?

    c.   Was his vision or hearing impaired?

    d.   Was his full attention on what he was doing?

    e.   Was his mind on something else?

    f.   Did he think the driver would see him?

    g.   Did he misjudge the vehicle's speed?

C3.012   What is the pedestrian's attitude in regard to his personal responsibilities in traffic? Does he think that it is entirely the responsibility of the driver to protect him? How well does he understand the problems and limitations of drivers and vehicles?

C3.013 Children, particularly the very young, are frequently the victims of traffic accidents. Because of excitement and general lack of attention, they may run into the path of a moving vehicle. This often occurs in their neighborhoods, where they have a false sense of security. Young children, because of their small size, may not be seen by a driver as readily as taller persons. A child playing in front of a car parked along the street would likely not be seen by a passing driver until such time as he or she darted out onto the roadway in front of the driver.

Reaction and Perception

C3.014 *Perception* is defined as the comprehending of a situation, such as a hazard, by means of the senses and mind. Reaction times of drivers in traffic are quite correctly referred to as *perception-reaction* times, because perception of a situation is usually involved. Inattention or distractions may cause a delay in perception. When there is a known *perception delay*, it should be added to the reaction time. In many instances, *actual perception* immediately follows the point of possible perception and there is no perception delay.

C3.015 *Reaction* is a person's voluntary or involuntary response to a hazard or other situation that has been perceived.

C3.016 *Reaction time* is the length of time from when a person perceives a given situation as being a hazard to when he reacts to his perception. When a person's reaction time is unknown, a reaction time of 1.6 seconds may be used for investigation purposes. This figure accounts also for any unknown perception delay and is therefore a perception-reaction time. (See NOTE following C2.004b for a more thorough discussion of perception-reaction time.)

C3.017 *Reflex Action* is involuntary action caused by a stimulus direct to a nerve or muscle, e.g., drawing away of the hand upon touching a hot stove.

C3.018 *Simple reaction* is response to an expected situation, such as braking when a traffic light turns red.

C3.019 *Simple reaction time* involving an uncomplex response, such as touching the horn, may be as low as 0.25 seconds. The reaction time to apply the brake pedal after a situation requiring braking has been perceived is from 0.50 to 0.70 seconds for most people.

C3.020 *Complex reaction* is reaction involving a decision, such as takes place when the driver has to decide quickly whether to press the accelerator or step on the brake pedal. Reaction time in such instances can be as high as 3.0 seconds or more.

C3.021 *Reaction distance* is the distance traveled during reaction time. To calculate reaction distance, use Formula C3-1:

United States	Metric
$d = S \times 1.466 \times t$	$d = S \times .278 \times t$

where d = distance in feet (meters)

S = speed in mph (km/h)

t = time in seconds

The number 1.466 (.278) is a constant used in converting speed in miles (kilometers) per hour to velocity in feet (meters) per second, and vice versa.

Example

A vehicle was traveling 50 mph (80 km/h). The driver perceived a hazard -- a child running out onto the roadway in front of his car -- and reacted. The driver had a perception-reaction time of 1.6 seconds. The distance the vehicle traveled during his perception-reaction time was:

$$d = S \times 1.466 \times t \qquad\qquad d = S \times .278 \times 1.6$$
$$d = 50 \times 1.466 \times 1.6 \qquad\quad d = 80 \times .278 \times 1.6$$
$$d = 117.28 \text{ ft} \qquad\qquad\quad d = 35.58 \text{ m}$$

Impaired Driving/Driving While Intoxicated (DWI)

C3.022 More than two percent of American drivers actively contribute to the *DWI* problem, which includes drugs as well as alcohol. DWI, sometimes referred to as *DUI* (driving under the influence), is a crime committed by a substantial segment of drivers. It has been and remains a **popular** crime, one that many from all walks and stations of life commit.

C3.023 Driving characteristics that sometimes may be associated with a person who is under the influence of alcohol or drugs are often observable, e.g., recklessly high speed, erratic steering. The investigator arriving at the scene of a crash should attempt to interview witnesses regarding the manner in which the vehicles involved were driven before the crash occurred.

C3.024 There are five major classes of conditions that may impair a person's ability to operate a vehicle.

1.   Carbon monoxide poisoning

2.   Pathological disorders

3.   Alcohol

4.   Drugs

5.   Medical impairment

C3.025 *Carbon monoxide* is an odorless, colorless, gradually poisoning gas. Suicides using this gas are common. Symptoms of carbon monoxide poisoning vary considerably in individuals. Some persons can go almost to the point of collapse without warning signs. In its early stages, carbon-monoxide poisoning has many symptoms in common with alcohol impairment, such as momentary exhilaration; overconfidence; and impaired vision, decision-making and judgment. In later stages, it is usually characterized by dizziness, tremor, headache, weakness, dilated pupils, muscular rigidity, and ultimately unconsciousness or death.

C3.026 A complete and thorough examination should be made of the exhaust system. Carbon monoxide can escape through damaged or corroded parts of an exhaust system and then find its way into the passenger compartment through holes in the underportions of the vehicle body, trunk openings or ill-fitting floor matting and interior upholstery.

C3.027 *Pathological disorders* include brain damage and some diseases of the inner ear. However, these pathological disorders occur in very few people and in even fewer drivers, as persons suffering from these disorders are rarely able to drive.

C3.028 *Alcohol* is a depressant and acts as an anesthetic or sedative. When consumed in any quantity, it affects an individual's vision, judgment and motor skills. Crashes involving driver alcohol use are about nine times more likely to result in death than crashes not involving driver alcohol use.

C3.029 *Drugs* affect the body in predictable ways with different categories of drugs affecting the body differently. As you conduct your investigation, you may see signs and symptoms indicating that a driver is under the influence of drugs rather than alcohol.

C3.030 It is likely that the experienced investigator will have encountered drivers under the influence of drugs rather than alcohol. Depending upon the specific type(s) of drug(s) used, some of these drivers may have appeared similar to persons under the influence of alcohol. Others will have looked and behaved differently from alcohol-impaired drivers.

C3.031 *Medical Impairment.* It is essential for the investigator to be able to recognize medical impairment. Medical impairment may be misinterpreted as alcohol and/or drug intoxication. Some impaired conditions are:

a. Impairment of normal respiration resulting in ears and lips becoming bluish in color and resulting in a very pale face.

b. Lack of muscle coordination caused by lead poisoning, carbon monoxide poisoning or head injury.

c. Lack of bodily control caused by an epileptic seizure.

d. Traumatic injury to the brain as a result of an accident or a fall.

e. Diabetic overdose of insulin or a requirement for insulin.

f. Flushed face caused by arteriosclerosis (hardening of the arteries), diabetes, emotions (blushing), or poisoning such as from carbon monoxide.

g. Speech impairment caused by mouth injuries or disease, loss of teeth, facial paralysis or mental deficiencies.

h. Drowsiness caused by carbon monoxide poisoning, head injury resulting from an accident, overdose of insulin or lack of sleep.

i. Loss of memory caused by epilepsy or head injury.

j. Eye disorder caused by glaucoma, hay fever and other allergies, concussion or fright.

k. Dizziness caused by head injury, Meniere's disease (congestion of the inner ear), or motion sickness.

When medical impairment is suspected, the investigator should refer the person to an appropriate medical facility for care.

C3.032 Face-to-face observation and interview of the driver allows you to use three senses to gather evidence of alcohol or drug influence:

1. Sight
2. Hearing
3. Smell

C3.033 *Sight.* There are a number of things you might see during the interview that would be describable clues or evidence of alcohol or drug influence. Among them are:

    a. Bloodshot eyes
    b. Soiled clothing
    c. Fumbling fingers
    d. Alcoholic beverage containers
    e. Drugs or drug paraphernalia
    f. Bruises, bumps or scratches
    g. Unusual actions

C3.034 *Hearing.* Among the things you might hear during the interview that would be describable clues or evidence of alcohol or drug influence are these:

    a. Slurred speech
    b. Admission of drinking
    c. Inconsistent responses
    d. Abusive language
    e. Unusual statements

C3.035 *Smell.* There are things you might smell during the interview that would be describable clues or evidence of alcohol or drug influence. Typically these include:

    a.   Alcoholic beverages

    b.   Marijuana

    c.   Cover-up odors like breath sprays

    d.   Unusual odors

C3.036 *Required Abilities.* Proper face-to-face observation and interview of the driver demands two distinct but related abilities:

1.   The ability to recognize the sensory evidence of alcohol or drug influence

2.   The ability to describe that evidence clearly and convincingly

Developing these abilities requires practice.

C3.037 The well-trained investigator will be able to temporarily remove an alcohol- or drug-impaired driver from our highways by using proper examining techniques and exercising good judgment in forming an opinion as to a driver's condition. The investigator should take the following into account:

1.   The relevant conditions on the *Psychophysical Observations Checklist* at the end of the Impaired Driving section

2.   Performance on the Standardized Field Sobriety Tests (divided attention tests)

   a.   Horizontal gaze nystagmus
   b.   Walk and turn
   c.   One leg stand

Major source for the Impaired Driving section: U.S. Department of Transportation, National Highway Traffic Safety Administration, *DWI Detection and Standard & Field Sobriety Testing*, Washington, D.C., 1992.

PSYCHOPHYSICAL OBSERVATIONS CHECKSHEET

SUSPECT'S BREATH
_____Odor of alcohol
_____Chemical odor
_____Cannabis odor

OBSERVATION OF FACE
_____Normal
_____Flushed
_____Pale
_____Other (describe)

GENERAL APPEARANCE
_____Clean
_____Orderly
_____Disarranged
_____Bloody
_____Vomit
_____Urine

EYES
_____Normal
_____Watery
_____Bloodshot
_____Pink/Red

ATTITUDE
_____Anxious
_____Restless
_____Agitated
_____Excited
_____Combative
_____Disinterested
_____Uninhibited
_____Disoriented
_____Drowsy
_____Confused
_____Hallucinating
_____Loss of memory
_____Cyclic mood swings
_____Polite
_____Antagonistic
_____Stuporous
_____Cooperative/indifferent
_____Laughing
_____Insulting
_____Argumentative
_____Fumbling

SPEECH
_____Talkative
_____Thick, slurred
_____Incoherent
_____Rapid
_____Slow
_____Non-communicative
_____Repetitive

PHYSICAL ACTIONS
_____Facial itching
_____Dry mouth
_____Nodding
_____Droopy eyelids
_____Low, raspy voice
_____Body tremors
_____Muscle tone - rigid
_____Muscle tone - flaccid
_____Muscle tone - normal
_____Grinding of teeth

OTHER
_____Nasal redness
_____Runny nose
_____Track marks
_____Perspiring
_____Warm to touch
_____Intense headaches
_____Residue of paint on
      person
_____Debris
_____Pills
_____Vials
_____Syringes
_____Drug paraphernalia

C3.038 These Standardized Field Sobriety Tests (SFST's) provide the investigator with a means to evaluate a driver for neuromuscular coordination, equilibrium and mental awareness. When a test is performed, the investigator should determine if the driver performs the test as instructed.

C3.039 **The investigator must always be aware of the driver's safety when conducting a check for impaired driving and be in compliance with NHTSA's approved Standardized Field Sobriety and Testing procedures.**

Interviews and Statements

C3.040 In serious accidents, such as those involving serious personal injury or death, interviews should be conducted and statements taken as soon as possible. Sometimes these duties have to be carried out after the at-scene investigation is completed.

C3.041 When trying to detect drivers and witnesses, remember that:

a. Drivers may be seen writing down information from a witness or another driver or be found standing near their damaged vehicles.

b. Witnesses may be heard or seen describing to others how the accident happened.

c. Drivers and witnesses may come forward and volunteer information or stand by when the investigator is questioning other drivers or witnesses.

d. It may be necessary to question persons at the scene as to whether they are drivers, witnesses or just passersby.

C3.042 Bear in mind that passengers and friends or relatives of a driver may give biased, or slanted, information. Some witnesses may provide information to confirm their own interpretation of how the accident occurred, and this information may not be factual.

C3.043 The investigator must be objective, understanding and tactful. He must exhibit a professional attitude and demeanor. He should:

a. Ensure that an individual is in proper condition, both physically and mentally, to be interviewed, i.e., not suffering from serious physical injury, shock or emotional disturbance to the extent that he may not comprehend what is expected of him.

b. Interview each driver separately, giving him or her an opportunity to express without interruption his or her own version of how the accident occurred.

c. Consider bringing the drivers together to compare their stories when the drivers' views do not agree. Each driver should then be requested to repeat in the presence of the other driver(s) his or her version of how the accident occurred so that conflicting areas can be clarified. When the drivers' stories agree and when the investigator is satisfied he knows how the accident occurred, he should bring the drivers together and tell them his version of the accident. He might also invite clarification on certain points at this time if he feels it is necessary.

d. Relate the drivers' versions of how the accident occurred to the physical evidence and other evidence that is available.

e. Have witnesses describe where they were and what they were doing at the time of the accident.

f. Give at the appropriate time an appropriate warning or caution -- in compliance with the requirements of local legislation, procedures and policies -- to individuals being interviewed.

C3.044 Interviews and statements should support, not replace, a thorough investigation for facts and physical evidence.

Driver, Passenger and Witness Information to Be Obtained

Driver

a. Full name and address
b. Birth date
c. Telephone number
d. Driver's license number
e. Driver's license restrictions, if any
f. Compliance with driver's license restrictions, e.g., eyeglasses, hearing aid, etc.

g. General health

h. Occupation

Passenger

a. Full name and address

b. Birth date or apparent age

c. Telephone number

d. Occupation

e. Seated position

Witness

a. Full name and address

b. Birth date or apparent age

c. Telephone number

d. Occupation

e. General health (particularly hearing and eyesight when these are factors)

Injuries

C3.045 In many traffic accidents, the impact is from the sides or front. When such impact occurs, the driver and passenger(s) may be forced from their seated positions. They often strike various parts of the vehicle's interior or are ejected from the vehicle and are injured, particularly if they are not wearing their seat belts.

C3.046   Drivers, passengers, and pedestrians who are involved in serious personal-injury accidents often are unable to recall many of the details of the actual collision and of the post-collision events.   Therefore, it is important for reconstruction purposes that the investigator be able to:

a.   Identify those who suffered injuries.

b.   Describe the nature and extent of driver and passenger injuries.

c.   Determine and describe how the injuries were received, e.g.,

i   Chest contusion, as from the chest being propelled into the steering wheel or dashboard

ii   Head contact with the windshield

iii   Injured ribs caused by the passenger or driver striking objects in the vehicle interior

iv   Legs, knees forced into the dashboard

d.   Describe the nature of pedestrian injuries and the means by which those injuries were received, e.g., legs were injured when struck by the car bumper; head and chest were injured when struck by the car hood or windshield.

C3.047 Investigators must complete reports and be able to relate injuries to the vehicle parts that caused them. In order to accomplish this, they must be knowledgeable regarding the human skeleton and soft body tissues and be able to identify vehicle body parts that can cause injuries to the human body.

C3.048 Relating the type and location of injury to the vehicle part that caused the injury will often help to establish the seating positions of vehicle occupants.

C3.049 The subsequent pages present:

    a.   The Human Skeleton Diagram

    b.   Injury Descriptions Table

    c.   Vehicle Interior Diagram

    d.   Occupant Contact Chart

    e.   Occupant Ejection Chart

    f.   Soft Tissue and Skeletal Injuries Diagrams

Following these are Projects A-1, A-2, and A-3.

The Human Skeleton

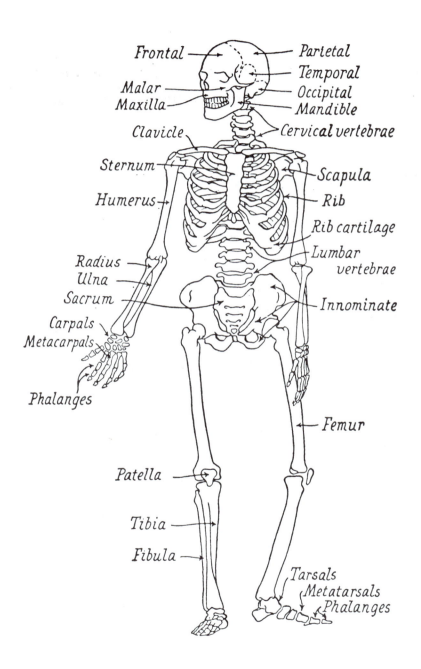

Frontal — Parietal — Temporal — Malar — Occipital — Maxilla — Mandible — Clavicle — Cervical vertebrae — Sternum — Scapula — Humerus — Rib — Rib cartilage — Radius — Lumbar vertebrae — Ulna — Sacrum — Innominate — Carpals — Metacarpals — Phalanges — Femur — Patella — Tibia — Fibula — Tarsals — Metatarsals — Phalanges

*Injury Descriptions

Body Region

Head - skull

Head or neck

Face

Neck - cervical spine

Shoulder

Upper limbs (whole or
   known part)

Arm (upper)

Elbow

Forearm

Wrist - hand

Chest

Abdomen

Back - thoracolumbar spine

Pelvic - hip

Lower limb(s) (whole or known part)

Thigh

Knee

Leg (lower)

Ankle - foot

Aspect of Injury

Right

Left

Bilateral

Central

Anterior (front)

Posterior (back)

Superior (upper)

Inferior (lower)

System/Organ

Teeth

Brain

Spinal cord

Ears

Nose

Lungs

Eyes

Arteries, veins

Heart

Spleen

Trachea

Skin (name region)

* Source: Transport Canada, Road and Motor Vehicle Traffic Safety

Lesion

Laceration	Amputation
Contusion	Burn
Abrasion	Fracture and dislocation
Fracture	Total severance, transection
Concussion	Strain
Avulsion	Detachment, separation
Rupture	Perforation, puncture
Strain	Crushing
Dislocation	

Injury Scale

Minor injury	Serious injury
Moderate injury	Critical injury
Severe injury	

Injury Sources - Exterior of Striking Motor Vehicle

Bumper	Hood edge
Windshield	Hood
Header rail	Hood ornament
A-pillar	Side surface
Side mirror	Other side protrusions
Undercarriage	Specify_____

Other Contacts

Ground	Other sources (Specify)
Other vehicle	_____
Other object	_____

Vehicle Interior

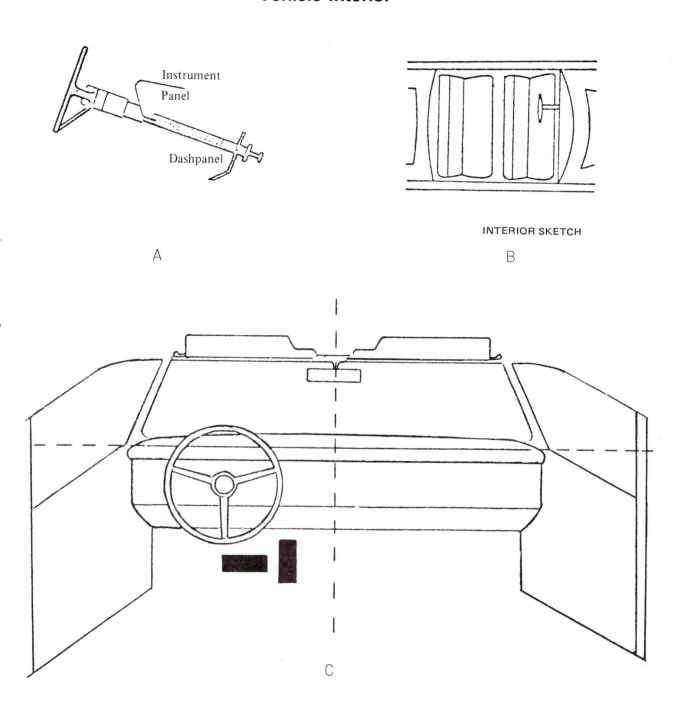

A

B

INTERIOR SKETCH

C

Sketch all occupant contact points. Dash lines indicate center
of instrument panel-windshield area for measurement purposes.

Source: Transport Canada, Road and Motor Vehicle Traffic Safety

Indications of Occupant Contact

Note indications or suspicions of occupant contact.

○ NO INJURY

FRONT

- ○ - Windshield
- ○ - Mirror
- ○ - Steering Assembly (Including transmission selector lever when column mounted)
- ○ Add - on Equipment (e.g. C.B., tape deck, etc)
- ○ Instrument Panel (Excluding foot control, parking brake, and hood release)

SIDE

- ○ - Side Interior Surface (Excluding hardware or armrests)
- ○ - Side Hardware or Armrests
- ○ - Roof Pillar Supports
- ○ - Window Glass or Frame
- ○ - Other Side Object (Specify)

INTERIOR

- ○ - Seat, Back Support
- ○ - Belt Restraint System
- ○ - Head Restraint
- ○ - Air Cushion
- ○ - Other Occupants
- ○ - Interior Loose Objects
- ○ - Other Interior Object (Specify)

ROOF

- ○ - Front Header
- ○ - Rear Header
- ○ - Roof Side Rails
- ○ - Roof or Convertible Top
- ○ - Other Roof Object (Specify)

FLOOR

- ○ - Floor
- ○ - Floor or Console Mounted Transmission Lever, Including Console
- ○ - Parking Brake Handle
- ○ - Foot Controls Including Parking Brake
- ○ - Hood Release

REAR

- ○ - Backlight (Rear window)
- ○ - Backlight Storage Rack, Door, Etc.
- ○ - Other Rear Object (Specify)

EXTERIOR THIS VEHICLE

- ○ - Hood
- ○ - Outside Hardware (e.g. mirrors, antenna, etc.)
- ○ - Other Exterior Surface or Tires (Specify)
- ○ - Unknown Exterior Objects

NON - CONTACT INJURY

- ○ - Non - Contact Injury Source (Impact force)
- ○ - Injured, Unknown Source
- ○ - Unknown if Injured

Comments:

Source: Transport Canada, Road and Motor Vehicle Traffic Safety

132

Indications of Ejection

Note indications or suspicions of occupant ejection.

◯ NO EJECTION

EJECTION APERTURE

◯ - Door

◯ - Windshield

◯ - Roof

◯ - Window

◯ - Floor

EJECTION REGION

◯ - Front

◯ - Left

◯ - Right

◯ - Cent

◯ - Rear

EJECTION APERTURE STATUS
(At time of accident)

◯ - Closed

◯ - Open

◯ - Partially Open

◯ - Separation

Comments:

Source: Transport Canada, Road and Motor Vehicle Traffic Safety

133

Soft Tissue and Skeletal Injuries

Indicate the nature and location of all injuries.

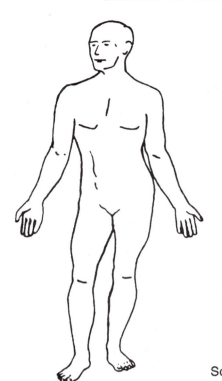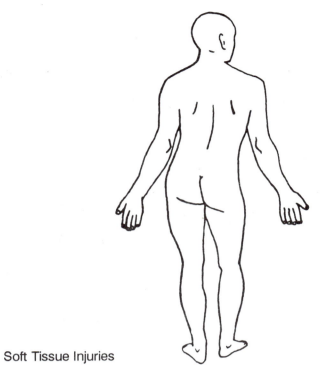

Soft Tissue Injuries

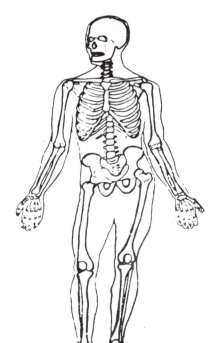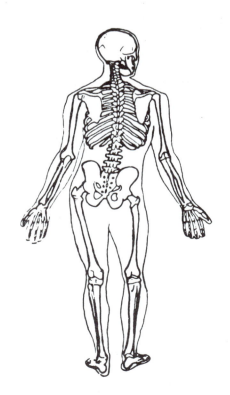

Skeletal Injuries

Lesson 3
THE HUMAN ELEMENT

PROJECT A-1

See Figure C3-A-1-1.

Complete the name for each letter designation. The first one has been done for you.

U   Ribs_____   E _____

D^1 _____   R _____

D^2 _____   C _____

J _____   M _____

A _____   H _____

P _____   S _____

F _____   G _____

K _____   O _____

B _____   Q _____

L _____   I _____

T _____

135

Project A-1, cont'd

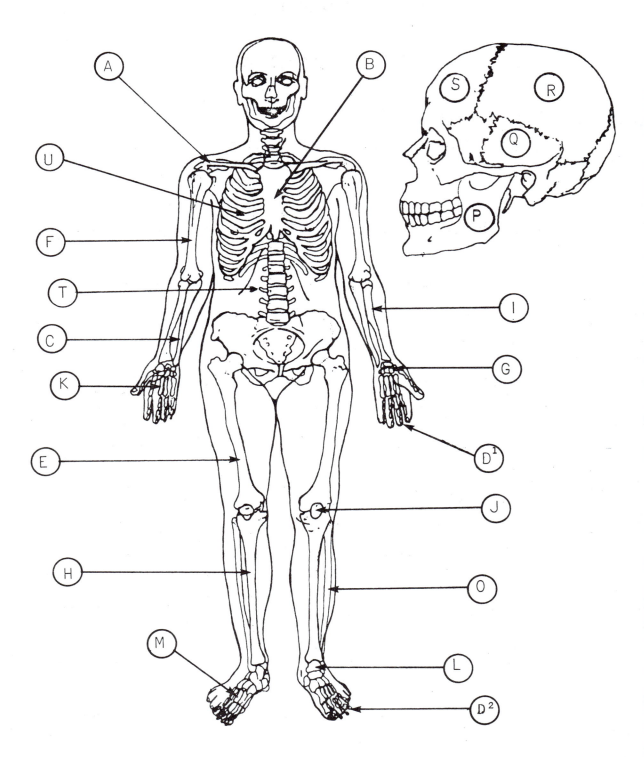

Figure C3-A-1-1

Lesson 3
THE HUMAN ELEMENT
Project A-2

a.   Review Lesson 2 -- Series of Events.

b.   See Figure C3-A-2-1.

Vehicle 1 was traveling north on A Street and was approaching a side street called General Laneway. The speed limit was 40 mph (65 km/h). The driver was traveling at the speed limit. Both he and his only passenger, who was seated in the front seat, were wearing seat belts.

At General Laneway, Driver 1 could have seen Vehicle 2 approaching from his right on 1st Avenue. However, because of the distraction caused by a child riding a bicycle erratically on the sidewalk near the south-west corner of the intersection (on his left), he did not notice Vehicle 2's approach.

At a sign stating *Intersection Ahead*, which was 300 feet (91 meters) from Vehicle 2's line of travel through the intersection, Driver 1 became aware of Vehicle 2 and of the fact that Driver 2 had apparently not seen him either and was not going to stop. Driver 1 also realized that the only evasive action he could take would be to apply his brakes, which he did at the mail box, intending to bring his vehicle to a full stop before the intersection.

Vehicle 1 skidded 80 feet (24 meters) in a straight line. Vehicle 2 traveled in a straight line, crossing Vehicle 1's line of travel.

137

Project A-2, cont'd

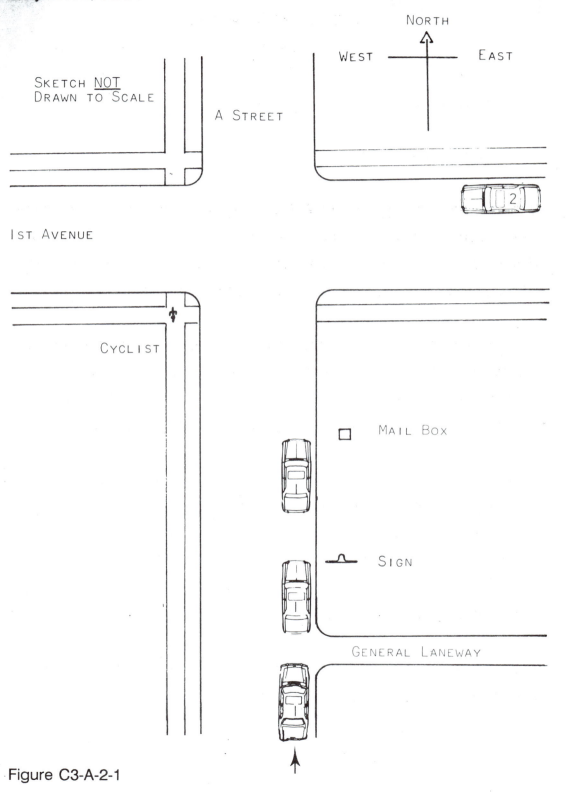

SKETCH <u>NOT</u> DRAWN TO SCALE

A STREET

NORTH

WEST — EAST

1ST AVENUE

CYCLIST

MAIL BOX

SIGN

GENERAL LANEWAY

Figure C3-A-2-1

Project A-2, cont'd

1. Where was the Point of Possible Perception?

   _____

   _____

2. Where was the Point of Actual Perception?

   _____

   _____

3. There was a perception delay.

   True ___   False ___

4. His was a (circle the correct answer):

   a. Simple reaction

   b. Complex reaction

5. With the information given, Driver 1 could be considered to have a reaction time of:

   a. 0.22 seconds

   b. 0.70 seconds

   c. 3 seconds

   d. 1.6 seconds

   e. 0.55 seconds

Project A-2, cont'd

6.   What was the distance from the sign to the mail box?

    _____ feet   or   _____ meters

7.   There was a collision between Vehicles 1 and 2.

                    True ____   False ____

8.   The passenger advised the investigator that as the result of this
     incident he suffered severe injury to his ribs (right side) -- the type
     injury most often suffered from a side impact. The truthfulness of the
     reported injury is borne out by the circumstances of the case.

                    True ____   False ____

9.   The child's presence needn't be considered in the investigation.

                    True ____   False ____

10. Driver 1 probably did not violate any law.

                    True ____   False ____

Lesson 3
THE HUMAN ELEMENT
Project A-3

See Figure C3-A-3-I

Vehicle 1 was traveling west on Main Highway at the speed limit of 55 mph (90 km/h). There were two passengers sitting in the front seat beside the driver. None of the occupants was wearing a seat belt.

The vehicle veered to its right and struck the left rear corner of a parked car (Vehicle 2). Vehicle 1 rotated clockwise and came to rest against the curb and facing the opposite direction.

While Vehicle 1 was rotating, one passenger fell out of the vehicle onto the roadway.

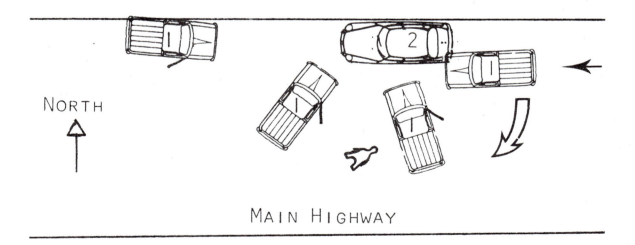

NORTH

MAIN HIGHWAY

Figure C3-A-3-1

When the investigator arrived, all vehicle occupants were sitting on the curb.

The investigator noticed or learned of the following injuries:

Occupant 1

Lacerated forehead

Occupant 2

Injured knees and complaint of sore chest

Occupant 3

Abrasions and bruises on all exposed parts of body; torn clothing; and skin torn away from left shoulder

An examination of Vehicle 1 revealed that the right front door had been sprung open. There was an indication of interior contact with the middle or center area of the windshield, and a piece of flesh was found on the right-front door latch.

All three vehicle occupants were brothers. Only Occupant 3 held a driver's license. All occupants said that Occupant 3 had been driving the vehicle at the time of the collision.

Using the limited information available, show the seated positions of Occupants 1, 2 and 3 on Figure C3-A-3-2.

Project A-3, cont'd

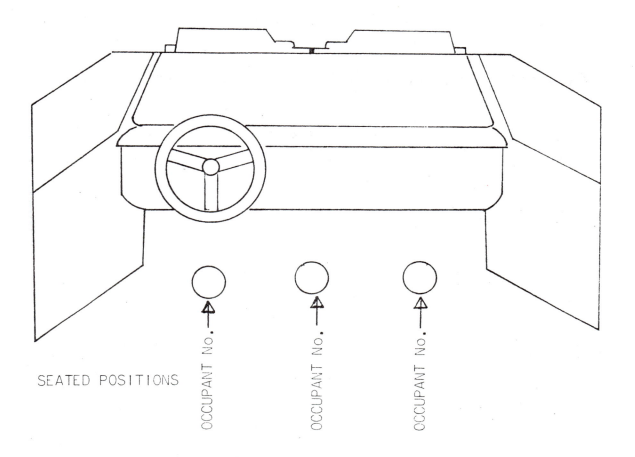

Figure C3-A-3-2

INTRODUCTION

Lesson 4

SUBJECT: Environmental and Trafficway Factors

Traffic accident investigators determine weather and trafficway conditions and their effects on traffic accidents and locate, identify and interpret marks, damage and other evidence found on the roadway and other parts of the trafficway.

This lesson will familiarize the student with the various environmental and traffic engineering factors involved in traffic accident investigations. The student will learn what kinds of evidence to look for during an at-scene investigation, how to recognize and interpret evidence found at the scene or obtained elsewhere, and how environmental and trafficway factors affect drivers and pedestrians who are either directly or indirectly involved in a traffic accident.

Lesson Contents

This lesson covers the following topics:

    a.   Environmental and trafficway factors, including

           i   Physical elements of the roadway

           ii   Informational factors

           iii   Special informational factors

b.   At-scene evidence

c.   Traffic and highway engineering

d.   Factors considered in traffic and design

e.   Roadway

f.   Obstructions

g.   Weather and light

h.   Glare

i.   Trafficway marks and damage

j.   Damage to fixed objects

k.   Roadway marks and damage, including

   i   Chips and gouges
   ii   Grooves
   iii   Holes
   iv   Scrapes
   v   Scratches

l.   Debris

m. Tire marks, including

    i   Tire prints

    ii   Acceleration marks

    iii   Striation marks

    iv   Underinflated tire marks

    v   Overinflated tire marks

    vi   Ruts

    vii   Trenches and furrows

    viii Skid marks

    ix   Scuff marks

    x   Scrub marks

n. Yaw or sideslip marks

o. Environmental Investigation Guide

p. Regulatory and warning signs

Lesson Objectives

Upon completion of this lesson, the student will be able to do the following to the satisfaction of the instructor:

1. State the trafficway conditions and characteristics that affect the safe operation of a motor vehicle and/or the safe passage of a pedestrian.

2. State the weather or atmospheric conditions that affect the safe operation of a motor vehicle and/or the safe passage of a pedestrian.

3. Discover, recognize, identify and interpret the various kinds of trafficway marks and damage found at an accident scene and state how each was caused.

4. Discover, recognize, identify and interpret the various types of debris found at an accident scene and state the source of each type.

Lesson 4

ENVIRONMENTAL AND TRAFFICWAY FACTORS

Environmental Factors

C4.001 Environmental factors contribute to highway safety in several important regards. Safe transportation requires, in addition to a properly functioning vehicle and operator, an accommodating roadway which permits the driver-vehicle combination to traverse it without incident. This demands that the environment provide not only a roadway surface compatible with the driver-vehicle combination, but also the information needed by the operator to maintain himself on his desired path. In this view, the environment consists of:

a. The *physical elements* of the roadway itself and all other physical entities on the roadway and the roadside which affect the safety of movement of the vehicle.

b. The *informational factors* which provide the vehicle operator the information about his location on the road and the instructions for his continued travel.

c. A *special set of informational factors* concerned with traffic control.

C4.002 Ideal characteristics and *non-ideal characteristics* of the trafficway are both of interest, e.g., a dry roadway surface as opposed to a wet, snow-covered or oily surface; delineation markers by night or in fog as

148

opposed to delineation markers only by day and with unrestricted visibility; a roadway with as opposed to without artificial illumination. Such features influence highway safety, i.e., facilitate or hinder, as the case may be, travel uninterrupted by events causing damage, injury or death.

The Roadway Factor

C4.003 The features of the roadway believed to be important are:

       a.   Surface properties

       b.   Surface materials

       c.   Surface condition

       d.   Surface construction

       e.   Topological features

            i   curvature
            ii   gradient
            iii   alignment and width
            iv   obstructions, including vehicles, pedestrians, litter and animals
            v   surface defects, e.g., bumps and potholes

C4.004 Roadways intended for vehicle travel are frequently constructed so as to constrain the vehicle to the roadway, e.g., with guard rails, and to prevent it from accidentally straying beyond the roadway edges, either into the off-highway roadside or across the line separating the opposing flows of traffic. In addition to these purposeful roadside features, there are other objects on the roadside edges, some of which are intended to aid traffic, such as light poles and sign posts, and some which are not so intended, such as trees. However, all roadside features may become factors contributing to an accident event and its severity.

Informational Factors

C4.005 To maintain the vehicle in its intended path, the driver requires information that permits him to perceive the intended path. He must have an unobstructed view of the roadway far enough ahead to permit him to maneuver his vehicle within the limits of his motor response capabilities and his vehicle's turning and handling capabilities.

C4.006 The alignment of the road and the roadway and roadside structures must not block the motorist's view of the roadway to which his present movement commits him. To see this roadway, there must be adequate illumination, natural or artificial. On the other hand, the glare of sunlight, the headlights of other vehicles and other extraneous illumination sources must not interfere. We place the separate factors of physical obstruction of view, inadequate illumination and interference with illumination all under the heading of visibility factors affecting highway safety.

Operational Traffic Control Factors

C4.007 Street signs and other devices for the control and regulation of speeds and other traffic flow characteristics constitute a class of factors affecting highway safety. Inadequacies in the control system can even create hazards which might not exist if the control system were absent.

Traffic control is exercised essentially through:

1. Control of speed (maximum and minimum)

2. Control of direction (one-way streets and ramps; turns)

3. Limitations on vehicle types (exclusion of trucks, motorcycles, etc.)

4. Right-of-way specifications (stop-signs, lights, etc.)

C4.008 Each of the foregoing forms of traffic control is intended to expedite the flow of traffic with minimum hazard to that traffic. Traffic control becomes of concern to safety in two situations:

1. In cases of poor design of the control systems, such as improperly set speed limits, poorly placed signs or signals, and

2. In cases of failure to conform to regulation, such as driving below or beyond the posted speed limit or traveling the wrong way on one-way roads and ramps.

At-Scene Evidence

C4.009 The at-scene investigator should examine the scene for the adequacy of highway signs and traffic signals, road conditions, engineering deficiencies, view obstructions, etc. The surrounding area should also be

151

checked for such structures as billboards. The weather conditions prevalent at the time of the accident should be noted.

C4.010 The roadway and roadside generally leave some form of physical signs or evidence of what happened. It is very important that these signs be recognized and correctly interpreted. For example, evidence of yaw marks, skid marks, or damage suffered by or found on vehicles and highways may establish a vehicle's (or pedestrian's) direction of travel, place, position and behavior during pre-collision and post-collision times.

C4.011 Although extremely important and helpful, physical evidence at the scene can rarely explain all that happened. However, it can often supplement as well as prove or disprove statements of drivers and witnesses as well as prove or disprove theories of what happened. Also, it quite often can indicate the direction that further investigation should take.

C4.012 Physical evidence, or the lack of it, is perhaps the most important part of accident-investigation evidence gathering. Properly preserved, documented and interpreted physical evidence will make the difference between positive knowledge and guesses, fact and fantasy, or proof of and speculation about the accident *series of events*. It is the responsibility of the investigator to locate, document (he should not rely on memory), provide, interpret and use all available evidence to the best of his ability. Properly gathered and preserved evidence can be used later by a specialist to reconstruct the accident.

Traffic and Highway Engineering

C4.013 The at-scene investigator must be particularly careful to examine the trafficway for all forms of evidence. The roadway, shoulders and adjacent areas should be examined for:

a. Roadway alignment

b. Inadequate or improper roadway design

c. Adequacy of advance warning signs or signals

d. Maintenance of traffic control devices, such as restoration of obliterated wording and repair of non-functioning signals

e. Placement of traffic control devices

f. Signs, vegetation, parked vehicles, etc., in locations that obstruct the clear view of traffic control devices

g. Location, visibility, maintenance and adequacy of roadway surface markings such as shoulder and lane markings, center lines and stop lines

h. Position, height and distance from the roadway of traffic-control devices

i. View obstructions

j. Shadows cast by buildings, overhead wires, etc., that might obscure or impair a driver's view of a pedestrian or other object

k. Highway defects or obstructions

l. Inadequate street lighting

m. Glare from fixed lights

n. Roadway conditions

C4.014 Traffic engineering and geometric design must also be considered when relating human limitations and behavior to traffic accidents.

1. Traffic engineering improvements should improve driver and pedestrian behavior in respect to the following:

 a. Speed reduction where warranted (by means of signs)

 b. Lateral placement (ability to get into the proper lane and to pass safely)

 c. Routing

 d. Movement at points of conflict, e.g., merging, yielding right-of-way, stopping

 e. Paying attention (degree of alertness)

2.   Driver limitation factors

   a.   *Complexity of driving*, including

      i   Operating vehicle, steering, accelerating, braking, keeping in line, etc.

      ii   Watching traffic

      iii   Seeing and comprehending traffic control devices

      iv   Distractions such as signs, lights, persons on sidewalks and in cars or shops, etc.

      v   Keeping on route

   b.   *Type of driver*
      Young or old, man or woman, experienced or inexperienced, commuter, shopper, physically impaired, etc.

   c.   *Driver willingness to comply with regulations*
      Drivers and pedestrians often do not do what is lawfully required unless it appears reasonable and easy to do.

Factors in Traffic Engineering and Highway Design

C4.015 The investigator is in a position to make recommendations to the proper authorities in respect to what he believes to be deficiencies in the highway system.   In order to make reasonable recommendations, the investigator should have some knowledge of the factors considered in traffic engineering. These include:

a. *Time factors*

Time factors are used in:

   i   Computing *sight distances* for passing and stopping

   ii Computing sight distances at intersections

   iii Computing *warning distances*

b. *Visibility*

Visibility data is useful in reflectorization, sign legibility and sign design, illumination, pavement brightness and headlighting.

c. *Stubbornness*

Human stubbornness must be considered in all traffic engineering.

d. *Human limitations*

Human limitations should be considered in design:

   i   Physical elimination of unnecessary conflicts

   ii Better design of curves, grades, lane width

   iii Reduction in the effect of grades

   iv Adequate stopping sight distances

v   Frequent opportunities for passing

vi   Elimination of distractions

vii   Channelizing and other design practices to reduce to only one or two the number of choices confronting a driver at one time

e.   *Traffic controls*

Traffic controls should simplify the problems of driving by providing warnings, directions, and notices of regulations in a uniform manner, and should do so sufficiently in advance and with repeat warnings where necessary. They should cut the complexity of decisions.

Roadway

C4.016   The roadway surface conditions must always be examined. Slipperiness, for example, is one of the most common surface conditions which contribute to accidents. Determine if:

a.   Slipperiness contributed to the accident.

b.   Slipperiness prevented evasive action.

c.   Slipperiness contributed to the extent or seriousness of the accident.

C4.017 Conditions that make a roadway surface slippery include:

    a.   Moisture--especially when mud or traffic film is present

    b.   Ice or snow

    c.   Oil or grease

    d.   Soft asphalt or tar joints, especially during hot weather

C4.018 When examining the roadway, it must be remembered that many factors may cause a driver to lose control of the vehicle. These include:

    a.   A change in the alignment of a straight and level road

    b.   Superelevation or bank

    c.   Sudden narrowing of the roadway

    d.   Off-sets

    e.   Dead ends

    f.   Lack of signs to warn of danger or changes

    g.   Traffic signal malfunction, misplacement, non-visibility, etc.

    h.   Pavement markings

    i.   Control devices of varying types

    j.   Holes, ruts or large grooves in the roadway (see Fig. C4-1)

    k.   Curbs, lip at the edge of the pavement (see Fig. C4-2)

    l.   Soft shoulders

    m.   Misplaced traffic-control signs (see Fig. C4-3)

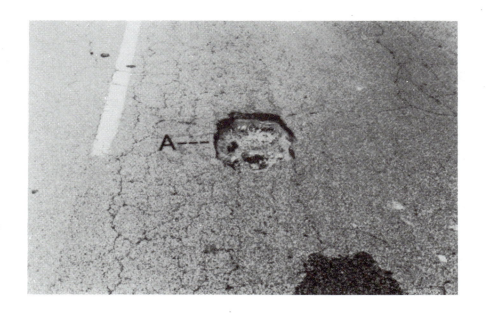

Figure C4-1 Roadway defects such as the hole shown at **A** can cause the driver of a vehicle to lose control. (Photo by IPTM, 1994)

Figure C4-2 When a wheel drops off a pavement edge, the driver may be unable to steer the vehicle back onto the roadway normally; if he over-steers, the vehicle may veer across the road out of control. (Photo by IPTM, 1994)

Obstructions

C4.019 Various types of obstructions can keep a driver from seeing another traffic unit, a control device or a hazard. The investigator should obtain evidence to confirm or disprove a driver's statement that his view was obstructed.

C4.020 Do not confuse view obstructions with reduced visibility. In reduced visibility, the object gradually becomes visible as it looms up in the distance.

C4.021 View obstructions in or on the roadway include:

a. A parked vehicle hiding a pedestrian who steps out in front of a moving vehicle. The parked vehicle is a view obstruction to both the driver and the pedestrian.

b. A vehicle which is stopped or slowing at an intersection and which hides traffic on a cross street. Large vehicles, especially, fall into this category.

c. A pedestrian screening a taillight from view.

d. Disabled vehicles on the roadway.

C4.022 Horizontal view obstructions include:

a. Embankments, hedges, trees, crops, weeds (see Fig. C4-4)
b. Buildings
c. Billboards, signs, etc.

160

Figure C4-3 Improperly placed traffic-control signs can affect a driver's ability to safely approach or enter an intersection. (Photo by IPTM, 1994)

Figure C4-4 Vegetation may partially or totally block traffic-control signs. (Photo by IPTM, 1994)

C4.023 Partial view obstructions include:

a. Crests of hills
b. Bridges
c. Hollows in the roadway

C4.024 Vertical view obstructions as well as horizontal view obstructions can affect drivers but can sometimes be at least partially overcome.

a. Due to the illumination of headlights during darkness, a driver may be able to detect the approach of a vehicle before it crests an intervening hill, lessening the danger posed.

b. The size of vehicle and a driver's seated position have an effect. In large vehicles, such as trucks, the driver may be able to see over and beyond a view obstruction.

Weather and Light

C4.025 Adverse weather and darkness reduce visibility by lessening the distance at which a driver can see objects. Factors to be considered are:

a. Lack of lights
b. Pedestrians in dark clothing
c. Overdriving headlights

C4.026 Accidents involving either adverse weather or darkness result from driving too fast for conditions. Factors to be considered are:

162

a. Fog and smoke

b. Rain and snow

c. Combinations of these, plus darkness

Glare

C4.027 *Glare* is a factor in many traffic accidents. It may go undetected because it may be gone when the investigator arrives. Drivers often fail to mention glare as a factor. It is therefore important for the investigator to view the accident scene as quickly as possible. If there is any delay, attempts should be made to return on another day which has the same weather and light conditions and view the scene for any indication of glare.

C4.028 There are three kinds of glare which are of particular importance in accident investigation:

1. *Headlight glare.* This typically occurs at night. It is rarely the cause of collisions with other moving vehicles. It is most likely to be a factor in:

   a. Pedestrian accidents

   b. Running off the road

   c. Striking fixed objects or striking vehicles which are parked or stopped in the lane of travel or on the shoulder

2. *Glare from fixed lights or backlighting.* This includes glare from street lights, advertising signs, etc. Fixed-light glare will most likely contribute to accidents when the lights line up in a driver's field of vision alongside something he should see, such as:

    a. Traffic signals

    b. Traffic signs

3. *Sun glare.* Sun glare will often make things invisible to the driver (see Fig. C4-5).

Figure C4-5 Glare from the sun in some positions and glare of other kinds can obstruct a driver's view of traffic-control devices such as a traffic light. (IPTM Photo)

Trafficway Marks

C4.029 Marks on or along the trafficway can tell much of what happened. Use this information as a catalyst for further investigation and to prove or disprove other information gained during the investigation. Do not rely totally on information supplied by witnesses.

C4.030 In fatal accidents, there is often no one to tell the investigator what happened. Even when there are survivors, they often refuse to give any information, or they are inclined to be somewhat untruthful in order to protect themselves or someone else from possible prosecution or civil liability. It is therefore important for the investigator to examine the scene thoroughly, analyze what he sees, and then form his own opinion as to what happened based on all the information and physical evidence that comes to his attention.

C4.031 Physical evidence at the scene will often help to:

a. Establish the positions of vehicles, pedestrians and other objects involved in the accident prior to, during, and after the accident.

b. Indicate from debris such as vehicle parts, paint chips, etc., the kinds of vehicles or even particular vehicles involved in an accident.

c. Establish who the drivers were.

d. Identify victims.

e.   Support, prove or disprove statements and other information relating to the circumstances of the accident.

Damage to Fixed Objects

C4.032   Fixed objects that can be damaged include trees, guard rails, fences, signs, posts, bridges, curbs and other structures on or next to the roadway. Some fixed objects may show repeated damage. It is therefore important to examine them for new damage that can be related to the accident under investigation.

C4.033   The types of damage include:

a.   Breaking of roadside objects such as:

i   Hedges

ii   Trees

iii   Fences

iv   Mail boxes

v   Utility poles

vi   Buildings

b.   Scraping of roadside objects such as:

         i   Bridge abutments

         ii   Guard rails

         iii   Posts

         iv   Trees

         v   Traffic signs

         vi   Curbs

C4.034   Damage to fixed objects can help to show what happened. Therefore, it is important for the investigator to examine the scene for this type of evidence. A chipped or scraped curb may give clues as to the path of the vehicle or where the vehicle left the roadway and its direction of travel (see Fig. C4-6). Similarly, damage to another object will often help to establish a vehicle's path of travel at the time it struck the object and after it left the object. When an object is struck, the investigator should compare damage marks on both the vehicle and the object to establish the vehicle's position at the time of collision and should match paint scrapings on both the vehicle and the object which was struck.

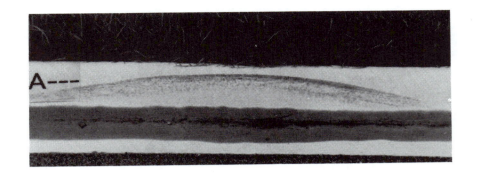

Figure C4-6 A vehicle's path of travel and movement may be traced from scratches, damages and marks left on highway or roadway fixtures by matching vehicle damages, scrapes or marks to those marks or damages. Such marks as shown at **A** will often answer the question of why a vehicle reacted as it did, e.g., veering into the opposing lane after striking a curb. (Photo by IPTM, 1994)

Roadway Marks and Damages

C4.035 During a frontal collision, a vehicle's front end pitches forward and there is an immediate weight shift from the rear to the front end. During a severe impact, the undercarriage will often strike the roadway surface, leaving marks and/or damages on or to the roadway surface. See Figure C4-7.

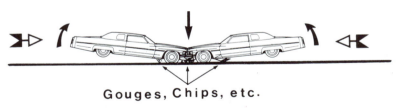

Gouges, Chips, etc.

Figure C4-7 Thin arrows indicate where marks and damages may be left on the roadway surface as the result of a collision.

It is important that measurements of the widths of vehicle parts or of the distances between parts be taken and matched to the damages or marks to or on the roadway surface. In this way, the vehicle's placement on the roadway at the time of collision can be established. Any such matching should also include examining the vehicle part that caused the damage or made the mark for road-material particles.

The investigator should look for these marks and damages at the scene:

a.   A *chip* or *gouge*, which is a concave, chip-like cavity in the pavement caused by a metal protrusion. Edges of the cavity may have striation marks that can be measured and matched to the object that caused them.

b.   A *groove*, which is a long, narrow indentation or furrow cut into the roadway surface, generally caused by a bolt or some similar type of protruding part on a vehicle. A groove may be straight or circular. Straight grooves indicate the direction of travel. Circular grooves indicate that the vehicle was rotating or spinning. A groove may be deep initially and become shallower toward its end (see Fig. C4-8, but see also Fig. C4-10).

c.   A *hole*, which is a round, smooth-walled cavity in a roadway surface and is usually caused by protruding bolts, broken rods or similar round objects.

d.   A *scrape*, which is a wide superficial wound or a wide, clean graze mark caused by a sharp or angular edge being passed over the highway surface, that is, a vehicle part sliding over the roadway.

e.   A *scratch*, which individually is a long, narrow, superficial wound on a highway surface. A scratch mark is usually left by a sliding vehicle part other than a tire. Scratches usually are not deep and often appear not individually but as a broad band of rough, parallel striations (see Fig. C4-9).

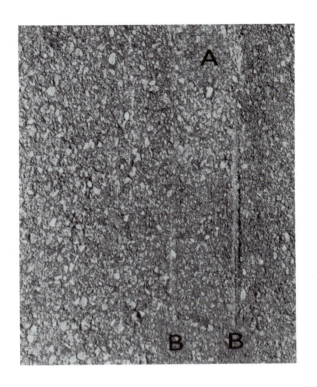

Figure C4-8 Grooves, scrapes and scratches at **A** and **B** correspond to vehicle parts in Figure C4-9. (Photo by IPTM, 1994)

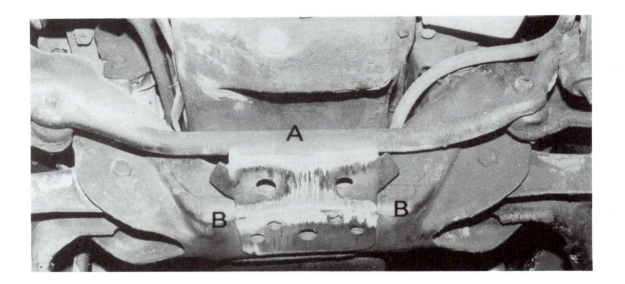

Figure C4-9 Undercarriage parts of a vehicle that can cause damage to roadway. Parts such as **A** and **B** will most probably cause grooves, scrapes or scratches. Many other parts of an automobile, such as tie rods or cross members, may cause various marks on the roadway when they are forced into contact with it. (Photo by IPTM, 1994)

170

Figure C4-10 Pavement grooves
(Photo by IPTM, 1994)

Figure C4-11 A groove at **A** leading
into a gouge at **B** (Photo courtesy of
Charles C. Thomas, Publisher)

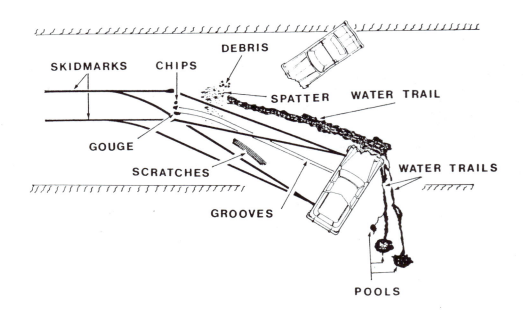

Figure C4-12 Debris is often present among the other types of evidence at an accident scene. (Courtesy of Charles C. Thomas, Publisher)

Figure C4-13 An assortment of debris may be found at an accident scene. (Photo courtesy of Charles C. Thomas, Publisher)

Debris

C4.036 *Debris* is a term encompassing fragments and loose materials strewn on the roadway as the result of a collision or having otherwise fallen from a vehicle. Debris may consist of solids or liquids. See Figures C4-12 and C4-13.

C4.037 When debris falls from a vehicle during collision, the forces of the collision will determine the direction in which the debris will travel. The manner in which debris is scattered can assist the investigator in determining a vehicle's direction of travel at the time of impact and can assist in determining the approximate point of impact. The investigator must determine whether certain articles of debris were actually deposited at the location where he found them or whether they were moved there after the collision by someone at the scene. This is particularly important with larger articles that might have been moved to allow safe or free passage of traffic.

C4.038 When a collision breaks a radiator, the pressure inside forces the coolant out immediately (see Fig. C4-14). Initially the coolant will spatter out onto the roadway as scattered drops *(spatter)*. After the pressure has subsided, the coolant will dribble out and, if the vehicle is moving, the *dribble* will form a *trail* on the roadway. When the vehicle is at rest, the liquid will dribble out to form a puddle or *pool*. If the puddle or pool is not absorbed quickly into the surface, there may be *runoff* in the form of rills or small streams. This type of evidence is very helpful in establishing the approximate point of impact and the vehicle's path of travel to its final rest position after impact.

C4.039 Although debris is useful in determining the approximate point of impact, debris itself is usually not satisfactory evidence for pinpointing the point of impact unless the speed of the vehicles involved is very slow, about 3 to 6 mph (5 to 10 km/h). Before a collision, the items that after impact will become debris are traveling at the same speed as the vehicle to which they are attached, or in which they are contained, or on which they are riding. When a vehicle suddenly decelerates due to a collision, the debris is knocked loose, falls, and makes contact with the roadway surface at some distance from the actual point of impact.

Figure C4-14 Spatter is the result of violent release of radiator water. Water trails form as water flows on the roadway surface. Any type of liquid trail from the vehicle often pools at the lower side of the roadway. (Photo by IPTM, 1994)

C4.040 As mentioned, debris can be useful in assisting the investigator to determine the approximate point of impact. In head-on collisions between vehicles of similar weight traveling at approximately the same speed at the time of impact, the underbody debris will often be found piled between the two vehicles. Sometimes, however, debris will be found scattered over a wide area. Metal and glass parts may be broken off and thrown many feet (meters) from the actual point of impact by the force of the impact. Other parts of the vehicle or parts of the cargo may roll or slide for a considerable distance from the point of impact. Rust, mud and vehicle undercoating materials will usually fall very close to the point of impact, generally in a fan-out pattern.

C4.041 Underbody debris, e.g., mud, dust, rust, paint and road tar knocked loose from the underside of a vehicle, will usually fall in a fan-out pattern and after hitting the pavement will continue in the direction it was traveling as it hit the pavement. This may not be the same direction the vehicle was traveling. For example, if a vehicle traveling north is struck on the right side by a vehicle traveling west at a high speed, debris from the north-bound vehicle will be accelerated toward the west, and after hitting the roadway surface the debris will have a westerly component as well as a northerly component in its direction of travel.

C4.042 Baggage, clothing, bottles, papers and the like from a passenger car will help reconstruct what happened and help identify who was involved. This type of evidence may be found inside or outside of the vehicle. Liquor or wine bottles would suggest a possibly alcohol-impaired driver. Pills, needles and other such items would suggest possible use of a narcotic or stimulant. This type of evidence is very useful when a lone driver is involved, particularly if he is killed.

175

C4.043 From the definition of debris, we know that debris may consist of either liquids or solids. These may be classified as follows:

1. *Liquids*

    a. Vehicle *fluids*

        i   Radiator water or coolant

        ii   Crankcase oil

        iii   Transmission oil

        iv   Differential oil

        v   Brake fluid

        vi   Battery acid

        vii   Gasoline

        viii   Diesel fuel

    b. Liquid cargos

    c. *Blood*

        i   Blood may serve to locate the point at which a body came to rest inside or outside of a vehicle.

        ii   Blood may show the path a body traveled before coming to rest.

2. *Solids*

    a. *Underbody debris*

    Rust, mud, dust, road tar, underbody coating, paint, etc.

    b. *Vehicle parts*

    c. *Other types of cargo*

    Includes packaged materials, luggage and livestock

    d. *Granular cargo*

    Loose material such as grain, feed, fertilizer, gravel, etc. This type of cargo is usually carried high on a vehicle and will therefore tend to travel further and spread over greater areas than underbody debris.

    e. *Road materials*

    Debris such as gravel and pebbles scattered from their place by the force of the collision

    f. *Clothing*

    i   Clothing may indicate where the occupant of a vehicle actually struck the roadway.

177

ii   Shreds of clothing may show the path where a body slid or was dragged along the roadway.

iii   Sometimes a pedestrian's shoes come off right where he was standing when struck.

g.   *Paint*

i   Paint chips may be found among other types of debris on the roadway.

ii   Paint scrapings may be found as rub-off from a vehicle. They may be found on an opposing vehicle or on some other object such as a sign post or bridge abutment.

iii   Paint debris is a useful clue in determining the color and perhaps the year and make of a vehicle in hit-and-run accidents.

iv   Paint transfer may be found on the clothing of pedestrians that have been struck.

Tire Marks

C4.044 An investigator should be able to recognize and correctly interpret the physical appearance of tire marks left on a highway. Unless tire marks are examined and interpreted intelligently, the conclusions drawn from this evidence could be erroneous.

C4.045 It is important to determine whether or not tire marks found on the highway relate to the accident under investigation. If possible, each tire mark should be related to the tire that made it. In so relating a tire mark, it is often helpful to count the number of dark lines in the tire mark and compare that number to the number of tire ribs of the tire in question.

C4.046 An investigator must not confuse skid marks or other roadway marks resulting from a damaged vehicle being towed from the accident scene with marks that were made at the time of the accident. He must be able to interpret and explain the latter and all other marks found at an accident scene or appearing in photographs.

C4.047 A vehicle making skid marks or tire prints at an accident scene is sometimes found at rest a considerable distance from the tire marks. The tire marks left at the scene may be linked to the discovered vehicle in several ways, all of which reinforce each other. Matching may be done by the tire prints or tread ribs, or by witnesses' and drivers' statements, scrape marks, gouges, and so forth. Of particular importance, however, are specific tire-tread and tire-mark measurements.

C4.048 There will be illustrations of tire marks throughout the remainder of this lesson. Tire marks are classified by type as follows:

    a.   Tire prints

    b.   Acceleration marks

    c.   Striation marks

    d.   Underinflated tire marks (see Fig. C4-20 for underinflated tire)

179

e.   Overinflated tire marks (see Fig. C4-19 for overinflated tire)

f.   Deflated or blow-out tire marks

g.   Ruts

h.   Trenches or furrows

i.   Skid marks

j.   Scuff marks

k.   Scrub marks

C4.049 The various types of tire marks may be described as follows:

a.   *Tire prints* (see Figures C4-16 and C4-17)

    i   Tire prints are caused by a rotating tire leaving a print of the tire tread pattern on a highway surface.

    ii   Tire prints may result when a tire, after rolling through a liquid and wetting the tire tread, then rolls on a dry surface.

    iii   Tire prints may be found in soft materials such as snow, slush, sand, or mud.

    iv   Tire prints are an indication that the wheel was not sliding or braked.

v   Tire tread ridges, or *ribs*, will make a print on a roadway surface if the surface is slightly wet or dusty.

vi   If the surface is soft and wet, the tire tread will leave an impression of the tread pattern on the surface. The soft surface material squeezes into the tire tread grooves and is left standing above the surface as the tire passes over.

Figure C4-15 Striation marks at **A** caused by a vehicle sideslipping on gravel or gritty surface. The photograph also shows pavement grinding. (Photo by IPTM, 1994)

Figure C4-16 Tire print caused by a rotating tire. A tire print shows the tread pattern (**A**). The number of dark lines (**B**) indicates the number of tire tread ribs. Tire tread ribs often leave similar dark lines in a straight skid, but without the tread pattern. (Photo by IPTM, 1994)

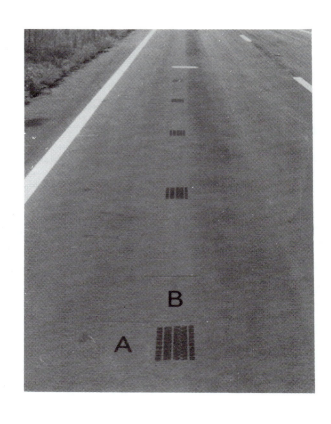

Figure C4-17 Close-up photograph of a tire print. Note the tread pattern. (Photo by IPTM, 1994)

182

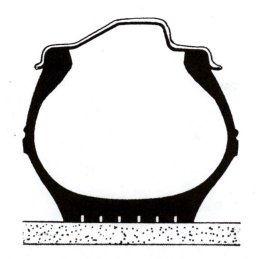

Figure C4-18 Properly inflated tire

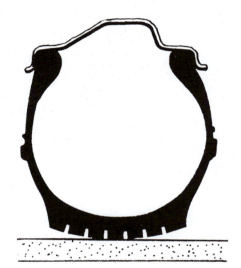

Figure C4-19 Overinflated tire

Figure C4-20 Underinflated tire

Figure C4-21 Forward acceleration mark beginning very dark, especially at the outer edges, and becoming lighter. (Photo by IPTM, 1994)

Figure C4-22 Vehicle has made reverse acceleration marks at **A**, forward acceleration marks at **B**. (IPTM photo)

b. *Acceleration marks* (see Figures C4-21 and C4-22)

    i   An acceleration mark is caused by extreme acceleration of the motor that in turn spins a drive wheel.

    ii   The beginning of an acceleration mark is dark with very dark side ridges, similar to an overloaded or underinflated tire mark.

    iii   Tire tread rib marks are often visible in an acceleration mark.

    iv   A clean tread for the full tire circumference is an indication that the tire had been spinning under acceleration.

    v   A tire tread will give an indication of scratches or striations when it has spun on a gravel or gritty type surface.

c. *Striation marks*

    i   Striation marks are a number of narrow, parallel scratches or tire marks caused by (a) tire sideslipping, (b) gravel-like particles caught between a skidding or sideslipping tire and the roadway.

    ii   Striation marks, properly interpreted, will show the direction of travel.

iii   Studded tires on a skidding, sideslipping or spinning wheel leave thin, parallel scratches or striation marks.

iv   Striation marks are very often evident in a mark from a tire that is rotating and sideslipping at the same time, as when the vehicle is in a yaw (see Fig. C4-15). In such a case, the striation marks are particularly evident in the leading outside tire mark.

Figure C4-23 Overloaded or underinflated tire marks from several different vehicles caused by a weight shift onto the tire. (Photo by IPTM, 1994)

Figure C4-24 Underinflated tire mark. Note its somewhat uneven edges at **A** and **B**. (Photo courtesy of Charles C. Thomas, Publisher)

Figure C4-25 Overloaded tire mark caused by an overloaded single wheel. (Photo by IPTM, 1994)

d.   *Underinflated (overdeflected) tire marks* (see Fig. C4-24)

  i   A rotating underinflated tire leaves two parallel marks appearing as fairly straight, dark, thin lines at the outer edges of the tire tread.

  ii   An underinflated tire mark may not necessarily result from tire air pressure of less than the recommended amount.

  iii   The concave or *cupped* appearance of the tire may also result from a shift in weight onto the front tires, as during braking action (see Fig. C4-33).

  iv   An underinflated tire mark can also result from a load shift when a tire on a dual wheel loses air pressure, forcing the remaining tire on that dual-wheel unit to carry the additional weight and creating in the remaining tire the effect of an underinflated tire.

e.   *Overinflated tire marks*

  i   An overinflated tire mark can appear as either a tire print or as a skid mark.

  ii   As a tire print, an overinflated tire mark appears as a somewhat narrower print than a properly inflated tire. Generally, the ribs of the outer tread are very faint or do not show at all.

iii   As a skid mark, an overinflated tire mark appears narrower in width in the same manner as a tire print.

iv   The narrow appearance of a skid mark from an over-inflated tire may result from a weight shift off that tire. For example, when there is a weight shift to the front during braking action, there will be less weight on each of the rear tires. Often, the resulting narrow rear-tire skid marks will overlap the front-tire skid marks and track within those front-tire skid marks. See Figure C4-33.

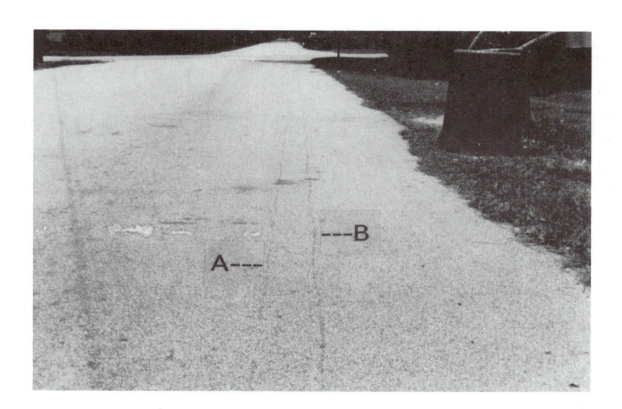

Figure C4-26 Flat tire mark with outer edges labeled **A** and **B**. When a tire is deflated, it *flops* as it rotates, leaving distinct outer-edge *flop marks*. (Photo by IPTM, 1994)

Figure C4-27 A rut in soft sand caused by a rotating tire. Note the tire tread pattern from **A** to **B** and the material thrown to the sides. By contrast, a skidding tire does not show a tread pattern, although it may show tread rib marks and throw material both to the sides and to the front. (Photo by IPTM, 1994)

Figure C4-28 Grass flattened by rotating non-sideslipping tires. (Photo by IPTM, 1994)

Figure C4-29 Furrows in grass caused by rotating sideslipping tires. Note the baring of the grass roots in the furrows. (Photo by IPTM, 1994)

f.   Deflated or blow-out tire marks

When a tire loses air pressure and becomes flat, as in the case of a blow-out, the tire begins to *flop* under the wheel rim. As the wheel rotates, the tire sidewalls as well as the tread come into contact with the roadway, leaving distinct *scalloped* or wavy marks (*flop marks*), usually from the outer edges of the tire (see Fig. C4-26).

g.   Ruts, trenches and furrows

i   A rotating tire traveling in soft material, such as mud or snow, causes a rut (see Fig. C4-27). A skidding or sideslipping tire traveling in soft material causes a trench or furrow, pushing the material in front of it.

ii   A rotating non-sideslipping tire traveling over grass merely causes the grass to flatten for the width of the tire (see Fig. C4-28), whereas a skidding or side-slipping tire causes grass roots to be bared and makes a furrow in the earth (see Fig. C4-29).

Skid Marks and Scrub Marks

C4.050 A skid mark is a tire mark that results from a tire sliding over a roadway surface or other surface. (Scuff marks--which involve side-slipping--will be discussed under a separate heading.) A skid mark is caused by:

192

a. A wheel that is not free to rotate because

i the wheel has become locked as a result of braking action by the driver, or

ii the wheel has suffered binding or become jammed as the result of a collision.

b. A wheel that is free to rotate but is being forced sideways, as occurs when the rear tires of a vehicle in yaw lose their remaining grip on the surface and break away.

C4.051 The type of surface affects the appearance of skid marks.

a. Most roadway skid marks are found on asphalt surfaces (excluding extremely cold asphalt surfaces) and are the result of smearing of the asphalt or tar caused by heat from the skidding tire.

b. Skid marks on a surface of a hard material such as cement are sometimes difficult to see. They may appear as a scraping or cleaning mark. Burned-off tire particles may also be seen adhering to the roadway surface for a very short period of time, but these particles may soon be blown away by the wind from passing vehicles or destroyed by adverse weather conditions.

c. Very cold asphalt surfaces normally do not soften or smear. Consequently, skid marks on such surfaces appear much the same as on cement surfaces.

d. Skid marks (and scuff marks) are not always visible at the time they are made on paved roadway surfaces that are wet. However, these marks may later become visible on asphalt once the pavement has dried. As a tire skids (or sideslips) on wet pavement, there is an erasing or cleaning action as the tire pushes the water away from its path. The evidence of such skids (or sideslips) is sometimes short-lived. Nevertheless, areas in question should be marked and examined as soon as possible for any evidence of skidding (or sideslip) action.

e. On paved surfaces covered with foreign material such as dust, dirt or sand, a skidding tire pushes the material aside and leaves a skid mark, but as the vehicle passes, the material may return to obscure the skid mark. The investigator should sweep away the material to determine whether there is a skid mark.

f. When examining a roadway surface for skid marks, the investigator should get as low and far back as possible. When circumstances permit, a better view may be had when the sun is behind the investigator. Polarized sun glasses also provide a clearer view of skid marks during daylight.

g. In a *straight skid*, a tire usually leaves a skid mark the width of the tire tread and often leaves parallel tread rib marks but no cross pattern. A skidding tire may leave a skid mark of a different width from that of the tire tread under certain circumstances, including the following:

i.   When the front wheels have been turned to either the right or left, a wider skid mark may appear.

ii   In a straight skid, when a rear tire leaves an overlapping skid mark that tracks within the front tire skid mark, the rear tire skid mark will appear as a slightly narrower skid mark similar to the skid mark of an overinflated tire (see Fig. C4-33).

h.   The end of a skid mark is generally the darkest part of the mark. It ends abruptly and there may be a deposit of dirt or other substance on the pavement where the wheel stopped as the vehicle slid to a stop and just before the place where the wheel began to rotate as the vehicle got underway again. See Figure C4-37.

i.   In a straight skid, the tire-tread pattern will not appear, but there may be enough grooves showing between the dark lines of the mark to allow their number to be counted (see Fig. C4-16).

j.   In a sideways skid or slide, neither the pattern nor grooves will show. However, there may be striation marks caused by the tire-shoulder ribs.

k.   Skid marks are useful in determining:

i   the minimum speed where the skid marks started.

ii   a vehicle's location on the roadway leading up to the point of a collision.

iii   the approximate point of collision if there is a deviation in the skid marks, e.g., as in offset skid marks.

iv   the path of travel before and after the collision.

v   the action of the vehicle, i.e., rotation, change of direction, etc.

l.   A tire may show a scraped area or flat spot on the tread where it made contact with the roadway while sliding (see Fig. C4-35).

C4.052 An *impending skid mark* is that portion of a tire mark that is left by a braked wheel just before complete cessation of wheel rotation.

a.   Braking effect is at its greatest during this time.

b.   An impending skid mark may lead into a skid mark as the braked wheel completely stops rotating.

c.   The transition from an impending skid mark to a skid mark is sometimes called *shadow* and may appear slightly darker than the impending skid mark. During this phase, cessation of tire rotation is complete and the tire is sliding, but the tire has not yet built up enough heat to produce a skid mark on the surface. See Figures C4-30 and C4-31.

d.   Another name for impending skid mark is *incipient skid mark*.

Figure C4-30 Shadow appears just before each dark skid mark. The point where it begins is labeled **A**. The shadow area is where the wheel is locked but the tire has not generated enough heat to mark the roadway. (Photo by IPTM, 1994)

Figure C4-31 A bumper gun detonator device can be used to place a paint dot on the pavement at the onset of braking and thereby assist in locating an impending skid mark and the shadow area. (Photo by IPTM, 1994)

Figure C4-32 Shadow area begins at the lower **A**. Dark skid mark begins at the upper **A**. Paint dot **B** from the bumper gun shows where the rear of the test car was located at the onset of braking. (Photo by IPTM, 1994)

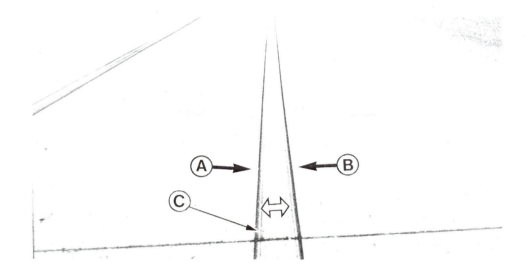

Figure C4-33 *Skidmarks*. Because of the forward shift in weight, the front tires *cup* with most of the weight being carried by their outer edges. Tire distortion is similar to that of an overloaded or underinflated tire. The outer edges generate greater heat, leaving two dark, thin parallel lines. At the same time, the rear tires lift slightly with tire distortion similar to that of an overinflated tire. In a straight skid, a rear tire leaves an overlapping skid mark that tracks within the front-tire skid mark, as indicated by the two-way arrow. (Photo courtesy of Charles C. Thomas, Publisher)

Figure C4-34 A crowned or superelevated roadway causes a vehicle in a skid to *drift* to the lower side, as shown here particularly by the longer, rear-wheel skid marks. (Photo by IPTM, 1994)

Figure C4-35 Braked wheel causes the tire to be cleaned or scraped on the area that was in contact with the roadway as indicated in **A** to **B** in each photo. (Photos by IPTM, 1994)

Figure C4-36 Burned-off tire particles are from a tire in a skid. These particles are short-lived evidence. (Photo by IPTM, 1994)

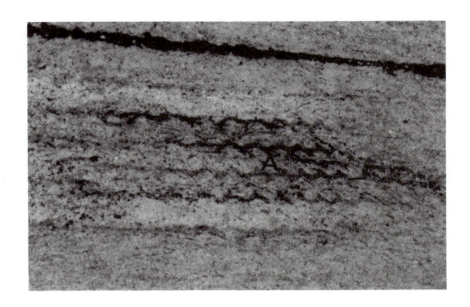

Figure C4-37 A skidding tire will pick up debris in its tread, e.g., dirt, and deposit it where the wheel stops, as indicated by **A**. The debris may be seen on the roadway after the vehicle again proceeds, but it is usually short-lived. This type of evidence is useful in determining the stopping point of the vehicle. (Photo by IPTM, 1994)

Figure C4-38 The point of impact may be established by following the skid mark to the place where the tires have dug into the roadway surface because of the downward force during collision, causing sometimes a gouge in the pavement. The change in direction at impact is revealed here by offset marks -- tire scrub marks. (IPTM Photo)

C4.053 In addition to the straight skid marks discussed above, other marks meeting the skid-mark criteria in C4.050 can be classified as follows:

a.   *Scrub marks*

   i   A scrub mark is a tire mark resulting from a wheel that is locked or jammed during collision so that the tire then slides along the roadway.

   ii   A scrub mark is most commonly caused by a sideways movement of a vehicle during collision (see Fig. C4-38).

   iii   The beginning of a scrub mark will often help in determining the point of impact.

   iv   When there is a sideways movement, striation marks may result from tire-shoulder ribs.

   v   When the direction of the skid is in alignment with the wheel, the scrub mark appears much the same as a straight skid mark.

b.   *Spin skid marks*

Spin skid marks result when:

   i   a vehicle rotates around its center of mass, as in cases where the rear wheels move in a manner so as to lead the front wheels.

ii   there is external force applied to a vehicle in a direction other than in direct line with the center of mass.

c.   *Skip skid marks*

i   Skip skid marks occur when a locked wheel bounces on the roadway. The blank spaces between the skid marks are usually 1 - 3 feet (1 m) long.

ii   Bouncing that results in skip skid marks is usually caused by:

    1.   a locked wheel striking a hole, bump, rut or body, or sliding on a washboard-type surface.

    2.   a vehicle colliding with another vehicle or object, causing the locked rear wheels to momentarily lift off the roadway.

    3.   an unloaded or lightly loaded trailer, the most common type being a semi-trailer adapted for a tractor-trailer braking system that locks the wheels of the trailer before locking the wheels of the tractor and thereby prevents jackknifing (see Fig. C4-39).

d.   *Intermittent skid marks*

i   Intermittent skid marks occur when locked wheels are released and relocked through braking action (see Fig. C4-40).

ii   Blank spaces or gaps between the intermittent skid marks are usually a minimum of 15 to 20 ft (4 to 6 m) in length.

iii   The investigator must take care not to confuse intermittent skid marks with skip skid marks.

iv   If the investigator is uncertain whether a tire mark is an intermittent skid mark or a skip skid mark, it may be helpful and important to ask the driver how he was braking.

v   Intermittent skid marks are sometimes referred to as *gap skid marks*.

Figure C4-39 A braked dual wheel of an empty or lightly loaded semi-trailer or similar vehicle will often bounce, causing a skip skid mark. (Photo by IPTM, 1994)

Figure C4-40 Intermittent or gap skid marks are caused by pumping the brake pedal with full application and release. (Photo by IPTM, 1994)

e.   *Offset marks*

   i   An offset mark occurs when one vehicle is in collision with another vehicle or some other object and is suddenly pushed or directed to one side as a result of the force from the other vehicle or object (see Fig. C4-38).

   ii   An offset shows:

      1.   the location of the tire at the point or time of collision.

      2.   the direction of the applied force that changed the direction of the vehicle.

   iii   An offset mark most often appears as a scrub mark.

Tire Action

C4.054   There are a number of terms that describe tire action on the roadway. An investigator should be familiar with those that follow:

a.   *Pavement grinding*

   i   Pavement grinding occurs when a collection of fine particles of stone, glass, or any gritty material embedded in or adhering to a tire surface is ground

206

against the roadway surface as the tire slides or *digs*, as in acceleration slippage (see Fig. (C4-42).

ii   Pavement grinding can occur on either wet or dry pavement.

iii   Pavement grinding results in various types of scratches on the roadway surface, the type of scratch depending upon the type of material abrading the surface.

iv   Pavement grinding most often occurs on a cold or hard pavement surface before the tire has built up enough heat to cause a smear.

v   *Studded tires* will leave scratches or striations (see Fig. C4-41).

vi   Pavement grinding on a wet surface will appear as scratches after the roadway dries.

b.   *Pavement erasing*

i   Pavement erasing occurs when a cool sliding tire erases or removes the dirt from a hard, smooth, dirty surface.

ii   Pavement erasing is very hard to see or to photograph except under certain lighting conditions.

iii   Pavement-erasing marks can be short-lived and are usually not visible on a wet roadway surface.

Figure C4-41 Studded tire has left scratches. (IPTM Photo)

Figure C4-42 Acceleration mark showing pavement grinding. Note the striations caused by this tire action. (Photo by IPTM, 1994)

c. *Smear*

  i   Smear will be found when a tire slides on a roadway covered with wet snow, slush or mud.

  ii Smear in soft materials normally does not leave a tire-tread pattern because the soft roadway material falls in behind the tire as it passes (but see Fig. C4-43).

  iii At the end of a skid, a tire print may be quite evident against a mound of material that is built up ahead of the sliding tire.

d. *Marks on asphalt* (tar)

  i   The marks on asphalt material occur only when the heat from friction between a sliding tire and the pavement surface is so great it actually starts to melt the asphalt or tar.

  ii Marks are left on the pavement surface by the ribs of the tire face, not the grooves between them.

  iii Marks on asphalt materials are long-lasting.

  iv Marks are not common on wet or damp surfaces because of the cooling effect of the moisture.

Figure C4-43 Tire smear from blacktop surface onto painted surface. (Photo by IPTM, 1994)

    e.   *Splatter*

        i   Splatter is that portion of the soft material that is squirted to the sides as a tire rolls through or over the material.

        ii   Splatter is most common at the edges of a tire imprint in mud, but can be seen in slush or other material to a lesser degree.

    f.   *Squeegee marks*

        i   Squeegee marks occur when a sliding tire rubs moisture off a paved surface.

ii   When the tire and roadway surface are warm and neither is very wet, the resultant skid mark may be dry enough to strike a match on.

iii   Squeegee marks are very short-lived and will frequently have disappeared before the investigator's arrival.

iv   When visible, a squeegee mark gives an appearance similar to that of a rolling tire print.

g.   *Stippling*

Stippling is the sticky material which a tire pulls up from the roadway surface and leaves standing in little points or ridges.

h.   *Tire grinding* (see Fig. C4-36)

i   Tire grinding occurs when a tire slides over a very gritty roadway surface and particles of rubber are ground off the tire surface.

ii   The particles ground off a tire appear as a dust which accumulates in the tread pattern and is then deposited on the roadway surface at the end of the skid when the wheels start to rotate.

iii   Tire grinding particles are very short-lived. They may be blown away by passing vehicles or be lost because of adverse weather conditions.

i. *Tire Ruboff* (see Fig. C4-36)

   i   Tire ruboff is rubber ground from a sliding tire rather than roadway material melted by such a tire.

   ii Most visible skid marks on roadways are the result of melting of asphalt material. Occasionally, however, a mark may be a combination of both melting and ruboff. A close examination of a mark is required to make this determination.

Scuff Marks or Sideslip Marks

C4.055 A *scuff mark* is a mark caused by a tire that is both rotating and sideslipping. There are various types of scuff marks, including:

   a.   Acceleration scuff marks

   b.   Flat tire scuff marks

   c.   Overloaded or underinflated tire scuff marks

   d.   Yaw marks

C4.056 A *yaw* or *sideslip mark* is caused by a rotating tire which is also sideslipping. When a vehicle is negotiating a curve normally--with no wheels sideslipping--each rear tire is said to track *inside* the path of its corresponding front tire, the tire on the same side of the vehicle. When a vehicle making a turn or rounding a curve goes into a yaw, however, each

212

rear tire may--if the centrifugal force on the vehicle is sufficient--cross over the path of its corresponding front tire and is then said to track *outside* the path of that front tire. Used with a curved front-tire path as a frame of reference, the terms *inside/outside* indicate that each rear tire tracks inside/outside of the curved path of its corresponding front tire (see Fig.'s C4-44 and C4-45). If the rear wheels come to track outside their corresponding front tires, which will also be sideslipping, it follows that the yaw marks left by the rear tires will appear outside the marks left by their corresponding front tires.

C4.057 The *critical speed* of a curve is the maximum speed at which a given vehicle can travel around the curve without having the centrifugal force on the vehicle exceed the frictional forces generated by the tires and the (roadway) surface, causing the vehicle to lose lateral stability and break out of the path it has been following in the curve.

C4.058 When the speed of the vehicle exceeds the critical speed for the curve, the rear tires will start to cross over the paths of the front tires and the vehicle will go into a *critical speed yaw* or *critical speed scuff*. Once the rear wheels begin tracking completely outside the paths of the front tires, the transition from yaw to critical speed yaw is considered complete.

C4.059 Only those rear-tire yaw marks that lie completely outside the front-tire yaw marks may be considered as *critical speed yaw marks* and only critical speed yaw marks may be measured for use in the Critical Speed Formula (presented in Lesson 6).

C4.060 *Yaw* is a term applied to the sideways rotation of a vehicle around its center of mass, such as occurs when the rear of a vehicle sideslips and moves in a direction other than the direction in which the vehicle is headed. At high speeds on curves, *centrifugal force (inertia)* attempts to overcome *centripetal force*--the frictional resistance or adhesion between the tires and the roadway--and causes the vehicle to want to break out of the curve in a straight path (see Fig. C4-46). If the vehicle's speed is great enough, the vehicle will sideslip into a yaw.

C4.061 *Inertia* defined: According to *Newton's First Law of Motion*, every body continues in its state of uniform motion in a straight line unless acted upon by external forces so applied to the body that the direction of motion is changed. The inertial tendency of a body to continue in a straight line is a common observation. The occasional sideslipping of a motor vehicle when attempting to round a corner is an illustration of the effect of inertia.

C4.062 As a vehicle is driven into a curve, centrifugal force (inertia) causes a weight shift onto the leading, outside front tire. The outer side of the tire tread of this lead tire carries the shifted, excess weight. At the beginning of a yaw, the outer edge of the lead tire leaves a very narrow, dark mark that first appears as a thin line and then widens to the width of the portion of tire tread that is in contact with the roadway surface as the vehicle goes into the yaw (see Fig. C4-47). It is this thin sideslip mark caused by the lead tire that is so important in calculating speed from sideslip or yaw. Striation marks caused by the side of the tire tread are often visible (see Fig. C4-49).

C4.063 Yaw marks are valuable as evidence. They can be used to:

a. Show the path a vehicle was traveling during the time it was sideslipping.

b. Make a determination of a vehicle's true average speed through the length of the yaw mark.

c. Establish that a vehicle was traveling too fast to safely negotiate a curve.

C4.064 A *side scuff mark* that appears very similar to a yaw mark can be caused by an underinflated or overloaded tire. Such a mark normally follows a proper path within the lane of travel of the vehicle and continues on for great distances. This type of mark may occur at relatively low speeds and should not be confused with a high-speed sideslip or yaw mark. A flat tire, on the other hand, leaves a scalloped scuff mark.

C4.065 An acceleration mark can become an *acceleration scuff mark* where there is lateral movement of the tire during acceleration.

Figure C4-44 Under normal conditions, the rear tires track inside the front tires on a curve. (Photo by Ned Stuart, 1993)

Figure C4-45 Entering a curve at excessive speed puts a vehicle into a yaw, causing the rear tires to track outside the front tires. (Photo by Ned Stuart, 1993)

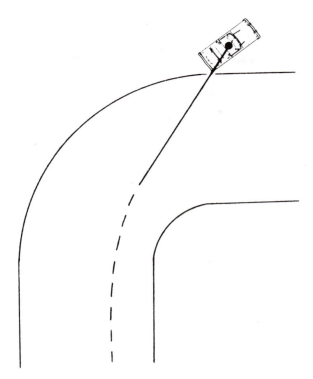

Figure C4-46 When there is insufficient centripetal force to hold a vehicle on the roadway in a curve, centrifugal force causes it to depart in a straight line from its curved path.

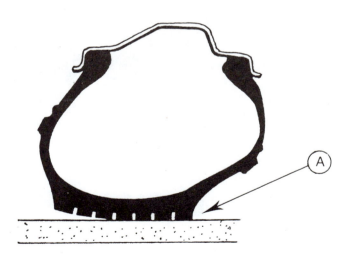

Figure C4-47 There is tire distortion when a vehicle is in a yaw. **A** indicates that portion of the outer side of the tread area making the very narrow, dark mark on the roadway as the vehicle begins to go into the yaw. This mark is most evident with the lead front tire. See Figures C4-48 and C4-49 for the yaw mark.

Figure C4-48 Beginning of the lead tire yaw mark at **A** and the crossover of the rear tire yaw mark at **B**. (Photo by IPTM, 1994)

Figure C4-49 Yaw mark showing striations (Photo by IPTM, 1994)

C4.066 An investigator must be able to identify each mark that appears at the scene or in a photograph of the scene and explain how the mark was made. He must take care not to confuse one type of mark with another type. He must not mistake shadows for tire marks nor mistake marks that are not part of the accident for marks resulting directly from the accident. See Figures C4-50, C4-51 and C4-52.

Figure C4-50 Tire prints caused by passing traffic must not be confused with skid marks. (Photo by IPTM, 1994)

219

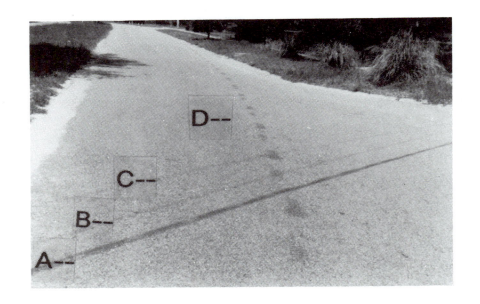

Figure C4-51 The shadows at **A**, **B**, and **C** must not be confused with or interpreted as tire marks as at **D**. (Photo by IPTM, 1994)

Figure C4-52 During the follow-up investigation, a skid mark caused by a locked wheel on a towed vehicle must not be confused with an accident skid mark. (Photo by IPTM, 1994)

Lesson 4
ENVIRONMENT AND TRAFFICWAY FACTORS
PROJECT A-1

See Photograph No. 8035.

Circle the most appropriate answer.

In Photograph No. 8035, the letter **A** indicates:

a.   A skid mark

b.   A tire print

c.   A scrub mark

d.   Striations

e.   An acceleration mark

This particular tire mark was caused by:

a.   An underinflated tire

b.   A tire that was rotating and sideslipping

c.   A locked wheel

d.   A flat tire

e.   Tire grinding

Photograph No. 8035

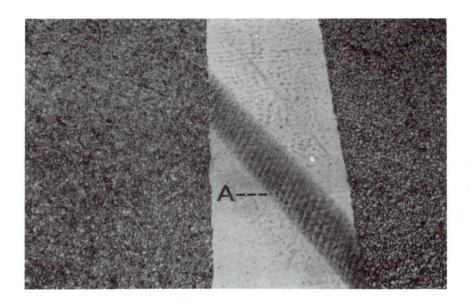

Lesson 4
ENVIRONMENTAL AND TRAFFICWAY FACTORS
PROJECT A-2

See Photograph No. 8037.

Circle the most appropriate answer.

In Photograph No. 8037, the letter **A** indicates the following:

a.   A flat tire mark

b.   An overloaded tire mark

c.   A yaw mark

d.   A striation mark

e.   A scrub mark

This particular tire mark was probably caused by:

a.   A locked, skidding wheel and tire

b.   An overload on the tire

c.   A sideslipping tire

d.   Tire grinding

e.   A flat tire

Photograph No. 8037

Lesson 4
ENVIRONMENT AND TRAFFICWAY FACTORS
PROJECT A-3

See Photograph No. 8039.

Circle the most appropriate answer.

In Photograph No. 8039, the letter **A** indicates:

a.   A gouge

b.   A scratch

c.   A chip

d.   A groove

e.   A hole

This particular mark was probably caused by:

a.   A broken wheel rim

b.   An undercarriage bolt

c.   Tire grinding

d.   Debris falling onto the roadway

e.   Traffic engineers

Photograph No. 8039

Lesson 4
ENVIRONMENT AND TRAFFICWAY FACTORS
PROJECT A-4

See Photograph 8041.

Circle the most appropriate answer.

Photograph 8041 shows the marks left by a yawing vehicle. Which of the following statements would have been true once the vehicle had gone into the yaw?

a.   Rear tires were tracking inside their corresponding front tires.

b.   Rear tires were tracking so that they overlapped the front tire marks.

c.   Wheels of the vehicle were locked up.

d.   Rear tires were tracking outside their corresponding front tires.

e.   Centrifugal force was too weak to hold the vehicle in its path.

This particular type of mark is caused by:

a.   A rotating tire

b.   A sideslipping tire

c.   Excessive speed on a curve

d.   All of the above

e.   None of the above

Photograph No. 8041

Lesson 4
ENVIRONMENT AND TRAFFICWAY FACTORS
PROJECT A-5

See Photograph 8032.

Indicate the correct answer with an X or a ✓.

a.   The section of the tire mark between points **1** and **2** contains a shadow area.

     True_____   False_____

b.   The tire mark between the letters **A** and **B** was caused by a rear tire.

     True_____   False_____

Photograph No. 8032

INTRODUCTION

Lesson 5

SUBJECT: Vehicle Inspections

Traffic accident investigators physically examine vehicles for deficiencies, defects and damage.

This lesson will enable the student to systematically inspect all mechanical vehicular features that may have contributed to an accident. It will also enable the student to analyze a vehicle's damage, both interior and exterior, and relate that damage to damage suffered by other vehicles or objects and/or injury suffered by persons or animals.

Lesson Contents

This lesson covers the following topics related to vehicle nomenclature and vehicle inspection:

    a.   Accelerator
    b.   Brakes
    c.   Steering systems
    d.   Suspension systems
    e.   Tires
    f.   Exhaust systems
    g.   Trailer connections
    h.   Gear shift lever
    i.   Vehicle glass

j.   Horn

k.   Lamps and reflectors

l.   Wheels

m.   Windshield wipers and defrosters

n.   Radio

o.   Mirrors

p.   Speedometer

q.   Seat belts

r.   Interior damage

s.   Door locks

t.   Vehicle loads

u.   Vehicle fires

v.   Contact damage

w.   Induced (incidental) damage

x.   Imprints

y.   Ruboff

z.   Thrust

a[1]   General equipment

b[2]   Damage classifications

c[3]   Follow-up examinations

d[4]   Mechanical Inspection Guide

e[5]   Checklist of Physical Evidence

f[6]   Glossary

Lesson Objectives

Upon completion of this lesson, the student will be able to do the following:

1.   Upon examining a vehicle at an accident scene or given a photograph or sketch of a defective, damaged or broken item or

232

part from a vehicle involved in an accident, state whether the damage contributed to or was caused by the accident.

2. Upon examining a vehicle at an accident scene or being given a photograph or sketch of a damaged vehicle part *and* another object, state whether the object caused the vehicle-part damage.

3. Upon examining various vehicle parts at an accident scene or being given a photograph, sketch or diagram of various vehicle parts (over 15 parts), identify at least 15 of those parts and relate the function(s) or purpose(s) of each part to the operation of a vehicle.

Lesson 5

VEHICLE INSPECTIONS

General

C5.001 The at-scene investigator must examine all vehicles involved in an accident. An examination must determine whether a vehicle's structure, equipment, accessories or load was defective or hazardous, and/or whether they in any way interfered with the safe and lawful operation of the vehicle.

C5.002 A very important task in a vehicle inspection or examination is to determine whether an abnormal *vehicle condition* existed before the accident occurred, and how and to what extent, if at all, the condition contributed to the accident. If it can be shown that the accident would not have happened if the condition had not been present, the condition can then be considered as the cause of the accident or at least a contributing factor. In many instances, it will be found that a vehicle condition in combination with a driver error is a primary factor in an accident.

C5.003 The severity of an accident will often dictate the extent to which a vehicle inspection must be conducted and reported. In a very minor accident, only the information needed to complete the report might be required. However, in severe accident situations, a detailed vehicle examination is necessary, including a complete description of damages, measurements of damages and photographs.

C5.004 Whenever possible and with due regard for an individual's rights under Miranda (in the U.S.A.), an immediate statement (verbal or written) as to how the accident occurred should be obtained from the driver of each vehicle involved. Frequently, a driver will claim that a vehicle condition or defect caused the accident. Such a statement will assist the at-scene investigator in pinpointing problem areas and also areas on which to focus an investigation to prove or disprove the driver's claim. When it is suspected that neither the driver nor the vehicle was the primary cause, some other condition should be looked for, such as a road defect.

C5.005 The at-scene vehicle examination should include:

a. Observations of the general, overall condition of the vehicle, including mechanical defects and apparent damage.

b. The final resting place of the vehicle.

c. A good series of photographs.

C5.006 Vehicle inspections should cover the following items with a view toward relating their condition, position and existence to the accident:

a. Accelerator

b. Brakes

c. Door locks

d. Exhaust system

e. Gadgets, window or windshield stickers, ornaments, etc., both inside and outside the vehicle

f. Gear shift lever/shifter

g. Horn

h. Lights, e.g., headlights, taillights, signal lights, reflectors

i. Loads and binders

j. Mirrors

k. Radio/cassette player/CD player

l.   Car telephone

m.   Shocks and springs

n.   Speedometer

o.   Steering

p.   Tires and wheels

q.   Windows and windshield

r.   Windshield wipers

It is not usual that a thorough examination or inspection can be made at the scene. When necessary, a more thorough examination should be carried out at a proper facility after the vehicle has been removed from the scene. See the Mechanical Inspection Guide and Evaluation and the Checklist of Physical Evidence from the Vehicle following C5.144 at the end of this lesson. The Checklist concentrates on items uncovered by the vehicle inspection that can be used as evidence.

C5.007 In-depth inspections or examinations of such items as braking systems or headlight filaments should normally be carried out by persons having the expertise to qualify them to testify as expert witnesses, such as mechanical engineers, laboratory technicians, and others who through experience are qualified.

C5.008 Although it is not necessary that an at-scene investigator be a qualified mechanic, it is essential that he be knowledgeable about (a) the construction of a vehicle and (b) a vehicle's primary parts and their purposes and functions and be able to apply this knowledge to at-scene and follow-up investigations.

Accelerator

C5.009 An accelerator on a motor vehicle is a mechanical device, usually a foot-operated throttle, for increasing the speed of the vehicle. An accelerator is comprised of a pedal and a series of linkage rods, each with a coupling and a return spring or mechanism.

C5.010 The accelerator and all its components should be checked at the scene. This check should determine the presence of any binding or sticking as well as return action after the accelerator pedal has been depressed. Examine the functioning of the accelerator both visually and manually from the foot pedal through to the carburetor. To conduct the manual examination, grasp the throttle linkage and open and close the throttle several times to check for obstructions or bindings that might have caused the throttle to stick open or otherwise malfunction. Check visually for bent linkage rods, worn connections, defective retrieval spring or evidence of binding that could have caused the accelerator to malfunction.

C5.011 To assist in determining who the driver was, care should be taken to look for shoe-sole imprints on the accelerator pedal which can be matched to a shoe worn by a suspected driver. (Similar imprints may be found on the brake pedal. The reverse also occurs--the pedals may leave their imprints on the sole.)

C5.012 Some modern vehicles may be equipped with automatic traction control or acceleration slip regulation (ASR). These systems are designed to limit power to accelerate during slippery or limited traction conditions. In the event of a suspected system failure, it is suggested that an expert in these systems be engaged. See Figure C5-1.

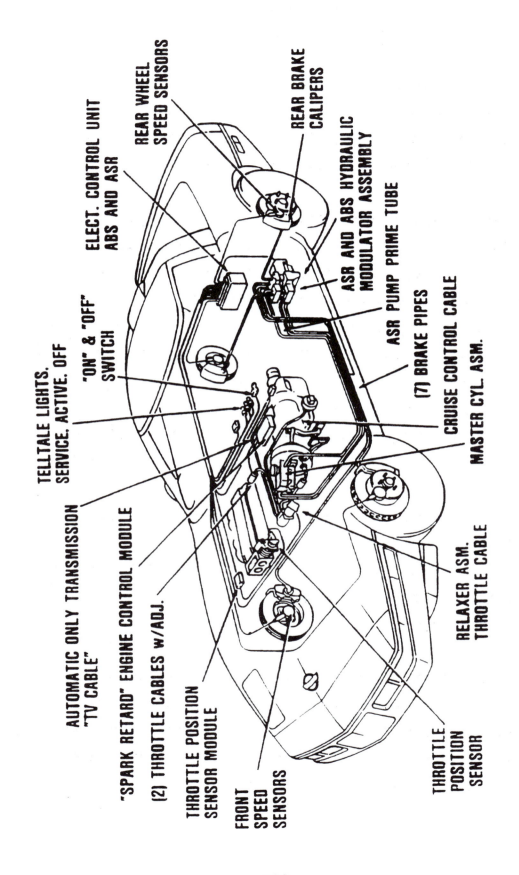

TELLTALE LIGHTS.
SERVICE. ACTIVE. OFF

"ON" & "OFF"
SWITCH

AUTOMATIC ONLY TRANSMISSION
"TV CABLE"

"SPARK RETARD" ENGINE CONTROL MODULE

(2) THROTTLE CABLES w/ADJ.

THROTTLE POSITION
SENSOR MODULE

FRONT
SPEED
SENSORS

ELECT. CONTROL UNIT
ABS AND ASR

REAR WHEEL
SPEED SENSORS

REAR BRAKE
CALIPERS

ASR AND ABS HYDRAULIC
MODULATOR ASSEMBLY

ASR PUMP PRIME TUBE

(7) BRAKE PIPES

CRUISE CONTROL CABLE

MASTER CYL. ASM.

THROTTLE
POSITION
SENSOR

RELAXER ASM.
THROTTLE CABLE

Figure C5-1 Controls, sensors, cables and assemblies utilized in acceleration slip regulation (ASR) and an anti-lock braking system (ABS)

238

Brakes

Types of Brake Systems

C5.013 There are two types of brake systems on modern vehicles:

1. Drum brake
2. Disc brake

A vehicle can have drum or disc brakes or a combination of both (see Fig.'s C5-2 and C5-3). Both systems use *hydraulic fluid* to activate the brakes.

C5.014 Some large commercial vehicles are equipped with *air brakes*. While air is used to activate their brakes, these vehicles still use drum or disc wheel systems.

C5.015 When a driver presses the brake pedal of a hydraulic system, pressure is transferred through the hydraulic fluid from the *master cylinder* to the *wheel cylinders* of drum brakes and to the *calipers* of disc brakes. This pressure forces the *brake shoes* with their *brake linings* against the drums of drum brakes and the *brake pads* against the *rotors* or *discs* of disc brakes. Releasing the pedal releases the pressure to the wheel assemblies and releases the brakes.

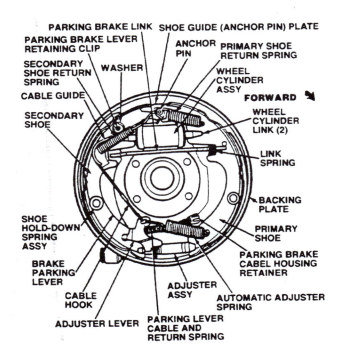

Figure C5-2 Typical drum brake

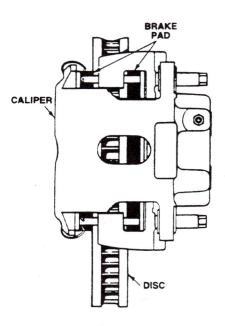

Figure C5-3 Typical disc brake

240

Dual Braking System

C5.016   Most modern vehicles have a dual braking system, i.e., two separate braking systems (see Figure C5-4). This is to safeguard against a brake failure. Should one system fail, the other will still provide adequate braking power to stop the vehicle. The diagonal configuration ensures that with only two wheels braking the vehicle will come to a stop in a reasonably straight path. See Figure C5-5.

Figure C5-4   Master cylinder for a dual braking system.   Note the two separate fluid reservoirs.

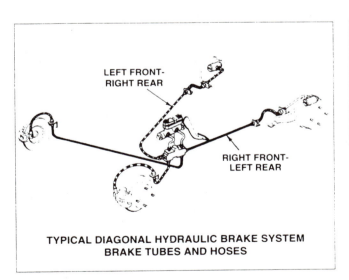

TYPICAL DIAGONAL HYDRAULIC BRAKE SYSTEM
BRAKE TUBES AND HOSES

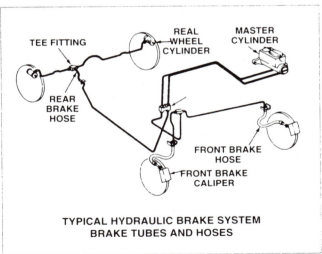

TYPICAL HYDRAULIC BRAKE SYSTEM
BRAKE TUBES AND HOSES

Figure C5-5   Hydraulic brake system configurations

Anti-Lock Brakes

C5.017   Vehicles equipped with an anti-lock braking system (ABS) decelerate at a different frictional level than vehicles having a standard braking system, so the investigator should inspect the vehicle to determine if it is equipped with ABS. Most vehicles have external markings (ABS) either on the vehicle body or sometimes on the wheels themselves. In the absence of such markings, check to see if the vehicle has an ABS fuse block in the engine compartment. If no such evidence exists, a check with the manufacturer's representative (dealer) may be required as to whether the make and model or, better still, the particular vehicle is so equipped. Because anti-lock brakes do not permit any wheel to lock up even under hard braking, but keep each wheel on the threshold of lock-up and thereby maximize braking efficiency, they are particularly useful in stopping the vehicle on wet and slippery surfaces. Anti-lock brakes have the additional advantage of permitting the driver to continue steering while braking hard, which would be impossible if the front wheels were to lock up, as they would be likely to do without ABS.

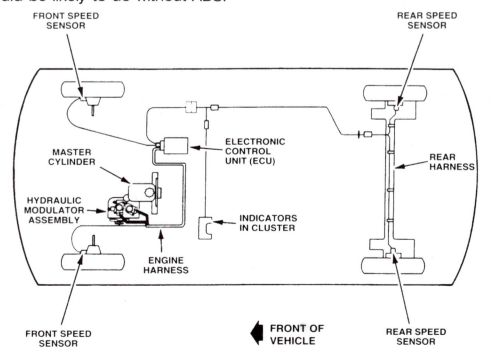

Figure C5-6 Anti-lock braking system (ABS)

Parking Brake

C5.018 A parking brake is usually operated by a lever, handle or small foot pedal. When the parking brake is applied, the rear wheels or drive shaft are locked through a series of cables and rods. Special attention to this system should be given in *runaway* vehicle accidents.

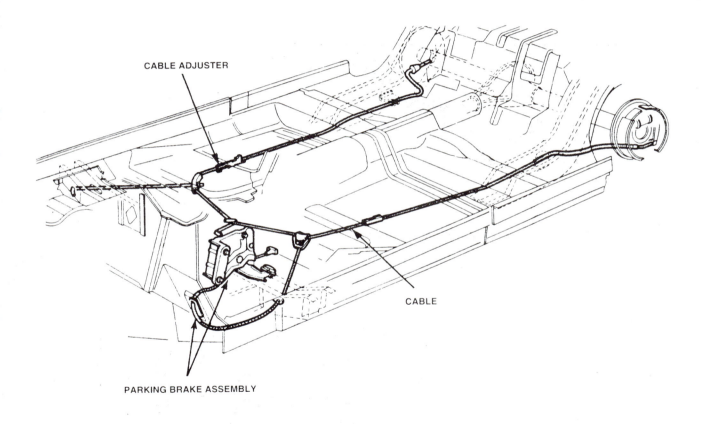

Figure C5-7 A typical parking brake system

Power-Assisted Brakes

C5.019 Power-assisted brakes utilize a diaphragm located between the master cylinder and the brake pedal. The diaphragm receives vacuum from the intake manifold and provides a boost or assist to the pressure applied to the brake pedal by the driver (see Fig.'s C5-8 and C5-9). To check the adequacy of a power-assisted braking system, carry out the normal hydraulic braking system inspection procedures, but also include the power-assist unit.

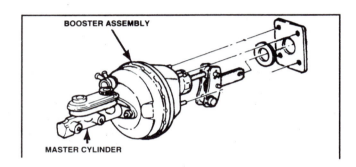

Figure C5-8 Typical vacuum assembly

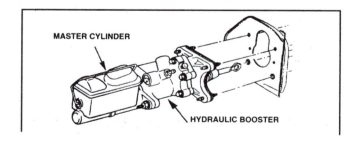

Figure C5-9 Typical hydraulic booster assembly

Badly Adjusted Brakes

C5.020   When the braking on one side of a vehicle is not of equal efficiency to the braking on the other side, the vehicle will pull to the side with the stronger braking. A check can be made at the scene or elsewhere by jacking up the vehicle and testing each wheel for turning resistance while the brakes are applied gradually.

C5.021   A check should also be made to determine how far the brake pedal can be depressed. As brake linings wear, it is necessary to depress the brake pedal farther in order to brake. Properly working automatic brake adjusters will take up this slack, however, and maintain proper or adequate brake pedal travel.

Brake Inspections

C5.022 Examine the braking system in an effort to determine whether the brakes were deficient prior to the collision. This is particularly important if there are no signs of braking on the roadway, i.e., no skid marks leading up to the collision point, when there is no apparent reason for the driver not to have applied the brakes.

C5.023 A skid mark is good evidence that there was braking capability on the wheel that left the mark. By itself, a single skid mark does not prove that the braking efficiency of the entire braking system was adequate. Other wheels that left no skid mark may have had defective braking. Or the vehicle may have been loaded far beyond its safe carrying capacity except on the one wheel that locked up and left a mark.

C5.024 Brake failure, when it occurs, is often the result of brake-fluid loss. There are, however, a number of tests that can be carried out to determine the cause of the failure and the general condition of the braking system without removing the wheels and other parts of the system.

C5.025 Brake fluid lines may crack through normal wear and tear, be broken by outside forces, as from rocks or collision, or be worn by rubbing against a wheel or other vehicle part. If brake-line failure is evident, check the roadway leading up to the point of collision for evidence of fluid loss caused through the application of brakes. Conversely, examine the collision point for fluid loss indicating that fluid lines were broken and fluid lost as a direct result of the collision.

C5.026 If there is low pedal reserve, determine whether full brake-pedal reserve can be restored and, if so, how many strokes are required to restore it to normal. The time necessary to restore braking efficiency by pumping the brake pedal could very well have a bearing on why the brakes were not activated. Check the fluid level in the master cylinder. Inspect the fluid lines from the master cylinder to all wheels. Inspect the inner side of each wheel for fluid stains. If stains are evident, the wheel cylinder has been defective or leaking for a longer period of time. Fresh fluid on the inside of a wheel indicates a recent break in the wheel cylinder or at least that the brakes were recently applied.

C5.027 Linings that are wet or damp from water, grease or oil often cause braking deficiencies due to reduced friction between the brake lining and brake drum. When there is evidence of pulling to the right or left, hard pedal effort, or brake fading, check immediately for wet or damp brake drums and tires on one or more wheels and for water on the roadway

246

leading up to the point of collision. A later examination can be made of the brake linings for oil or grease.

C5.028 When brakes are applied constantly over extended periods of time -- as on steep hills -- the brake linings become hot, causing a possible *fading* or loss of full braking efficiency without the usual evidence of brake failure being available to the investigator.

C5.029 In situations where a vehicle is badly damaged or where a detailed technical examination of the braking system is required, the investigator should obtain the services or assistance of a qualified mechanic.

Air Brake System

C5.030 An air-brake system consists of five main components:
1. Compressor
2. Reservoir
3. Foot valve (brake pedal)
4. Brake chambers
5. Brake shoes and drums

C5.031 The compressor pumps air into the reservoir, where it is stored. The foot valve draws the compressed air from the reservoir when the brake is applied. Upon brake application, the compressed air is directed through a series of lines and valves to the brake chambers, transferring the force exerted by the compressed air to mechanical linkages and the brake shoes and drums.

INVESTIGATING FOR BRAKE EQUIPMENT FAULTS

DRIVER'S CLAIM	TYPE OF SYSTEM	TRY VEHICLE	POSSIBLE ORIGINS OF CLAIM	INSPECT VEHICLE	OBSERVE SCENE	ADDITIONAL FACTS
BRAKES PULL	All Systems	Drive only after inspecting vehicle.	Wet Brakes	Look for wet brakes and tires. Wet front right brake for left pull and wet front left brake for right pull.	1. Look for deep puddles in roadway. 2. Look for angled skid marks. 3. Look for vehicle rotation.	1. Wet brakes are temporary condition and can disappear. 2. Power unit or master cylinder will not cause pull.
			Contaminated Brakes	Have linings inspected for contamination by qualified mechanic.		
			Over Adjusted Brakes	Have adjustment of brakes checked by qualified mechanic		
	Power Assisted Systems	1. With vehicle stationary, check pedal efforts with and without engine running. 2. On trucks with low air or vacuum warning, does light or buzzer stay on with engine running? Does gauge show a reading.	No Power Available	1. Look for disconnected or ruptured air or vacuum line.	Look for skid marks which show maximum braking occurred despite hard pedal.	Brakes can still be applied though harder pedal efforts are required.
HARD PEDAL EFFORT	Straight Air Systems	With vehicle stationary and engine running, does warning light or buzzer stay on? Does gauge show reading?	No Power Available	2. Look for loose or broken belt on vacuum pump or air compressor.	Look for skid marks by trailer of combination vehicle.	On most combination vehicles the trailer brakes can be operated by hand separate from the tractor brakes. In addition, they will come on automatically if air pressure is interrupted or drops too low.
	All Systems	Drive, but only after inspecting vehicle.	Wet Brakes	Look for wet brakes and tires.	Puddles in roadway.	Wet brakes are temporary.
			Brake Fade	1. Smell and feel for brake heat. 2. How is vehicle loaded? Is it towing a trailer without brakes which adds to load? 3. Is parking brake on? 4. Have linings inspected for wear by qualified mechanic.	1. Is terrain hilly or mountainous? 2. There should not be any skid marks.	1. Brake fade is temporary condition. 2. What is the speed of the vehicle and frequency of stops? 3. Did driver ride his foot on brake pedal?
PEDAL GOES TO FLOOR	All Hydraulic Systems, Either Manual or Power	Apply brake pedal with vehicle stationary.	Hydraulic Leakage	1. Check for fluid in master cylinder reservoir. 2. Check for visible fluid leakage at hydraulic hose and tubing.		1. Pedal should not go to floor with split hydraulic system, though stopping distance may increase with a failure. 2. Pedal may not go all the way to floor after brakes cool down from fade condition. This is because the system contracts as brakes cool.
			Brake Fade	See vehicle inspections above for brake fade.	1. Check fluid on ground. 2. There should not be any skid marks at point of stop.	
			Brakes Out of Adjustment	Have adjustment of brakes checked by qualified mechanic.	3. Failure of front (split hydraulic system) can cause vehicle rotation.	
			Brake Fluid Boil	Check for fluid spill-over from master cylinder reservoir.		Brake fluid boil is temporary condition
BRAKES WONT RELEASE	All Systems	Drive vehicle to check for freedom of movement under engine power.	Bind in Brake Pedal	Pull on brake pedal to see if it is fully released.	Skid marks should continue to point of stop.	
			Master Cylinder Linkage Improperly Adjusted	Have adjustment of master cylinder linkage checked by qualified mechanic.		
			Stuck Control Valve in Power Unit	Have air or vacuum power source disconnected by qualified mechanic to see if brakes release.		

Figure C5-10 Investigating for brake equipment faults

248

C5.032 An air-pressure gauge indicating air pressure in the main reservoir system is usually mounted on the dashboard of the vehicle cab. Federal and state legislation usually governs the minimum and maximum amounts of air pressure required for vehicle operation.

C5.033 Slack adjusters take up the slack in the brake linkages. If slack adjusters are not properly adjusted, braking efficiency can be substantially reduced or be totally destroyed.

C5.034 When possible, an at-scene air-brake system examination should include a check for:

      a.   Reservoir pressure

      b.   Pushrod travel on all chambers

      c.   Audible air leaks

      d.   Damaged or broken lines and connections

      e.   Moisture in reservoirs

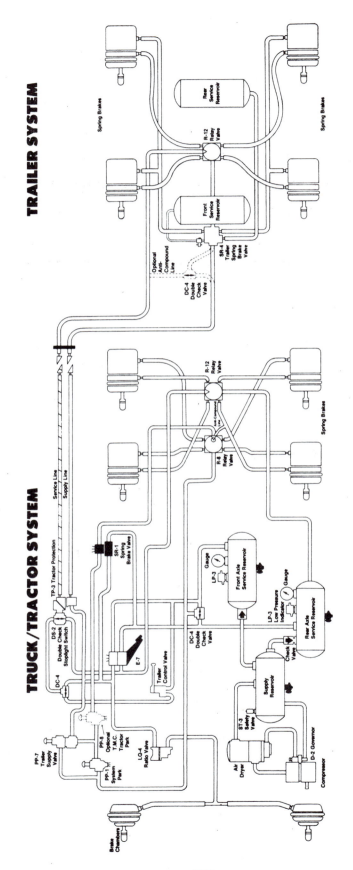

TRAILER SYSTEM

Spring Brakes

Rear Service Reservoir

R-12 Relay Valve

Front Service Reservoir

Spring Brakes

SR-4 Trailer Spring Brake Valve

DC-4 Double Check Valve

Optional Anti-Compound Line

TRUCK/TRACTOR SYSTEM

Service Line

Supply Line

TP-3 Tractor Protection

DS-2 Double Check Stoplight Switch

DC-4

SR-1 Spring Brake Valve

E-7

Trailer Control Valve

DC-4 Double Check Valve

R-12 Relay Valve

Anti-Compound Line

R-8 Relay Valve

Spring Brakes

Gauge

LP-3

Front Axle Service Reservoir

LP-3 Low Pressure Indicator

Gauge

Rear Axle Service Reservoir

Check Valve

PP-7 Trailer Supply Valve

PP-8 Optional T.M.C. Tractor Park

PP-1 System Park

LO-4 Ratio Valve

Supply Reservoir

ST-3 Safety Valve

Air Dryer

D-2 Governor

Compressor

Brake Chambers

Figure C5-11 Typical dual tractor/trailer air-brake system

Steering Systems

General

C5.035 A worn or defective steering assembly may cause loss of vehicle control. Check the condition of the steering assembly by turning the steering wheel as fully as possible in each direction. Quick, short turns on the steering wheel will often indicate loose or worn parts. Check all steering parts for continuity and the steering column for loose mountings. An examination can be made most effectively when a tow truck lifts the vehicle in removing it from the accident scene.

C5.036 When a *power-assisted steering system* is involved, check for broken or disconnected hoses; check the drive belt for tension, slippage or breakage; and check the pump reservoir for fluid. If the power-steering drive belt is missing, check the engine compartment and the roadway leading up to the point of collision for the belt or its remnants. Belt breakage may have caused loss of steering and braking control.

C5.037 Raise and rotate each wheel separately to check for *binding*. Check for *wheel-bearing play* by grasping either side of the tire of a raised wheel with both hands (one on each side) and attempting to move the wheel in and out. Worn or loose bearings can cause steering difficulty, particularly at high speeds.

C5.038 Damaged or improper *wheel alignment* causes a vehicle to steer hard, causes it to pull to one side or the other and may cause it to wander on the roadway. Worn tires often indicate improper wheel alignment and front suspension problems.

C5.039 It is necessary that a vehicle be kept in proper alignment in order to steer and maneuver properly. There are several possible causes of steering defects: bad design, accidental damage, worn components, amateur modifications or fitting of larger diameter tires than proper for the vehicle. Any of these conditions will affect the self-centering action of the front wheels.

C5.040 Check the free play of the steering wheel. Steering-wheel play in excess of one inch (2.54 cm) is a possible indication of a worn or defective steering linkage or steering box.

C5.041 Major parts of the *front end* of a truck and a car, respectively, are listed below, followed by an explanation of the function of several parts that often affect alignment and tire wear.

Truck	**Car***
Solid axle	Upper A frames
King pins and bushings	Lower A frames
Brake drums	Spindle support arms
Brake shoes	Upper and lower ball joints
Spindles	Spindles
Main bearings	Main bearings
Small bearings or bushings	Small bearings
Hubs	Rotors and calipers (disc brake)
Wheels	Brake drums and shoes (drum
Rims	brake)
Tires	Wheels

*with independent front suspension

252

Steering gear	Tires
Cross-shaft	Steering gear
Pitman arm	Cross-shaft
Drag link	Pitman arm
Idler arm	Idler arm
Tie rod	Center link
Tie rod ends	Tie rods
Tie rod arms	Tie rod ends
	Tie rod arms

Following is an explanation of how replacing certain parts can solve misalignment and tire wear problems.

IDLER ARMS

Idler arms hold the steering linkage in place. By replacing worn idler arms you can reduce vehicle wander, excessive play in the steering wheel and abnormal tire wear.

TIE ROD ENDS

Tie-rod ends connect the steering arm to the linkage. By replacing worn tie rod ends you can reduce front-end looseness, vibration, misalignment and excessive tire wear.

BALL JOINTS

Ball joints are the pivot points on which the front wheels turn. By replacing worn ball joints you can reduce front-end noise, looseness and abnormal tire wear.

BUSHINGS

Bushings help dampen front-end movement, keep body roll to a minimum and help dampen wheel shock and vibration. Replacing worn bushings helps eliminate noise and play, and makes handling safer and more predictable.

Steering Gear Design

C5.042 The following discussion of the steering system and the steering gear is based on the National Automobile Manufacturers Association Inspection Guide.

The steering system changes the rotary motion of the steering wheel into side-to-side turning motion at the front wheels. The steering gear is enclosed in a housing at the end of the steering column and mounted to the vehicle chassis.

All steering gears except rack and pinion have some kind of *worm gear* on the end of the steering wheel shaft. The steering gear also contains a *cross-shaft*, or *sector shaft*, which turns the rotary motion of the steering-wheel shaft 90 degrees. A short lever called a *pitman arm* is connected to the cross-shaft. Rotary motion of the cross-shaft becomes side-to-side or front-to-rear motion of the pitman arm and is relayed to the front wheels by the steering linkage.

Steering gears are classified by the device used to engage the cross-shaft with the worm gear. The types in general use are:

1. Cam and lever
2. Worm and roller
3. Worm and sector
4. Recirculating ball

At one time, a common steering gear on U.S. vehicles was the recirculating ball type. A ballnut is mounted on the worm gear and moves up and down the worm as the steering shaft, or worm shaft, turns. Ball bearings roll between the threads on the worm and the internal threads of the ballnut to reduce friction and ease steering effort. External teeth on the ballnut mesh with a sector gear on the cross-shaft to turn the cross-shaft as the ballnut moves.

A slight amount of looseness may develop in the steering gear during the life of a vehicle. All steering gear types have provisions to adjust worm-shaft endplay and *backlash* between the worm and the cross-shaft gear. Manufacturers provide specific instructions for various designs.

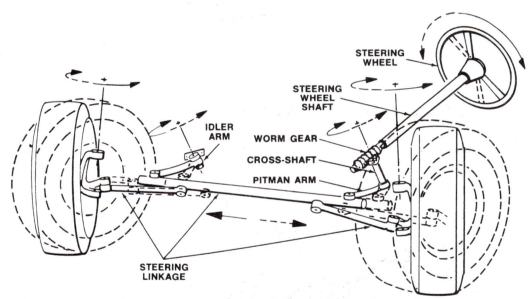

Rotary motion of the steering wheel is changed into turning motion at the front wheels by the steering gear and linkage.

Figure C5-12   Manual steering gear (Courtesy of National Automobile Manufacturers Association)

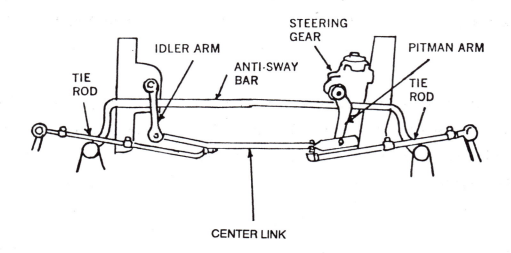

Figure C5-13 Typical steering system

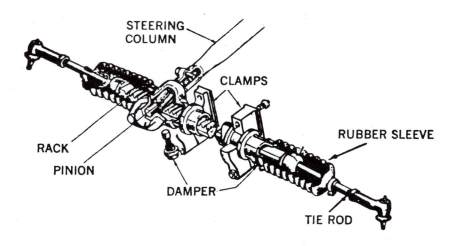

Figure C5-14 Rack and pinion steering system

C5.043   If there is evidence of rear-wheel displacement or improper alignment, check the rear-axle positioning arms and/or struts, rear axle and drive shaft for breakage or worn supports.

C5.044   A broken or weakened metal part should be examined to determine whether it might have contributed to the accident.   These examinations should pay particular attention to the steering, drive shaft, braking and wheel assemblies and any other metal part such as the windshield wiper assembly that might have malfunctioned because of breakage or weakness.

C5.045 Broken metal has a gritty or rough surface. Old breaks or cracks such as those that often occur as the result of metal fatigue are discolored. New breaks give a shiny appearance. A combination of discoloration and shiny metal in a break usually indicates an old crack and a fresh or recent break (see Fig. C5-15). If a part is broken as the result of impact, the part normally shows damage where it was struck.

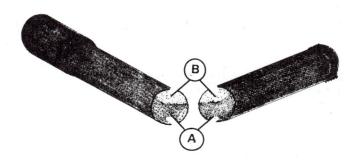

Figure C5-15 A broken tie-rod. Note the discoloration of the old crack **A** and the shiny, gritty appearance of the new break **B**. (Courtesy of Charles C. Thomas, Publisher)

Front Wheel Drive (FWD)

C5.046 A vehicle referred to as a front-wheel-drive vehicle is one in which the front or steering-axle wheels, rather than the rear wheels, provide power to move the vehicle. A FWD vehicle has no drive shaft connecting the engine and transmission through a rear differential and rear axles to the rear wheels, but has a transmission and differential assembly mounted to the engine in the engine compartment and connected through the front axles to the front wheels. A 4-wheel-drive or all-wheel-drive (AWD) vehicle combines front-wheel drive with rear-wheel drive so that power can be supplied to all wheels. Many such models permit the front wheels to be disengaged when they are not needed for traction.

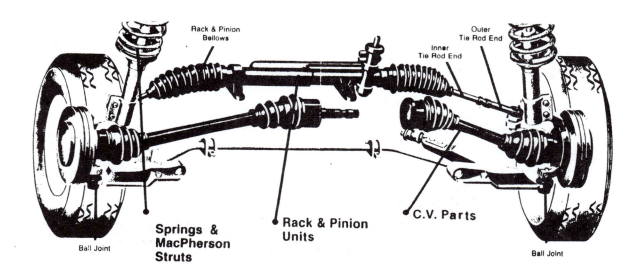

The front wheel drive system is primarily made up of:
1. The suspension system (MacPherson struts)
2. The steering system (rack & pinion)
3. The drive line (constant velocity parts)

Figure C5-16 Front-wheel-drive system (with rack & pinion steering)

TROUBLE SHOOTING CHART FOR INVESTIGATION OF STEERING EQUIPMENT FAULTS

Driver's Claim	Type of System	Try Vehicle	Possible Origins of Claim	Inspect Vehicle	Observe Scene	Additional Facts
Steering Pulls	Manual and Power Systems	Drive the vehicle unless a tire is flat.	Unbalanced air pressure in front tires	Check for low tire or flat tire.		
			Front wheel misalignment	Have front wheel alignment checked, and inspect front tires for irregular wear.		
			Weak or broken suspension spring	Have springs checked by qualified mechanic.		
Hard Steering Effort	Manual and Power Systems	1. Rotate steering wheel with vehicle stationary and then moving to check for difference in efforts. 2. Check steering effort with front wheels off the ground.	Bind in gear or column	1. Check gear box for lubricant. 2. Check gear box for foreign objects.		
	Power Systems	With vehicle stationary, check steering efforts with and without engine running.	No Power Available	1. Check pump reservoir for fluid. 2. Check pump drive belt for looseness and breakage. 3. Are there ruptured or disconnected hoses which show leakage?	1. Broken pump belt may drop to roadway. 2. Check for fluid on ground.	It will still be possible to steer though harder efforts are required.
Road Wheel Won't Turn Or Return	Manual and Power Systems	Check steering wheel lash.	Looseness in steering system			
			Disconnected linkage	Inspect for disconnection of linkage joints.		
					Check for skid marks.	Steering will not respond if front wheels are locked by braking.

SYMPTOM	CAUSE
Thumps and Knocks from Front Suspension	Loose or worn ball joints Loose front suspension attaching bolts Missing adjusting shims Loose shock absorber mountings
Groans or Creaks from Front Suspension	Loose attaching bolts Bent control arm or steering knuckle Ball joints galled or in need of lubrication
Squeaks from Front Suspension	Control arm shaft bushings need lubrication Coil spring rubbing on seat
Wander or Shimmy	Loose or worn ball joints Control arm shaft bushings worn Loose suspension attaching bolts Weak Shock absorbers Weak front springs Incorrect front end alignment
Frequent Bottoming of Suspension on Bumps	Weak front springs Weak shock absorbers
Front End Sag	Weak front springs
Irregular or Excessive Tire Wear	Incorrect front wheel alignment Loose or worn ball joints Loose front suspension attaching bolts Weak shock absorbers Weak front springs Bent control arm or steering knuckle Control arm shaft bushings worn
Floating, Wallowing and Poor Recovery from Bumps	Weak shock absorbers Weak front springs
Pulling to One Side While Braking	Loose or worn ball joints Loose suspension attaching bolts Bent control arm or steering knuckle Weak front springs Weak shock absorbers
Rough Ride and Excessive Road Shock	Damaged shock absorbers Weak shock absorbers Weak springs Control arm shaft bushings need lubrication Ball joints galled or in need of lubrication
Excessive Steering Play	Loose or worn ball joints Loose suspension attaching bolts Worn control arm shaft bushings Weak front springs
Car Pulls to One Side	Loose or worn ball joints Loose suspension attaching bolts Worn control arm shaft bushings Weak front springs Incorrect wheel alignment Bent control arm or steering knuckle
Hard Steering	Ball joints galled or in need of lubrication Incorrect front end alignment Bent control arm or steering knuckle

Suspension Systems

C5.047 Most automobiles use a ball-joint independent front suspension. The wheel *spindle* is attached directly to the suspension arms by the ball joints.

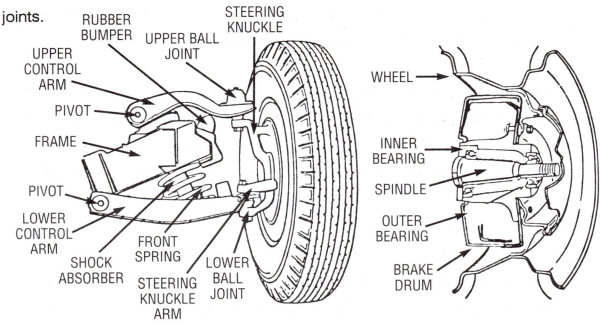

Figure C5-17 Front wheel mounting

The wheel itself turns on *ball* or *roller bearings* mounted on the wheel spindle. The *cone*, or inner part of the larger bearing, fits against the spindle and is sealed in place to prevent loss of lubrication. The bearing adjustment nut, located on the spindle, pushes against the outer, smaller bearing and can be turned with a wrench to provide correct bearing adjustment. A *cotter pin*, passed through openings in this nut and a hole in the spindle, serves to lock the bearing assembly in place. The outer parts of the bearing fit into machined recesses in the hub of the wheel. The dust cap fits over the outer end of the spindle and seals the bearing against dust, dirt and water. See Figure C5-17.

C5.048 Various types of suspension systems have been used to reduce shocks, absorb side thrusts, and improve riding comfort. Early cars used *leaf springs* of various types. Later, *coil springs* were introduced. Still later, *torsion bars* were used by some manufacturers. Most modern automobiles use either a combination of coil springs in front and *semi-elliptical* leaf springs in back or coil springs in front and back.

C5.049 It is important to distinguish between independent suspensions and non-independent suspensions. Essentially, the difference is that an *independent suspension* allows one of the wheels on an axle to move vertically without imposing any corresponding movement on the other wheel.

C5.050 For many years most cars have had independent front suspension. Today many cars have independent suspension front and rear. Independent rear suspension in its various forms is becoming more popular as efforts are made to improve roadability.

C5.051 Most commercial vehicle manufacturers use semi-elliptical leaf springs all around. The configurations of these springs in rear tandem suspensions vary with the particular manufacturer's ideas and the uses for which a vehicle has been designed.

C5.052 Altering suspension systems -- by raising or lowering a vehicle from its designed height, for example -- can adversely affect the stability and handling characteristics of the vehicle.

Independent Front Wheel Suspension

C5.053 All modern automobiles use some type of independent front-wheel suspension. Each wheel assembly, which is attached separately to the frame by means of an upper and lower *control arm*, operates in connection with a coil spring.

C5.054 Each wheel is free to move up and down without causing any action in the other wheel. Frequently, a *stabilizer bar* is used. This bar passes through *bushings* attached to the frame and is attached to the lower arms of the wheel assemblies. When one spring is deflected by a sudden load or bump, the stabilizer bar acts to transfer some of the force to the opposite side of the car and prevent body sway. See Figure C5-18.

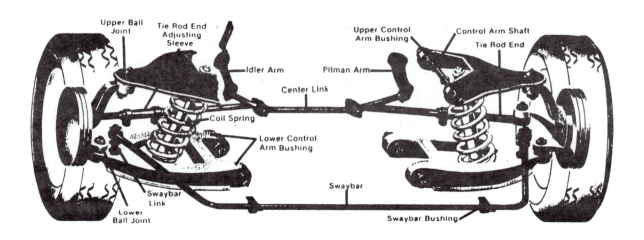

Figure C5-18 Independent front-wheel suspension on a rear-wheel-drive car

Independent Rear Wheel Suspension

C5.055 This suspension suspends the rear-wheel assemblies and, in rear-wheel-drive vehicles, the drive axles (but not the differential or drive shaft). It also absorbs side to side thrust and vibration by means of the larger rubber cushions with which the suspension is attached to the car. The rear wheels in suspension systems like this must be aligned for toe-in and camber in much the same manner as the front wheels. As in independent front-wheel suspension, independent rear-wheel suspension permits either of the wheels to move up or down without directly influencing the other wheel.

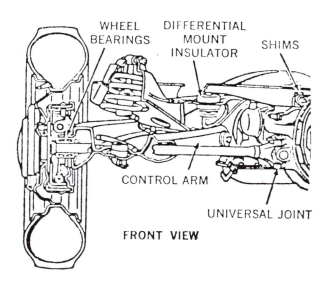

Figure C5-19 Independent rear-wheel suspension on a rear-wheel-drive car. Note the drive axle with universal joint. The differential is mounted to the car body.

Leaf Springs

C5.056 A leaf spring is composed of a number of flat steel strips, each one somewhat shorter than the other (see Fig. C5-20). A *U-bolt clamp* holds the leaves together, and *spring clips* are located at various points along the spring. The *main* or longest leaf has an eye fashioned at each end for attaching the leaf to the frame.

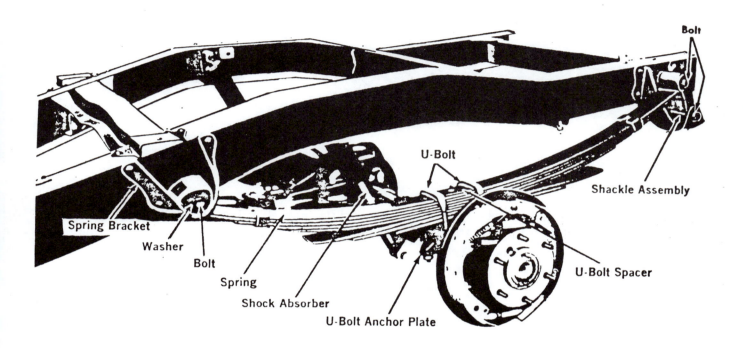

Figure C5-20 Leaf spring and attachments

C5.057 Usually one eye of the main leaf is bolted to the frame, and the other is attached by means of a swinging connection called a *shackle*. When the spring is deflected under a load, the leaves slide upon each other, causing friction which acts to lessen the vibration and reduce the bouncing action. This deflection causes the total length of the spring to be increased. As the load is removed and the leaves slide back into normal position, their friction upon returning also reduces the severity of sudden shocks.

265

C5.058 When a vehicle handling problem is suspected in an accident, check for loose or broken spring leaves and for loose, missing, or broken U-bolts, spring shackles, or spring clips.

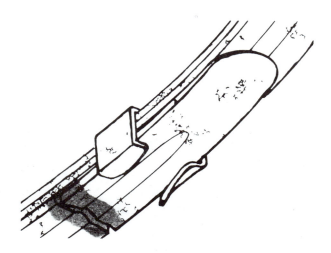

Figure C5-21 Broken spring leaves and damaged spring clip (Courtesy of National Automobile Manufacturers Association)

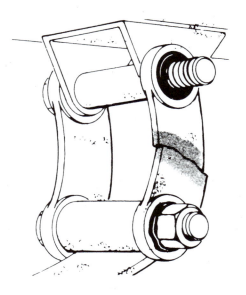

Figure C5-22 Broken spring shackle and missing nut on upper bolt (Courtesy of National Automobile Manufacturers Association)

Trailing Arm (Link)

C5.059 An independently suspended rear wheel may be held in position by means of a metal piece known as a *trailing arm* or *link* which is attached at one end to the wheel assembly and at the other end to a cross-member of the body of the car.

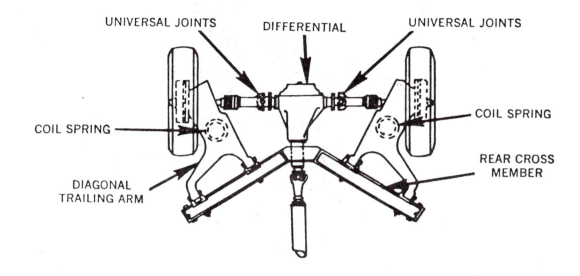

Figure C5-23 Independent rear-wheel suspension showing trailing arms (top view)

Coil Springs

C5.060 *Coil springs* are widely used in independent front-wheel suspensions and often in rear suspensions (see Fig.'s C5-17, 18, 19 and 23). They are efficient as load carriers, but they cannot absorb the driving and braking side thrusts imposed by the operation of the car. Coil springs operate noiselessly and require no lubrication.

Torsion Bars

C5.061 Some makes of cars employ independent front-wheel suspension through the use of *torsion bars*. Under this suspension system, road shocks are absorbed through a torque (twisting) action of the bar.

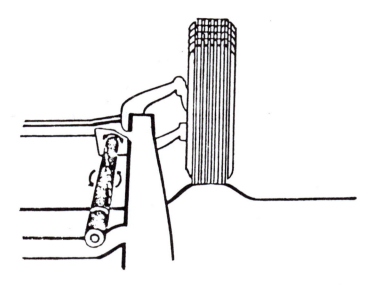

Figure C5-24 Torsion bar

Air Suspension

C5.062 In an *air suspension system*, columns of air support the vehicle in rubber and nylon-diaphragm air springs, replacing metal coil or leaf springs. Using a compressor, air reservoir, leveling valves, and regulators requiring assorted plumbing connections, air springs overcome certain shortcomings of the metal springs. The objective is a level, stabilized ride with proper road clearance under all road conditions.

Shock Absorbers

C5.063 A *shock absorber* is installed on each front and rear wheel to prevent excessive spring rebound. A shock absorber operates very much like the hydraulic check installed on doors to prevent slamming. It contains a piston or fan, which moves in a hydraulic fluid. When the normal distance between the wheel and frame of the vehicle is increased or decreased, the piston or fan presses against the fluid, forcing it through small restricted openings. Resistance to this flow creates a back pressure on the piston or fan and slows down its movement. This in turn absorbs sudden shocks to the car frame and reduces vibration.

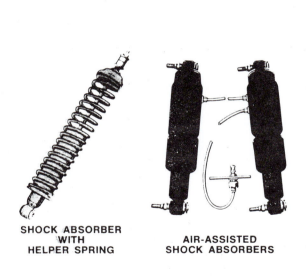

SHOCK ABSORBER
WITH
HELPER SPRING

AIR-ASSISTED
SHOCK ABSORBERS

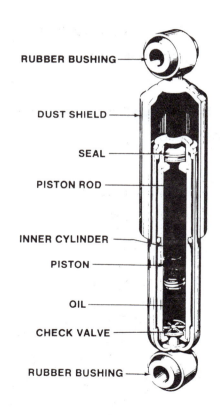

RUBBER BUSHING

DUST SHIELD

SEAL

PISTON ROD

INNER CYLINDER

PISTON

OIL

CHECK VALVE

RUBBER BUSHING

Figure C5-25   Shock absorbers   (Courtesy of National Automobile Manufacturers Association)

Tires

Types

C5.064 Tire construction and tire condition are obviously crucial to safe vehicle operation and performance. Therefore, tire knowledge by an investigator is essential to a thorough investigation.

C5.065 There are basically two types of tire construction:

1. Bias-ply construction
2. Radial-ply construction

Three basic types of tires are manufactured using these two types of construction:

1. Bias-ply tires
2. Bias-belted tires
3. Radial tires

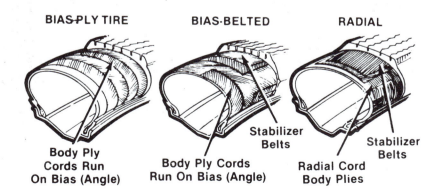

Figure C5-26 Tire types and construction

Bias-Ply Construction

C5.066 There are in turn three basic types of tires of *bias-ply* construction:

1. Textile
2. Steel
3. Belted

C5.067 The casing of a *textile* tire is made up of two or more plies (layers) of textile cords (rayon, nylon, polyester, etc.) set on a bias (at an angle) from bead to bead. The cords of each ply are laid crosswise to those of the next ply. Depending upon tensile strength of the cord used and the required size of the tire, there could be up to 44 plies in a tire casing.

C5.068 *Steel* construction involves the use of steel cords rather than textile cords.

C5.069 Some years ago tire manufacturers introduced *belted* tires with cross-ply casing in the passenger-car tire line. The casing of such a tire is the same as for a full cross-ply tire, but two or more belts with cords made of rayon, steel, fiberglass or other high-grade material form a layer around the circumference of the tire between the casing and the tread to reinforce the casing and stiffen the tread.

Radial-Ply Construction

C5.070 A *radial tire* is designed to function as two completely independent working parts:

1.   The casing (for cushioning power)

2.   The tread (for adequate contact area)

That is, in radial construction a pneumatic tire is made to perform its two basis functions in the most efficient manner by separating the provision of *cushioning power* from the provision of *contact area* so that a minimum of heat is generated by the tire. This is done by laying casing plies radially (archwise) from bead to bead with cords at right angles to the direction of travel of the tire and then bracing the crown area with stabilizing belts laid on top of each other circumferentially with cords running at an angle. The number of plies can vary from as few as two to as many as six, depending upon the type and size of the tire. The radial configuration of the cords enables the walls to work independently of the tread. Such action is not possible with other types of tire construction, where there is a direct connection between wall and tread movement. See Figure C5-27.

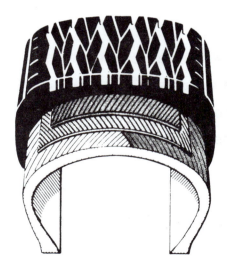

Figure C5-27 Note the lay of the cords in the casing plies of a radial tire as opposed to a belted bias-ply tire. The belts in both tires have a similar cord lay, however. (Courtesy of National Automobile Manufacturers Association)

272

C5.071 Radial tires should not be mixed with other types of tires. To do so can cause vehicle directional instability.

Inspection

C5.072 Tires should be checked for:

a. Fabric or rubber deterioration

b. Tread wear

c. Breaks in the casing

d. Cuts

e. Valve stem breakage

f. Nails, glass or other foreign objects embedded in the tire tread or walls

g. Tread separation

h. Bead failure

i. General condition (for wear)

C5.073 A vehicle showing overall neglect often has one or more tires showing abnormal tire wear (see Fig. C5-28). The pattern of this tire wear can sometimes point to the reason why the driver failed to control his vehicle properly and became involved in an accident.

C5.074 Tire tread wear can indicate whether a tire has been operated *underinflated* or *overinflated*. In accidents where tire failure appears to be a contributing factor, examine the air pressure of all remaining tires to determine whether the driver habitually operated the vehicle on underinflated or overinflated tires.

C5.075 An underinflated tire overheats rapidly. As heat increases, it melts the tire rubber and weakens tire fabrics. Under these circumstances, particularly on a long trip or at high-speed travel, the tire may burst.

C5.076 When being slammed into a pothole or driven at excessive speed around a curve, an underinflated tire may momentarily pull loose from the wheel rim along part of the rim's circumference, causing air loss and consequent loss of vehicle control.

C5.077 Uneven tire wear can be caused not only by improper inflation but also by incorrect wheel alignment (toe-in and camber). See Figures C5-28 and C5-29.

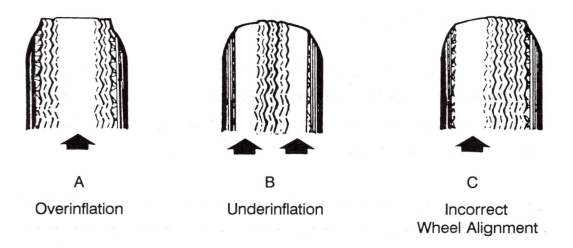

A
Overinflation

B
Underinflation

C
Incorrect
Wheel Alignment

Figure C5-28 Tire tread wear patterns

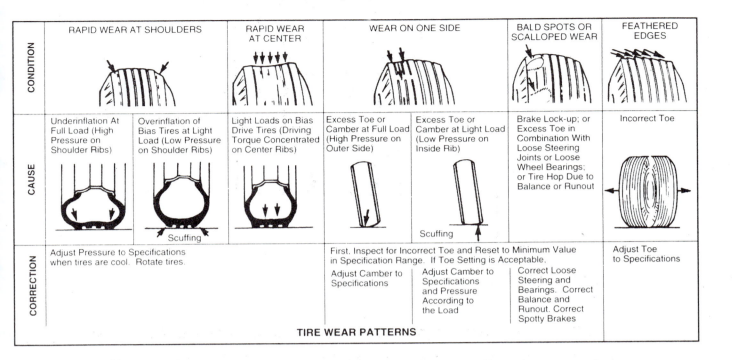

	RAPID WEAR AT SHOULDERS		RAPID WEAR AT CENTER	WEAR ON ONE SIDE		BALD SPOTS OR SCALLOPED WEAR	FEATHERED EDGES
CONDITION							
CAUSE	Underinflation At Full Load (High Pressure on Shoulder Ribs)	Overinflation of Bias Tires at Light Load (Low Pressure on Shoulder Ribs)	Light Loads on Bias Drive Tires (Driving Torque Concentrated on Center Ribs)	Excess Toe or Camber at Full Load (High Pressure on Outer Side)	Excess Toe or Camber at Light Load (Low Pressure on Inside Rib)	Brake Lock-up; or Excess Toe in Combination With Loose Steering Joints or Loose Wheel Bearings; or Tire Hop Due to Balance or Runout	Incorrect Toe
		Scuffing			Scuffing		
CORRECTION	Adjust Pressure to Specifications when tires are cool. Rotate tires.			First. Inspect for Incorrect Toe and Reset to Minimum Value in Specification Range. If Toe Setting is Acceptable.			Adjust Toe to Specifications
				Adjust Camber to Specifications	Adjust Camber to Specifications and Pressure According to the Load	Correct Loose Steering and Bearings. Correct Balance and Runout. Correct Spotty Brakes	

TIRE WEAR PATTERNS

Figure C5-29 Diagnostic chart for tread wear patterns

C5.078 Premature tread wear is a sign of tire, vehicle or driver neglect. Groove edges provide traction, cornering and braking grip. On wet roadway surfaces, tread *grooves* channel water off to the rear and out to both sides of the tire. When tread bars are worn down, the grooves become too shallow to disperse surface moisture effectively, causing the tire to lift from the road and ride on a film of water. This *hydroplaning* takes place at a certain critical speed and diminishes or eliminates vehicle control.

C5.079 A tire tread has built-in *wear indicators*. When these appear level with the tread surface, insufficient tread remains for safe driving. Worn treads are also more puncture-prone (90% of tire failures occur when only 10% of the tread remains). See Figure C5-30.

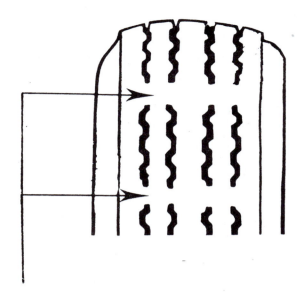

Figure C5-30 Tire tread wear indicators

C5.080 Poor quality *recaps* on tires may become loose and fail or tear away from the casing. This will cause difficulty in vehicle control. When a tire indicates this type of failure, the highway should be examined for tire fragments leading up to the point of collision to determine whether the tire damage or failure occurred before or resulted from the collision.

C5.081 If loss of air pressure is caused by damage such as a cut or tear, attempt to determine what caused the damage -- a broken body part that punctured the tire, a foreign object struck by the tire on the roadway, and so on. Where a tire loses air pressure because of cuts or holes resulting from the collision, the damage should be matched to the item that caused it. The item may be found on either vehicle involved in the collision or on any other object that the vehicle may have come into contact with. Such matching evidence eliminates any argument or suggestion that the tire was damaged or lost air pressure before impact. See Figure C5-31.

Figure C5-31 Air-pressure loss from a tire puncture caused by a broken body part during collision.

C5.082 Very often a driver will claim that his vehicle suffered a *blowout*, when actually a deflated tire visible at the scene went flat as the result of the collision. It is important to determine whether the air loss occurred prior to or after the collision. Prior air loss can be a contributing factor in a vehicle's going out of control. When there are no roadway marks indicating an air pressure loss leading up to the point of impact, check the tire closely for damage *before* any vehicles are moved and attempt to determine what damaged the tire or otherwise caused the loss of air pressure.

C5.083 When it is necessary to remove a tire from the wheel rim to conduct a deeper analysis of tire failure, mark the tire and rim in such a way that any tire damage can later be related to rim damage or defects (see Fig. C5-32).

C5.084 The investigator may need to record the descriptive data for a tire that will be used as an item of evidence. This information, found on the sidewall of the tire, is explained in Figure C5-33.

Figure C5-32 Use of a white crayon to mark the mounting position of the tire on the rim before the tire is removed for examination

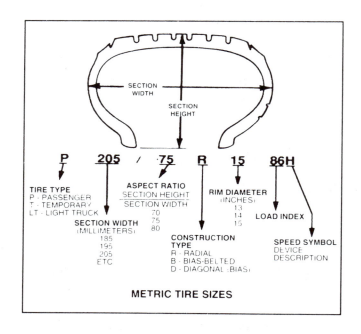

Figure C5-33 Interpretation of the label P205/75 R15 86H

Exhaust System

C5.085 The basic exhaust system on motor vehicles consists of the:

a. Exhaust manifold(s)

b. Front exhaust pipe (engine pipe)

c. Catalytic converter (modern vehicle)

d. Rear exhaust pipe (with catalytic converter)

e. Muffler(s)

f. Tailpipe

C5.086 The exhaust system carries engine exhaust from the exhaust manifold to the rear of the vehicle. In the case of many commercial type vehicles, it may be carried to other outside locations, such as alongside the cab.

C5.087 Engine exhaust contains *carbon monoxide*, which is an odorless, colorless, poisonous gas. This gas can escape through damaged or corroded exhaust system parts or improperly fitted connections. It will often find its way to the passenger compartment through holes in the under-portions of the vehicle body caused by erosion or other damage, trunk openings or ill-fitting floor matting and interior upholstery.

C5.088 Some automobile air conditioners do not draw in clean, fresh outside air when set for *maximum cooling*. Rather, they recirculate air within the vehicle and at the same time suck in carbon monoxide gas through openings in the vehicle body. When there is an indication that a driver or passenger has suffered the effects of carbon monoxide poisoning, a thorough follow-up examination of the air conditioning unit should be made.

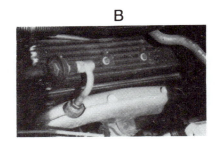

A

B

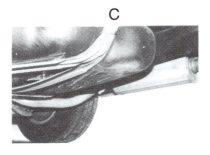

C

Figure C5-34 An exhaust system
  A. Exhaust pipes from manifolds; catalitic converters; exhaust pipes to mufflers; mufflers
  B. Left exhaust manifold
  C. Exhaust pipe from right-side muffler; resonator; tailpipe

Figure C5-35 Body erosion allows exhaust fumes (carbon monoxide) to penetrate the passenger compartment.

Other Parts Critical to the Investigation

Trailer Connections

C5.089 There are various devices for connecting a trailer or towed vehicle to a towing vehicle (see Fig.'s C5-36 and C5-37). The most common and acceptable devices are:

    a.   Couplings

    b.   Couplers and hitches

    c.   Fifth-wheel connections, used primarily by tractor and semi-trailer units

    d.   Auxiliary breakaway connections, such as *safety chains*, used to back up couplings and couplers and hitches.

C5.090 When there is evidence of a *breakaway* of the trailer or towed vehicle, examine for:

    a.   Sheared bolts

    b.   Bent parts

    c.   Abrasions

    d.   Worn or rubbed parts

    e.   Apparent *direction of force* at the time of and after breakaway

COUPLER—Attaches to Trailer

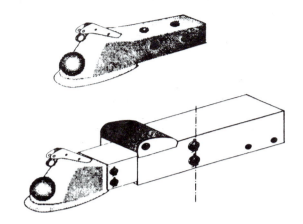

HITCH—Attaches to Tow Vehicle

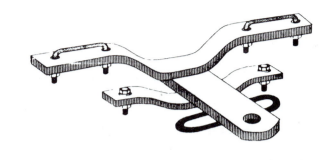

Figure C5-36 Coupler and hitch

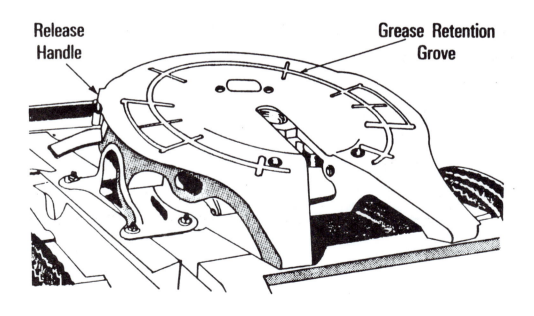

Release
Handle

Grease Retention
Grove

Figure C5-37 Fifth-wheel assembly found on large commercial vehicles

282

Gearshift Lever

C5.091 The *gearshift lever* position may corroborate other evidence regarding the speed of a vehicle prior to collision. In automatic-shift vehicles, a low range indicates a slower speed, whereas a high range or drive indicates the possibility of higher speeds.

C5.092 If the investigator is not totally familiar with the shifting mechanism in certain manual-shift vehicles (for example, large commercial trucks or farm tractors), he should have the gearshift lever position explained to him by a competent operator.

C5.093 The investigator should bear in mind that the gearshift lever might have moved from its pre-impact position to another position as a result of the collision.

Glass

C5.094 The *windshield* and *windows* of a vehicle involved in an accident should be examined to determine whether or not their condition contributed or could have contributed to the accident. Dust, dirt, mud, ice, snow, drops of water or fog on the outside surfaces of windshields or windows can obstruct the driver's view as can stickers, mist, condensation or a heavy smoke film on the inside surfaces.

C5.095 The cause of chips, gouges or cracks in a windshield should be determined. A damaged windshield or window can block the driver's view of other traffic on the highway and cause glare from sunlight, headlights or other bright lights, also obstructing his view. When the existence of glass damage prior to the collision is suspected, a driver's seated height should be established and his sight line related to the windshield and/or window damage.

C5.096 Glass may sustain *contact damage*, where a force acts directly upon the glass, or *induced damaged*, where a force acts directly upon another part which then transmits some portion of the force, sometimes through one or more other parts still, to the glass. Contact damage appears in a *spider-web* pattern, induced damage in a *checkerboard* pattern.

Figure C5-38 Contact damage caused by a person's head striking the windshield from inside the vehicle. Note the spider-web pattern.

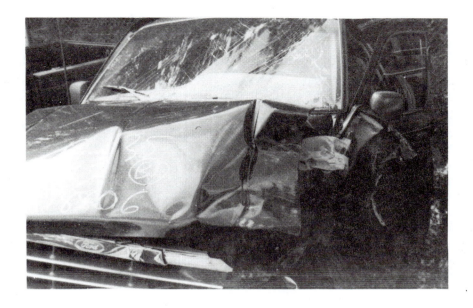

Figure C5-39 Induced damage to glass generally makes at least two sets of parallel cracks crossing each other in a checkerboard fashion.

C5.097 The positions of all windows, including air-vent windows, should always be examined. This is particularly important when there is inside *mist* or *condensation* on the windshield or windows. When windows are closed, condensation is not allowed to dissipate as readily as it would with fresh air. It is also important to determine whether windows were or were not open or partially open as it might be claimed that an insect or some other object entered the vehicle, striking or distracting the driver, or that a siren or horn of another vehicle was not heard.

C5.098 The inspection of the windshield and windows should also include checking the adequacy of the defrosters when inside mist or condensation is a factor.

285

Horn

C5.099 The adequacy of the horn is important in motor vehicle-pedestrian accidents, pullout and sideswipe accidents and all other types of accidents where a horn warning might have prevented a collision.

Lamps and Reflectors

C5.100 Examine the headlamp switch to determine whether it is in the *on* or *off* position. (CAUTION: see C5.106) Check all lights to see if they are in working condition. If the switch is in the *on* position and a lamp that is not broken does not work, check the attached electrical wires to determine if they are broken or disconnected, or whether there is some form of short circuit as a result of the collision.

C5.101 Determine the position of the high-low beam switch and whether the high-beam indicator light was working. This is important in accidents involving oncoming vehicles being forced off the roadway because of *bright* lights, accidents involving pedestrians and accidents attributable to a driver overdriving his headlights or driving too fast for conditions, e.g., darkness, fog, slick pavement.

C5.102 Some push-pull type headlamp switches will change positions (in or out) as the result of forces exerted during rear-end or front-end collisions. Nevertheless, there are experts who can determine by examination whether a light bulb was lighted at the time of collision. It is important that a complete examination of bulb *filaments* be made in instances where there might be some doubt as to whether a lamp was in fact on at the time of collision. This includes traffic-control signal lights as well as all vehicle lamps. In the case of traffic-control signal lights, it is possible to determine which phase the signal was in at the time it was damaged.

C5.103 Check brake lights and taillights in rear-end collision accidents and all other accidents that can be attributed in some way to a driver's sudden braking or deceleration.

C5.104 To determine if a light bulb was on or off at the time of impact will often require a microscopic examination of the filaments by a fully qualified laboratory technician. Such an examination should be carried out by someone who can qualify himself as an expert in lamp examination.

C5.105 Bulb filaments are very fragile. Extreme care must be taken in their removal, handling and storage. Nondamaged bulbs or lamps may be removed at the scene and transported elsewhere for examination. Where such removal might present a problem, a *qualified examiner* should be requested to attend the scene and remove the bulbs and/or carry out the examination.

C5.106 Careful notes should be made of lamp examinations or inspections at the scene or elsewhere and should indicate whether the bulbs were

    a.   on,

    b.   unbroken and off, or

    c.   broken.

A note should also be made on whether the *headlamp switch* is in the on or off position. If the switch is in the off position, DO NOT TURN IT TO THE ON POSITION to see if the lights will work. To do so may damage the filaments and thereby destroy the only physical evidence available that, through examination, will determine whether a lamp was displaying a light at the time of collision.

C5.107 Commercial and oversize vehicles require clearance lights and reflectors at their outer extremities. Additionally, commercial trailers manufactured after December 1, 1993 must display reflective sheeting or tape in specified places in order to be operated in the U.S.A. When involved in accidents, particularly sideswipe, underride and intersection accidents, vehicles of these types should be checked for the presence and serviceability of such equipment and markings.

Windshield Wipers and Defrosters

C5.108 Windshield wipers and defrosters that are either inadequate or not working can be a contributing factor in many accidents, particularly during rain, snow or other inclement weather conditions when the windshield must be kept clean in order for the driver to have proper visibility. During inclement weather, visibility problems become especially acute on secondary and dirt roads. Darkness further complicates visibility on any class of road.

C5.109 Examine the condition and adequacy of the windshield wiper and defrosting or defogging devices. Check the wiper blades and blade arms. Damaged, deteriorated or improperly adjusted wiper blade arms can cause inadequate wiper-blade contact with the windshield, resulting in impaired vision. Additionally, check the condition and position of the windshield-wiper control switch and the condition and position of the defroster (AC) controls.

Wheels

C5.110 Loose *wheel lug nuts* allow the *wheel rim* to move back and forth and cause the lug-nut holes to become elliptical. The lugs eventually wear through and break off. Loose lug nuts can lead to breakage of the wheel rim and loss of the wheel. When this occurs, the vehicle may go out of control and possibly overturn.

Figure C5-40 A broken-off lug resulting from loose lug nuts. Note the elliptical shape of the lug-nut hole.

Radio, Cassette Player, CD Player

C5.111 Determine whether the car radio, cassette player or CD player was turned on or off. If the radio was on, the station it was tuned to should be noted. The driver or passenger should be able to recall what was being broadcast when the accident occurred. This information can be useful in determining the exact time of the accident if the time is essential to know and not otherwise available. Additionally, a radio, cassette player or CD player turned to high volume might be the reason the driver did not hear a siren or horn.

Car Telephone/CB Radio

C5.112 An increasing number of vehicles are equipped with a car telephone that can be operated by the driver while he is operating the vehicle. Determine whether the driver was using the telephone when the accident occurred and if preoccupation with punching in a telephone number or carrying on a telephone conversation might have been a contributing factor. Give corresponding attention to possible use of a CB radio.

Mirrors

C5.113 Mirror positioning is very important in pullout, sideswipe and back-up accidents. Lack of or incorrect adjustment of rear-view mirrors may be why a driver did not see a parked vehicle when he was backing up, or why he did not see an overtaking vehicle as he attempted to change lanes. An examination of both inside and outside mirrors should include checking their positions in relation to the driver's seated height.

Speedometer

C5.114   The speedometer reading should be noted and recorded. Generally the reading will be zero. Occasionally, however, the needle will stick at the speed being registered at the time of collision because of impact damage. In some cases, this evidence corroborates other evidence of speed such as witnesses' statements.   It should be remembered, however, that a speedometer needle is quite sensitive and can *jump* during the first stages of collision and then jam, giving a false reading or indication of speed.

Figure C5-41 A stuck speedometer needle does not necessarily show the impact speed.

Occupant Protection Systems

C5.115 Most modern automobiles have occupant protection systems of the first or of the first and second categories below:

1.   Seat belts

    a. Active

    b. Passive

2.   Air bags

Seat Belts

C5.116 Active seat belts require the occupant to manually engage the system by fastening a buckling device.

C5.117 Passive seat belts have a part of the system that engages automatically (see Fig. C5-42). With some of these systems, some manual operation is required.

C5.118 The investigator should look for obvious indicators in establishing whether a seat belt was used by a vehicle occupant. Indicators that a seat belt was *not* used are:

    a.   Belts buckled together in front of, behind or under the seat

    b.   Shoulder belt stowed away

    c.   Belts not accessible, e.g., pushed down behind seat

d. Vehicle deformation caused by impact which intrudes, compressing the belt anchorage against the seat. (If the belt was worn, could it have retracted? If not and if the belt is not visible, it was probably not worn.)

e. Windshield impact damage, such as a spider-web pattern and bulge toward the outside of the vehicle. (The damage was probably caused by incorrect or nonuse of a seat belt.)

f. Damaged steering wheel caused by driver impact

g. Occupant ejected from the vehicle

h. Damaged upper dashboard (instrument panel) caused by occupant

i. Occupant injuries which are not compatible with seat-belt use

C5.119 Indicators that the seat belt was used include:

a. Stretching or *loading* of the belt fabric

b. Marks on latching mechanisms

c. Transfer on clothing or belts

d. Compatible injury patterns to occupants

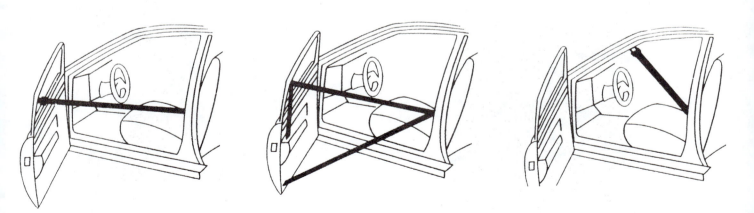

Figure C5-42 Some passive seat-belt restraints

Air Bags

C5.120   The air bag is a fabric bag mounted in the steering wheel on the driver's side (see Fig. C5-43) and on the dashboard on the passenger's side.   In a serious frontal crash, the bag will inflate at impact and deflate a fraction of a second after impact (see Fig. C5-44).

C5.121   The bag is controlled by *sensors* mounted in the vehicle.   Each air-bag manufacturer uses a slightly different system of sensors.

C5.122   If an air bag fails to deploy in a collision, the investigator should consult with an expert in air-bag technology before conducting an inspection.

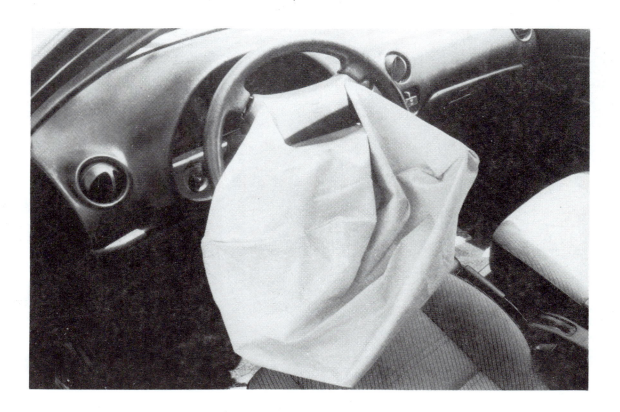

Figure C5-43   Driver's side air bag mounted in the steering wheel

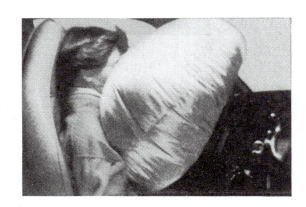

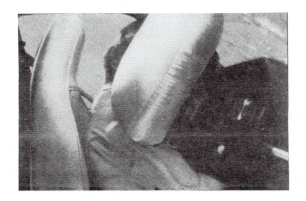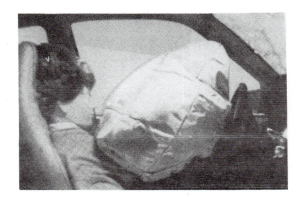

Figure C5-44 Air bag deploying (top left), inflating (upper right), cushioning driver's head (lower left), beginning to deflate (lower right)

Interior

C5.123 The interior of the vehicle should be examined for any mark or damage indicating that an occupant struck a certain point during impact. This type of evidence will often help ascertain the seated positions of occupants at the time of the accident. The mark or damage should be matched to any injuries suffered by the occupants, e.g., teeth marks on the dash matched to mouth injuries. You should look at all possibilities when attempting a match -- a rear-seated passenger might have been thrown to the front.

C5.124 The interior should also be examined for all forms of luggage or load. It is possible that an object being carried might have obstructed the driver's view or interfered with the driver's ability to steer or control his vehicle. At the same time, the number of passengers in a vehicle must be taken into consideration. Was there adequate room in the vehicle to accommodate everyone as well as everything being carried, both passengers and load?

Door Locks

C5.125 Inadequate or improperly adjusted door locks and latches may have allowed a passenger to be ejected from the vehicle. A thorough examination should be made of the (a) latches, (b) handles and (c) safety catches for general serviceability. Check manually for any binding or looseness that would suggest a possible malfunction.

C5.126 Examine the door for dents or bends of sufficient dimension to permit a door to unlatch.

Loads

C5.127 Loads on vehicles may contribute to accidents. Some common conditions are:

a. Load or part of the load falling from the vehicle as a result of failure of inadequate binders or other constraining devices, causing damage or injury to other highway users.

b. *Load shift*, throwing the vehicle out of control.

c. Driver's view or movements being obstructed by the manner in which the load is placed in or on the vehicle.

d. Load that extends too far at the sides, top, or rear of the vehicle, striking bridges, utility poles, utility wires, etc., or other highway users.

e. Load that is so high that it throws the vehicle off balance, causing it to tip over.

Vehicle Fires

C5.128 The at-scene traffic accident investigator must be able to recognize suspicious circumstances that would warrant additional investigation by himself or by an experienced arson investigator when a vehicle is damaged or destroyed by fire.

C5.129 When a vehicle is damaged or destroyed by fire, particularly in cases of single car accidents such as rollovers or running off the roadway, the investigator should consider the possibility that the driver or owner deliberately set the fire.

C5.130 The motives for setting a fire are many. A person may want to:
   a.   file insurance claims,
   b.   avoid costly vehicle repair, particularly when there is a large deductible clause in the insurance policy,
   c.   cover up a crime, etc.

C5.131 The vehicle and immediate area should be checked for *fire starters*, containers and supplies, and other evidence indicating that the fire was intentionally started. Check for the following:
   a.   Match packages

   b.   Gasoline or other *accelerant* containers

   c.   The ashes of rolls of cloth or paper inside the vehicle which may have been saturated with an accelerant

d. Places where an accelerant may have been spilled on the ground, saturating the soil

e. Evidence of an accelerant having been spread around inside the vehicle. This evidence may be in the form of ash trails caused by fast burning and intense heat.

f. Indications that all usual automobile parts and articles, such as radio, aerial, mirrors, spare wheel, tape deck, etc., had been removed before the fire started. (Or are they still in the vehicle and were they damaged or destroyed?)

g. Windows being partially or fully open. Fire requires oxygen to burn. If windows were open, particularly during adverse weather conditions, the possibility exists that they were opened to facilitate burning.

h. Noticeable sagging of the roof, trunk lid, and hood, and of the seat and axle springs. Did the tile glass and soft materials such as those found in radiators, fuel pumps, and carburetors, and the lead used in body repairs, melt and lose the original shape? When an accelerant is used, these materials usually suffer considerable damage because of the intense heat.

i. Evidence of a fire starting at places on or about the engine that cannot be connected with the usual sources of accidental fires under the hood: fuel pump, carburetor and electrical wiring. Such evidence would indicate that the fire was probably started by using an accelerant.

j.   Any indication that the fuel lines from the gas tank through to the engine had been tampered with, such as signs of breakage, disconnections, etc.

k.   Any indication that gas might have been drawn from the gas tank. For example, if the gas tank cap had been removed before the fire, so that gas could be siphoned, and not replaced until after the fire, there would likely not be any sign of scorching on the cap.

C5.132   Photographs should be taken of all damaged and suspicious areas. Photographs should be in color if possible.

Figure C5-45 A vehicle destroyed by fire

Vehicle Damage

Contact Damage

C5.133 *Contact damage* is caused by direct contact of a vehicle with some object which is not a part of the vehicle. There can be *external contact damage* and *internal contact damage*.

a. External contact damage is most useful in preparing damage diagrams and in determining *direction or force, collapse* and *overlap* (see Fig. C5-46). Contact damage on metal is generally indicated by the presence of scratches, paint rub-off, road materials, tree bark, a pedestrian's clothing, body tissue, etc., on or adhering to the area that struck or was struck by the other object.

b. Internal contact damage is damage suffered by the inside of a vehicle. Most often this type of damage is caused when vehicle occupants or parts of an inside load strike the dash, steering wheel, doors, windshield, windows, etc., during collision. By relating this internal damage to injuries suffered by the occupants, it is possible in some cases to establish the seated positions of the occupants.

Figure C5-46 External contact damage is useful in determining the angle of force for each vehicle. (Photos courtesy of Charles C. Thomas, Publisher)

Induced Damage

C5.134   Induced damage is damage of a vehicle part resulting from pressure or force exerted by engagement elsewhere on the vehicle.   For example, the trunk lid might be forced open when a vehicle is struck in the side and toward the rear, or the roof might buckle during either a rear-end or front-end collision.

C5.135   Induced damages are generally indicated by folds, creases or wrinkles rather than by scratches or crumbling.   Damage to the differential or to the universal joints is almost always induced damage, because these parts are seldom in contact with another object during collision.

C5.136   It is very important to distinguish between direct contact damage and induced damage.   To mistake induced damage for contact damage could very well lead to improper vehicle positioning at the time of initial contact.

Imprints

C5.137   *Imprints* are marks pressed onto or into vehicle body parts as a result of collision with some other object.   The shape and also pattern of the object, if any, is most often clearly delineated in the imprint.   Some objects that could leave imprints:

   a.   Tree or pole
   b.   Round headlamp, on an older vehicle, or a wheel, which leaves a mark that appears as a circle or part of a circle
   c.   Grille and bumper, in a rear-end collision.   When the damage to a striking vehicle is higher than the front bumper of the striking vehicle or the damage to a struck vehicle is lower

than the bumper of the struck vehicle, you have an indication that one or both of the vehicles were braking at the time of impact. Signs of skid marks should also be checked to confirm braking.

Ruboff

C5.138 *Ruboff* indicates contact of a minor degree. Although such damage may appear minor on a vehicle, the contact or impact could be fatal to a pedestrian. Signs of ruboff can be paint, rubber from tires, fabric particles from a pedestrian's clothing, skin, hair, blood, bark from a tree, road dust, mud, etc.

Direction of Force

C5.139 Contact damage shows the *direction of force* of a vehicle that has collided with another vehicle or another object. *Collapse* resulting from contact damage assists the investigator in judging where the force, which may have been applied over a large area, was centered.

C5.140 The direction of force is usually best determined by considering the direction of movement of some specific part of the vehicle, as indicated by collapse. A study of damage will indicate the direction of force at *maximum engagement*, when collapse and the forces producing it are at their greatest.

C5.141 When the direction of force is known, much can be learned from it about the position of a vehicle with respect to another vehicle or object at the time of initial contact and during engagement up to and including maximum engagement.

C5.142 Caution must be exercised in evaluating damage evidence when determining the direction of force, because after initial contact the direction can be altered as a vehicle rotates, especially before maximum engagement has been reached.

Damage Classification

C5.143 Some pre-conditions or vehicle defects are difficult to distinguish from collision damage. It is helpful to be familiar with the following classification of vehicle damage:

1. *Preceding but not contributing*

    This type of condition or damage is present in the vehicle before the collision but does not contribute to its occurrence.

2. *Preceding and contributing*

    This type of vehicle damage or defect is present before the collision and in some way contributes to its occurrence.

3. *During collision*

    This type of damage occurs during the collision. It is of the utmost importance that such damage be accurately interpreted and recorded for investigative and reconstruction purposes.

4.   *After collision and before final rest*

This type of damage can assist in determining the path of travel after collision. It is also useful in determining the angle of departure after collision.

It is important not to confuse collision damage (including that which occurs before the vehicle comes to final rest) with the kinds of post-collision damage described below.

5.   *After collision and final rest at scene*

This type of damage is often caused during rescue operations or is the result of thefts, vandalism, etc.

6.   *Removal and storage damage*

Tow trucks sometimes cause damage to collision vehicles while removing them from the scene. Damage can also occur at the yard where accident vehicles are being held. Care must be taken not to confuse this type of damage with other types of damage.

C5.144   There follows a Mechanical Inspection Guide and Evaluation (courtesy of Charles C. Thomas, Publisher) to aid the investigator in examining a vehicle, a Check List of Physical Evidence from the Vehicle to aid him in recording the evidence uncovered during his examination, and a Glossary to provide him with simple definitions of selected common automotive terms.

Mechanical Inspection Guide and Evaluation	

Examination Requested by_____

Date of Request:_____

Place of Examination:_____

Examination Conducted by_____

		am
Start: Date_____	Time_____	pm
		am
Finish: Date_____	Time_____	pm

Item	Findings, Conclusions and Comments
A. Vehicle Description License plate no. State or province Make Year Model/Type Color Registration no. Serial no. (VIN) Odometer mileage **B. Accelerator** Linkage Freedom of movement Retrieval (spring) Pedal tread **C. Brakes** Type 　Hydraulic 　Power assist 　Air Anti-skid device 　2-wheel 　4-wheel 　Not equipped Hydraulic pressure 　proportioning valve Wheel brake assembly 　Caliper movement 　Disc runout 　Drum surface 　Primary shoes 　Secondary shoes 　Wheel cylinder 　　(extension) 　Fluid pressure (psi)	

Item	Findings, Conclusions and Comments

Master cylinder
   Fluid level
   Fluid pressure (psi)
Hand brake
Emergency braking device
Pedal tread
   Good condition
   Worn condition
Lines (fluid, vacuum, air)
   Cracked
   Rock fractures
   Worn
   Leaks
   Collision damage
Pedal reserve
 	
D. Doors
 	
Latches
Handles
Safety catches
General operation
  (binding, loose)
 	
E. Exhaust System
 	
Manifold connection
Exhaust pipe
Muffler/catalytic converter
Tailpipe
Connections
 	
F. Air Conditioning Unit
 	
Defects (drawing in exhaust
  fumes, etc.)
 	
G. Frame
 	
Collision damage
Alignment
Cross members
"A" frame
 	
H. Horn
 	
Switch type (ring, button
  shroud, spoke)
Horn type (electrical, vacuum,
  air)
General condition
Audibility	

Item	Findings, Conclusions and Comments

I. Lights
 	
Switches
    Headlights
    Dimmer
    Back-up
    Brakelight
    Signal
Lights, general (type, color,
  number, location, condition)
    Headlights
    Taillights
    Signal
    Brakelights
    Clearance
    Fog
    Back-up
High-beam indicator
 	
J. Power Train
 	
K. Reflectors
 	
Reflectors, general (type, color,
  number, location, condition)
 	
L. Steering
 	
Type (power, manual)
Linkage, general
Tie-rods
Idler arm
Drag links
Steering box
Springs
King pins
Ball joints
Steering wheel free play
 	
M. Suspension
Springs
Control arms
Torsion bars
Shocks
 	
N. Tires
 	
Make
Name
Ply
Size
Serial number
Sidewall type
Load capacity
Pressure
    Recommended
    Actual	

Item	Findings, Conclusions and Comments
Tube or tubeless	
Tread type	
Summer	
Snow grip	
Mud grip	
Slick	
Original	
Recap	
Studded	
Chains	
Tread wear pattern	
Sides	
Center	
Uneven	
Tread depth	
New	
Percent worn	
General condition	
Cuts	
Abrasions	
Blowout	
Wear (light, medium, heavy, bald)	
Damage	
Type	
Location related to serial number	
Tire damage related to rim damage	
Tire damage related to vehicle damage	
O. Wheels	
Bearings	
Rotation	
Locking uniformity (brake application)	
Lugs (missing, loose, work)	
Seals	
Rim	
Condition	
Damage	
P. Windshield and Windows	
Clear	
Tinted	
View obstructions	
Damage	
General condition	
Q. Windshield Wipers	
Type (electrical, vacuum, mechanical)	
Blades and blade arms	
Switch	

310

Item	Findings, Conclusion and Comments
R. **Windshield and Window Defrosters** General Condition Type Switch	
S. **Speedometer** General condition Cable	
T. **Mirrors** Location Position Type	
U. **Vehicle** 　Overweight ☐ 　Overwidth ☐	
V. **Vision Obstructed** Driver's sight ☐ By passenger ☐ Window ☐ Windshield ☐ Load ☐ Mirror position ☐	
W. **Safety Equipment** Air bag Harness only Lap belt only Lap belt and harness Motorcycle helmet Vehicle equipped but 　not used Vehicle not equipped Ejected from vehicle 　Driver ☐ 　Passenger ☐	

Source: R. W. Rivers, *Traffic Accident Investigators' Handbook*, courtesy of Charles C. Thomas, Publisher.

311

Checklist of Physical Evidence from the Vehicle

1. **Identification**

   Make

   Size

   Model

   Owner

   Serial Number

2. **Damage Examination**

   A. Location of damaged areas

   B. Location of paint transfers

   C. Displacement of wheels, frame, etc.

   D. Contact damage

   E. Induced damage

   F. Glass damage

       1.   Contact

       2.   Induced

   G. Road or ground contact

       Match gouges in pavement with vehicle

       parts causing them

   H. Tires

       1.   Grass pinch

       2.   Abrasions

       3.   Scuffs

       4.   Inflated - deflated

   I. Wheels

   J. Lamps

       1.   Switch on or off

       2.   Condition of each external lamp

3.   Lamp held for further examination if necessary

K. Steering and suspension

L. Sources of injury to passengers

    1.   Internal contact

    2.   Ejection

        a.   Door failure

        b.   Roll over, partial ejection

        c.   Seat-belt usage

M. Pedestrian injuries

    1.   Contact with vehicle

    2.   Cloth marks or body tissue

N. Speedometer

O. Brakes

    1.   Pedal reserve

    2.   Fluid leaks

    3.   Condition of linings

Glossary

This glossary contains definitions of selected basic automotive parts and terms.

Accelerator

A mechanical device, usually a foot operated throttle, for increasing the speed of a motor vehicle.

Accelerator Pump

A carburetor pump which enriches the fuel-air mixture.

Air Filter

The assembly connected to the carburetor that filters out dirt and dust from the air as it is drawn into the engine.

Anti-Freeze

A chemical added to the cooling system to raise the coolant boiling point and lower the freezing point. Anti-freeze is a common term applied to the liquid containing the chemical that fills the radiator.

Battery

An electrochemical device that stores and provides electricity.

Battery Terminals

Round posts or bolt locations on a battery to which the battery cables are attached.

Bias-Belted Tire

A tire with plies that run diagonally from each side of the tire to the other, that is, *on a bias* to the tread's centerline.

Brake

A device that stops or holds a vehicle.

Brake Fluid

A special fluid used in the braking system.

Brake Shoe

An arc-shaped metal plate in a drum brake that is lined with high-friction material called brake lining.

Camber

The outward tilt of the top of the front wheels.

Carbon Monoxide

A colorless, odorless, tasteless, poisonous gas that is present in auto exhaust.

Carburetor

An engine component that mixes gasoline and air to meet engine operating conditions.

Caster

The front-wheel steering-axis tilt, forward or backward, that provides steering stability.

Catalytic Converter

The exhaust system device that helps to convert harmful gases into harmless gases.

Choke

A carburetor device that enriches fuel mixture.

Clutch

The mechanism that connects or disconnects the engine to or from the transmission.

Combustion Chamber

A space in the cylinder head of the engine where combustion of the air-fuel mixture takes place.

Cooling System

The system that circulates coolant and prevents engine overheating.

Crankshaft

The main rotating shaft of the engine.

Cylinder Block

The basic engine framework.

Diesel Engine

An engine that burns diesel fuel instead of gasoline.

Driveline

The connection of one or more driveshafts between the transmission and the rear axle.

Dual-Brake System

Two separate brake systems in the same vehicle.

Electrolyte

A sulfuric acid and water mixture used in batteries.

Electronic Ignition System

An ignition system that contains no contact points in the distributor.

Emission Control System

The system that cuts down air pollution from gases formed by the burned and partially burned mixture of fuel and air.

Engine

The vehicle power plant that converts heat energy into mechanical energy.

Exhaust Manifold

An assembly of connecting pipes between the engine and the exhaust pipe.

Expansion Tank

A radiator overflow tank which provides room for coolant to expand.

Fuel Filter

The fuel line device that removes dirt and other contaminants from fuel.

Fuel Pump

The device that pumps fuel from the fuel tank to the carburetor.

Ground

An auto's electrical connection to return the current to its source.

Ignition Switch

The switch that turns the ignition system on or off.

Ignition System

The system that consists of the battery, ignition coil, distributor, ignition switch, wiring and spark plugs.

Intake Manifold

The engine component that has passages from the carburetor to the cylinders for carrying the air-fuel mixture.

Master Cylinder

The fluid container of the braking system where pressure is developed when the brake pedal is depressed.

Muffler

The exhaust-system device that contains a series of pipes and/or chambers designed to lessen the sound of exhaust gases.

Oil Filter

The filter that removes impurities from the engine oil.

Parking Brakes

Mechanical brakes which can be set when the vehicle is parked.

Pollutant

Any gas or substance that contaminates the atmosphere.

Radial Tire

A tire with plies that run straight across the tire (not on a bias) from one side to the other and with two or more belts around the circumference of the tire under the tread.

Radiator

The cooling system component that removes heat from the coolant.

Refrigerant

The cooling substance used in an auto air conditioner.

Shock Absorber

The device that softens and reduces the motion of the springs.

Solenoid

An electrical switch that protects wiring from heavy electrical surges.

Spark Plug

An ignition component that ignites the engine's fuel-air mixture.

Spring

A vehicle device that absorbs road shock by flexing.

Starter

The electric motor that rotates the engine to initiate internal combustion.

Steering Gear

The gear that carries the rotary motion of the steering wheel to the steering linkage.

Steering Linkage

The system of arms, levers, and joints that control the direction of the wheels.

Tachometer

The device that measures engine speed in revolutions per minute (rpm).

Thermostat

A control device that regulates temperature.

Throttle

The carburetor valve that permits the driver to vary the amount of air-fuel mixture that enters the carburetor (see accelerator).

Tire Tread

The grooved tire portion that contacts the roadway.

Lesson 5
VEHICLE INSPECTIONS

Project A-1

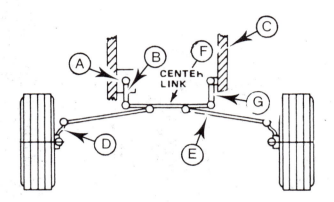

Bottom View

Using letters, relate the designations below to the appropriate parts in the diagram. (The first one has been done for you.)

    __F__   Center link

    _____   Tie rod

    _____   Steering-knuckle arm

    _____   Pitman arm

    _____   Steering gear (box)

    _____   Idler arm

Lesson 5
VEHICLE INSPECTIONS

Project A-2

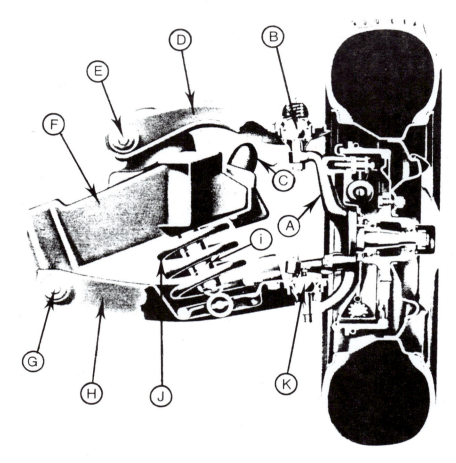

Relate the designations to the appropriate parts. (The first one has been done for you.)

__E__	Pivot	_____	Lower control arm
_____	Steering knuckle	_____	Front coil spring
_____	Lower ball joint	_____	Shock absorber
_____	Pivot	_____	Upper control arm
_____	Upper ball joint	_____	Rubber bumper
_____	Frame		

Lesson 5

VEHICLE INSPECTIONS

Project A-3

Relate the designations to the appropriate parts, referring to the diagrams on the next page. (The first one has been done for you.)

    __C__   Differential

_____ Rear leaf-spring assembly

_____ Ball joint front-suspension unit

_____ Universal joint (U-joint)

_____ Rack and pinion steering system

_____ Bent, damaged shock

Lesson 5 Project A-3 Diagrams

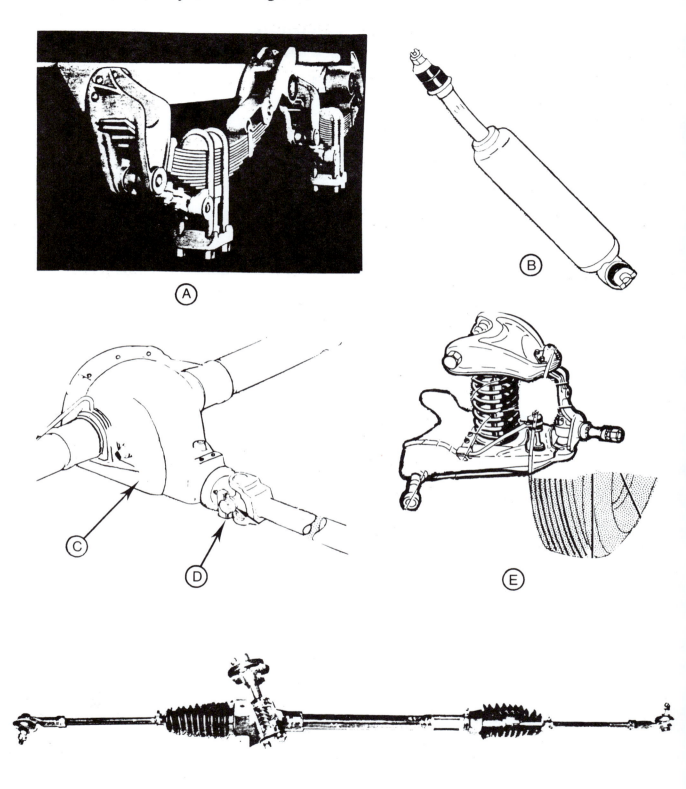

(A)

(B)

(C)

(D)

(E)

(F)

324

Lesson 5
VEHICLE INSPECTIONS

Project A-4

Relate the designations to the appropriate tire types and conditions, referring to the diagrams on the next page. (The first one has been done for you.)

__K__ Normal tire tread wear pattern

_____ Tire tread indicators

_____ Overinflated tire (shape)

_____ Underinflated tire tread wear

_____ Bias-ply tire

_____ Underinflated tire (shape)

_____ Tire tread wear (alignment or camber problem)

_____ Bias-belted tire

_____ Overinflated tire tread wear

_____ Radial-ply tire

_____ Normal inflated tire (shape)

Lesson 5 Project A-4 Diagrams

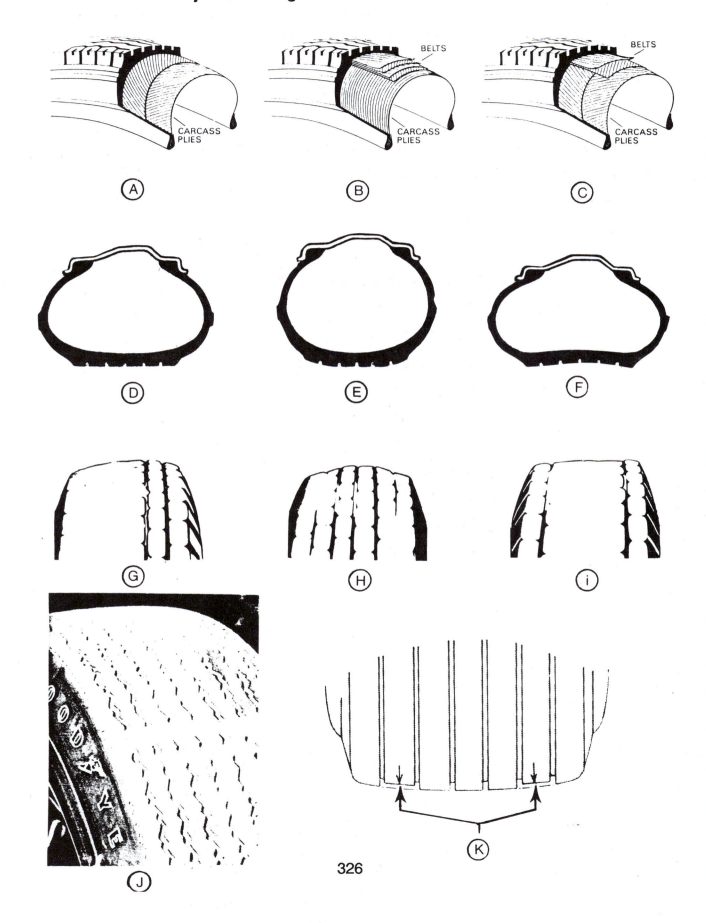

CARCASS
PLIES

(A)

BELTS

CARCASS
PLIES

(B)

BELTS

CARCASS
PLIES

(C)

(D)

(E)

(F)

(G)

(H)

(i)

(J)

(K)

326

INTRODUCTION

Lesson 6

SUBJECT: Speed Estimates

At-scene traffic accident investigators are required to calculate vehicle speeds from tire marks and other evidence found at a traffic accident scene.

This lesson will provide the student with the knowledge necessary to calculate speed from skids and yaw marks and to solve certain distance and time problems related to at-scene traffic accident investigation.

Lesson Contents

This lesson covers the following topics:

    a.   Speed estimates, general

    b.   Definitions

    c.   Abbreviations

    d.   Formulas

    e.   Speed and velocity conversions

    f.   Speedometer accuracy tests

    g.   Speed estimates from skid marks, general

    h.   Skid mark measurements

    i.   Coefficient of friction and drag factor

    j.   Speed from skid marks, calculations

    k.   Curve speed, yaw, sideslip, critical speed scuff

327

l.   Distance calculations

m.   Time calculations

Lesson Objectives

1.   Upon completion of this lesson, the student will be able to state and define to the satisfaction of the instructor:

    a.   Five circumstances under which speed estimates can be made.

    b.   At least twenty-five abbreviations and symbols used in an at-scene traffic accident investigations.

    c.   At least five speed estimated formulas.

    d.   At least eight different types of skidmarks and the correct method of measuring each.

    e.   At least two methods of determining coefficient of friction.

2.   Upon completion of this lesson, the student will be able to calculate to the satisfaction of the instructor:

    a.   Minimum speed from skidmarks

    b.   Speed from yaw marks

3.   Upon completion of this lessons, the student will be able to calculate to the satisfaction of the instructor the time required for a vehicle to skid to a stop when the skid distance and coefficient of friction are known.

4.   Upon completion of this lesson, the student will be able to calculate

to the satisfaction of the instructor the distance required for a vehicle to skid to a stop when the initial speed and the coefficient of friction are known.

Any test that the student wishes to conduct should be carried out under the strict supervision of a fully qualified and competent instructor. The student is cautioned, however, that neither the Institute of Police Technology and Management nor persons associated in any way with the Institute's instruction or training programs will accept responsibility for injury or damage resulting from any such test even though the test may be adequately supervised.

Because the Institute offers training on an international basis, all formulas and calculations are completed in both the United States and Metric measurement systems. The format used shows the U.S. figure first, followed by the metric equivalent in parentheses, e.g.,

30   (254)

Speed Constant   Metric Speed Constant

or, in many instances other than constants, only the *approximate* metric equivalent, in order to keep the metric calculations comparable in simplicity to the U.S. calculations.

The student should complete the projects at the end of the lesson in *either* the United States *or* the metric system -- but *not* in both. The choice is dependent on which system he will use in his course, or in his work, if he is studying independently.

Calculations are performed throughout much of this lesson. Values shown in the steps of a calculation are truncated after the *second* decimal place. If you use these values as a basis for calculating the final answer, in some instances your answer may differ slightly from the answer shown. This is because calculations for this lesson have been performed on a calculator with *all* decimal places left in the calculator up to the answer.

Lesson 6

SPEED ESTIMATES

General

C6.001 A complete and thorough review of Tire Marks, Tire Action, and Scuff Marks, Lesson 4, paragraphs C4.044 to C4.063, must be made before proceeding with this lesson.

C6.002 Speed estimates may be made from one or a combination of the following:

    a.   Skid marks

    b.   Yaw marks

    c.   Vehicle damage analysis

    d.   Reliable witness statements

C6.003 Speed estimates can be entered in both civil and criminal court proceedings. In many cases involving speed estimates based on skid marks, the investigator need not be an expert in order to testify. However, speed estimates from yaw marks and vehicle damage analysis are much more difficult to prove. Estimates in these cases should be given in court by a person who is or can be qualified as an expert. Nevertheless, a non-expert who is a competent investigator can often present evidence in court regarding what he saw and did at the scene of an accident, e.g., measure yaw marks, and this can then be interpreted for the court by a person who is qualified as an expert.

C6.004 This lesson is intended to give the student sufficient knowledge to enable him to testify with confidence that he properly identified, interpreted and measured certain types of tire marks and that he correctly determined the roadway coefficient of friction and calculated a minimum speed estimate from the evidence observed or gained during the course of his investigation.

C6.005 This lesson by itself is not intended to make of the student an expert in estimating speed from skid marks. However, the knowledge gained from the lesson, together with experience acquired from properly conducted field tests to prove various formulas used in this lesson, should enable the student to become qualified as an expert.

C6.006 Center of mass or center of gravity in a vehicle is located longitudinally at some point through the central axis, usually halfway between the front and rear axles. Vertically, the point is usually at about one third the height of the vehicle measured from the ground level. For practical investigation purposes, locating the center of mass in this manner is quite adequate.

C6.007 Distance is the extent of separation between objects and places. It is an ingredient in most calculations. Generally, speed calculations involve the distance traveled during a unit of time such as a second, this distance being of major importance in solving acceleration, deceleration and constant speed problems in the reconstruction of accidents.

C6.008 An expert is one who has a special skill or knowledge gained through training and/or experience.

C6.009 Gravity is the attractive force of a heavenly body, such as our planet earth, that acts on objects in proximity to that body. Gravity increases with the mass (see C6.010) of the body. Gravity is constant on earth and is expressed as an acceleration rate of 32.2 feet (9.81 meters) per second per second.

C6.010 Mass is the measure of the amount of matter present in an object and is independent of the strength of whatever gravitational force may be acting on the object. The mass of an object remains the same anywhere in the universe, whereas the weight of an object will vary greatly depending on the strength of gravitational attraction in each particular location. However, since gravity is constant on earth, weight may be substituted for mass in accident investigation formulas.

C6.011 Speed and velocity. In many texts and in this course, speed and velocity have the same meaning, i.e., the distance moved in a unit of time. It is important, however, that the student understand the difference between the terms speed and velocity. In a more exact sense:

a. Speed indicates rapidity without reference to direction of movement.

b. Velocity is a vector quantity where both rapidity and direction of movement are elements.

C6.012 Time may be measured in seconds, minutes or hours, or any part thereof. Speed is generally measured in miles per hour or kilometers per hour. When what is being considered is a vector quantity -- a quantity which has both magnitude and direction, e.g., acceleration, force, momentum or velocity -- that quantity should be measured in feet or meters per second.

SYMBOLS

Following are symbols commonly used in traffic accident investigation. Each is accompanied by the name of the term it stands for, and some terms are briefly defined. In many instances, definitions are given or enlarged upon elsewhere in this course.

C	=	Chord. A chord is a straight line measured from one end of an arc to the other.
CG	=	Center of gravity
CM	=	Center of mass
D	=	Distance
		Note: In some documents and texts, a small d is used to designate distance.
D_1	=	The small subscript 1 attached to a distance measurement identifies the measurement as the first of two or more such measurements. A small subscript 2 or 3 indicates a second or a third measurement, and so forth.
D_n	=	The small subscript n indicates that the distance variable to which it is attached can theoretically occur with an unlimited number of measurements.
e	=	Slope, bank or superelevation in feet per foot (meters per meter) of lateral distance
f	=	Coefficient of friction or drag factor
F	=	Force measured in pounds or kilograms
g	=	Accelerating force of gravity
H	=	Height
M	=	Mass

M   =   Middle ordinate. A middle ordinate is the distance measured at a right angle from the middle of a chord to the arc of a circle.

           Note: Mass and middle ordinate never appear in the same formula. Therefore, the same abbreviation can be used for both without causing confusion.

m   =   Grade in feet per foot (meters per meter) of horizontal distance

n   =   Braking capability or efficiency

R   =   Radius

r   =   Rise or fall over a known distance, either lateral or horizontal

S   =   Speed. Speed is a common term indicating the rapidity of vehicle movement. For the purpose of this course, speed and velocity have the same meaning. S = mph (km/h) unless stated otherwise.

S_c =   Combined speed. An overall minimum speed obtained by combining one or more speeds.

S_f =   Final speed. The small subscript f indicates the final measurement of the component to which it is attached.

S_o =   Original or initial speed. The small subscript zero indicates the original or first measurement of the component to which it is attached.

S_1 =   The small subscript 1 attached to a speed measurement identifies the measurement as the first of two or more such measurements. A small subscript 2 or 3 indicates a second or third measurement, and so forth.

$\bar{S}$ = Average speed. The overhead bar indicates an average speed.

S_n = The small subscript n indicates that the speed variable to which it is attached can theoretically occur with an unlimited number of measurements.

t = Time in seconds, minutes or hours

Note: In some documents and texts, a large T is used instead of a small t.

V = Velocity. A vector quantity. Movement measured in ft/sec (m/s) where rapidity and direction are elements.

V_f = Final velocity

V_o = Original or initial velocity

$\pm$ = Plus or minus

TABLE 6-1

Formula Summary

The following is a summary of the formulas used in this lesson. (If a constant or a conversion factor is not involved, the formula will be the same for both U.S. and Metric.)

United States	*Metric*

Formula C6-1 -- Conversion

mph x 1.466 = ft/sec   km/h x .278 = m/s

Formula C6-2 -- Conversion

ft/sec ÷ 1.466 = mph   m/s ÷ .278 = km/h

or

m/s x 3.6 = km/h

Formula C6-3 -- Speedometer Accuracy Test

$$S = \frac{3600}{t}$$

Formula C6-4 -- Coefficient of Friction Test when the weight of the object and the force (pull) to move the object are known

$$f = \frac{F}{W}$$

Formula C6-5 -- Coefficient of Friction using test skids

$$f = \frac{S^2}{30D} \qquad\qquad f = \frac{S^2}{254D}$$

| United States | Metric |

Formula C6-6 -- Grade or Superelevation

    m   =   grade -- horizontal rise or fall of the roadway every 100 feet (30 meters)

    e   =   superelevation -- lateral rise or fall of the slope or bank of a roadway every 100 feet (30 meters)

$$m = \frac{rise}{run} \qquad e = \frac{rise}{run}$$

Formula C6-7 -- Speed from skid marks

$$S = \sqrt{30Df} \qquad\qquad\qquad S = \sqrt{254Df}$$

Formula C6-8 -- Speed with partial braking capability or efficiency

$$S = \sqrt{30Dfn} \qquad\qquad\qquad S = \sqrt{254Dfn}$$

Formula C6-9 -- Speed from continuous skid on different roadway surfaces

$$S = \sqrt{30[(D_1 f_1) + (D_2 f_2)\ldots + (D_n f_n)]} \qquad S = \sqrt{254[(D_1 f_1) + (D_2 f_2)\ldots + (D_n f_n)]}$$

Formula C6-10 -- Speed when each side of the vehicle is on different surfaces

$$S = \sqrt{30[(D_1 f_1 n_1) + (D_2 f_2 n_2)]} \qquad S = \sqrt{254[(D_1 f_1 n_1) + (D_2 f_2 n_2)]}$$

Formula C6-11 -- Combined Speed Formula

$$S = \sqrt{S_1^2 + S_2^2 + S_3^2 \ldots S_n^2}$$

	United States		*Metric*

Formula C6-12 -- Distance required to stop when speed and drag factor are known

$$D = \frac{S^2}{30f} \qquad\qquad D = \frac{S^2}{254f}$$

Formula C6-13 -- Time required to slide (skid) to a stop when distance and drag factor are known

$$t = .249\sqrt{\frac{D}{f}} \qquad\qquad t = .45\sqrt{\frac{D}{f}}$$

Formula C6-14 -- Average velocity when distance and time are known

$$V = \frac{D}{t}$$

Formula C6-15 -- Time required for a vehicle moving at a known constant velocity to travel a known distance

$$t = \frac{D}{V}$$

Formula C6-16 -- Distance traveled at a constant velocity for a known time

$$D = V \times t$$

United States	***Metric***

Formula C6-17 -- Critical Speed Formula (for curve, critical speed yaw)

$$S = 3.86\sqrt{R(f \pm e)} \qquad S = 11.27\sqrt{R(f \pm e)}$$

Formula C6-18 -- Radius

$$R = \frac{C^2}{8M} + \frac{M}{2}$$

Speed and Velocity Conversions

C6.013 Traffic accident investigations often require the changing of speed (S) from miles or kilometers per hour to velocity (V) in feet or meters per second, or vice versa. The conversion formulas, included in the Formula Summary, are repeated below.

Formula C6-1

mph x 1.466 = ft/sec   km/h x .278 = m/s

Formula C6-2

ft/sec ÷ 1.466 = mph   m/s ÷ .278 = km/h

The conversion factors are not exact, but they are accurate enough for most traffic accident investigation calculations.

EXAMPLE 1

A vehicle was traveling at a speed of 30 mph (50 km/h). Convert from mph (km/h) to ft/sec (m/s).

Applying Formula C6-1:

30 x 1.466 = 43.98 ft/sec   50 x .278 = 13.9 m/s

EXAMPLE 2

A vehicle was traveling at 43.98 ft/sec (13.9 m/s). Convert from ft/sec (m/s) to mph (km/h).

Applying Formula 13 C6-2:

$$43.98 \div 1.466 = 30 \text{ mph} \qquad 13.9 \div 278 = 50 \text{ km/h}$$

C6.014 When conducting any form of speed test with a motor vehicle, it is essential that the accuracy or non-accuracy of the speedometer be known. To test a speedometer, travel at a constant speed over a distance of one mile (or one kilometer) and use a stop watch to determine the time that it takes to traverse the distance. Then, divide 3,600 (the number of seconds in one hour) by the number of seconds it takes to travel the mile or kilometer. Compare the constant speed (as registered on the speedometer) to the answer from your calculation. The difference will be the speedometer error.

Formula C6-3

United States

$$S = \frac{3600}{t}$$

Metric

$$S = \frac{3600}{t}$$

where S = actual speed traveled in mph (km/h)

t = time in seconds to travel the mile or kilometer at a constant speed

EXAMPLE

It took a vehicle 62 seconds to travel a measured mile/kilometer. The speedometer registered a constant speed of 60 mph/60 km/h.

341

Calculate the vehicle's actual speed and speedometer error.
Applying Formula C6-3:

$$S = \frac{3600}{62} \qquad\qquad S = \frac{3600}{62}$$

$$S = 58.06 \qquad\qquad S = 58.06$$

$$S = 58 \text{ mph} \qquad\qquad S = 58 \text{ km/h}$$

The speedometer error = 60 − 58 = 2 mph or km/h

C6.015 Skid marks may be used to calculate the minimum speed a vehicle would have been traveling at the beginning of its skid marks. To make this calculation, the following must be known:

a. Skid distance (slide to stop)

b. Coefficient of friction

c. Roadway grade or superelevation

d. The braking percentage

e. That the vehicle did not strike a substantial object before skidding to a stop

f. That the vehicle was not towing a trailer, unless the trailer was equipped with brakes which were applied and locked at approximately the same time as the brakes of the towing vehicle

Skid Mark Measurements

C6.016 In measuring the length of skid marks for speed calculation purposes, certain procedures must be followed in regard to the following:

a. *Accuracy.* Do not guess the length of any skid mark or other distance. Always use a tape measure or other accurate measuring device. The pace method is quite imprecise when used to measure skid marks and should be used only if there is no other way to make the measurements.

b. *Diagram.* In important or complicated cases, draw a preliminary diagram that may be used later to prepare a scale diagram to assist in the reconstruction of the accident.

c. *Measurements.* The purpose in measuring a skid mark is to find out how far the tire slid. If a tire leaves a curved skid mark, the measurement should be taken along the path of the skid mark to determine the distance over which the tire slid. If the vehicle spins, it is often better to measure the center-of-mass path.

d. *Recording.* Make measurements to at least the closest six inches (15 cm) and closer still if possible. Use an easily understood and explainable recording format for the measurements taken.

e. *Markers.* Use markers to show specific locations for photographic purposes, e.g., the beginning of an impending skid mark. When markers are to be used, photographs should be taken first without the markers in order to avoid any possibility of argument over their admissibility in court.

f.   *Longest skid mark in straight skids.* In a straight skid, the longest skid mark may be used as the skid distance when it is established that all wheels locked up at about the same time. It can be assumed that the longest skid mark is the total distance that the vehicle skidded, as otherwise the vehicle would not have skidded straight.   For record purposes, nevertheless, measure and record the lengths of all skid marks separately.

g.   *Nonsimultaneous lockup of wheels.* When all wheels do not lock up at the same time, or when there are considerable differences in skid-mark lengths, measure all skid marks separately and use the *average* length as the skid distance.

Figure C6-1 When wheels lock up at approximately the same time, use the longest skid mark as the skid distance. A conservative measurement of the skid distance may be made by averaging the lengths of all skid marks.

h.   *Skid marks.* Find the *beginning* and the *end* of each skid mark to be measured. Include an *impending* as well as the *positive* skid mark in the overall skid-mark length.

   i *Impending skid mark*

      An impending skid mark is that portion of a tire mark left by a braked wheel *just before there is complete cessation of rotation.* Braking is most effective at this time. The

344

impending skid mark may appear as a cleaning action on the roadway and will lead eventually into a positive skid mark.

ii   *Positive skid mark*

A positive skid mark is, for example, the long black smear left on the pavement. The measurement of such a skid mark cannot be questioned in court.

i.   *Separate measurement.* Measure and record separately the length of the skid mark or skid marks left by each wheel.

j.   *Overlapping skid marks.* Measure the total length of overlapping skid marks. The actual skid distance will be this length *minus* the length of the vehicle's wheelbase.

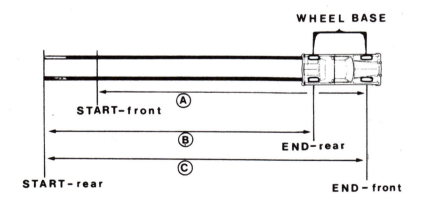

Figure C6-2 When rear skid marks overlap front skid marks, subtract the wheelbase distance from the total length of the overlapping skid marks, that is, the distance from the start to the end of the skid. In this example, *C* represents the total length of an overlapping skid mark. *A* and *B* are the distances the vehicle actually skidded.

k.   *Dual wheel skid marks.* Two tires on one wheel (a dual wheel) leave two skid marks. However, these skid marks are to be counted as one skid mark. Measure the *longest* of the two dual-wheel skid marks. If a truck, trailer or semi-trailer has, for example, eight wheels in contact with the roadway, measure and record separately the skid marks left by each dual wheel. Count each dual wheel as one wheel.

Figure C6-3 Dual-wheel skid marks. Skid mark *B* is the same length as skid mark *A* because the measurement of mark *B* is taken from the first indication of a skid to the last indication of a skid of that dual wheel unit.

l.   *Intermittent* or *gap skid marks.* Intermittent skid marks appear with gaps between them. These gaps occur when wheels are locked up, released and then relocked through braking action. Blank spaces or gaps between the intermittent skid marks are usually a minimum of 15 ft to 20 ft (5 m to 7 m), depending upon the speed of the vehicle and the driver's reaction time. Measure intermittent skid marks separately and in the same manner as a single skid. Use their sum (disregarding blank spaces or gaps) as the total skid distance. Include any impending skid mark in the measurement of each intermittent skid mark.

346

Figure C6-4 Intermittent or gap skid marks

m. *Skip skid marks.* Skip skid marks occur when a locked wheel bounces on the roadway. The blank spaces between the skid marks are usually not longer than 3 ft (1 m). Bouncing is usually caused by events such as the following:

i   A wheel strikes a hole or bump.

ii   An unloaded or lightly loaded trailer, particularly a semi-trailer, allows the wheels of one of the axles to lift momentarily off the roadway surface. A similar phenomenon occurs with a bobtail tractor.

Measure the skip skid marks for each wheel as one continuous skid mark from the beginning of the first skid mark to the end of the last skid mark.

Figure C6-5 Skip skid marks

n. *Curved skid marks.* Measure a curved skid mark by letting the measuring device follow the path of the skid mark around its curve. Do not confuse a curved skid mark with a yaw mark.

347

Figure C6-6 Curved skid marks

    o.   *Offset skid marks*. Measure the entire length of the skid mark, including the offset portion. If a skid mark is offset because the vehicle was struck while sliding, measure the length of the offset and the length of the lead-in skid mark separately.

    p.   *Motorcycle skid marks*. Measure each skid mark separately.

    q.   *Spin skid marks*. The length and exact position of each mark must be measured. An average of the skid-mark distances may be used as the skid distance, or the center of mass path may be plotted and its length used as the skid distance, which will yield a conservative value.

Figure C6-7 Spin skid marks

    r.   *Various surface skid marks*. When a skid mark traverses different kinds of roadway surfaces, measure the skid distance on each surface separately because each surface will usually have a different coefficient of friction value.

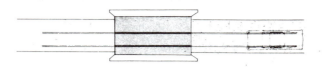

Figure C6-8 Skids on various surfaces

Coefficient of Friction and Drag Factor

C6.017 The coefficient of (sliding) friction, represented by the Greek letter mu (μ), is a numerical measure of the friction, traction, or adhesion developed when an object slides across the surface of another object. For the purposes of accident investigation, the coefficient of friction is the measure of the friction between a tire or some other object (e.g., a motorcycle on its side, a human body) and a level roadway surface or other level surface over which it is sliding.

C6.018 The drag factor (f) is based on the coefficient of friction value but includes adjustments for two important variables that must be considered in any actual situation:

1. Braking efficiency -- accounting for any wheels with defective brakes causing the tires on those wheels not to be sliding.
2. The slope of the surface if the surface is not level.

C6.019 In terms of a vehicle on a level highway or other surface, the coefficient of friction is the ratio obtained by dividing the horizontal force in pounds (kilograms) required to move the vehicle over the surface at a constant speed, with all its wheels locked so that all its tires are sliding, by the weight of the vehicle.

C6.020 The drag factor is the ratio obtained by dividing the force parallel to a highway or other surface required to move the vehicle at a constant speed over the surface, regardless of whether or not the surface has a slope and regardless of the braking efficiency when the brakes are set hard, by the weight of the vehicle.

EXAMPLE

If a horizontal force of 2000 pounds or kilograms is required to move a vehicle weighing 4000 pounds or kilograms over a level highway surface, and the vehicle has all wheels locked, either the coefficient of friction or the drag factor could be calculated using this formula.

Formula C6-4

United States	**Metric**
$\mu \text{ or } f = \dfrac{F}{W}$	$\mu \text{ or } f = \dfrac{F}{W}$

where μ = coefficient of friction

f = drag factor

F = horizontal force (pull), measured in pounds or kilograms, required to move the object at a constant speed

W = weight of the object being moved, measured in pounds or kilograms

$$\mu \text{ or } f = \frac{2{,}000}{4{,}000}$$

$$\mu \text{ or } f = .50$$

For present purposes, the symbol f can be used under conditions similar to those in the example to represent coefficient of friction as well as drag factor. This practice will be followed throughout the manual; the symbol μ will seldom appear. Wherever it is important to indicate that a friction value is not adjusted for the conditions of the particular situation, however, the term coefficient of friction will be used rather than the term drag factor even though the value is represented by f.

C6.021 *Influences*. Certain factors influence the distances tires will slide or skid on a roadway surface. Some of these factors have a noticeable effect. Others have a negligible effect and need not be considered in speed estimate calculations.

a. *Mud, snow, ice and dry surfaces*. These are important factors. These conditions will have considerable effect on the distance a tire will slide.

b. *Hot bituminous surface*. An important condition. A hot asphalt surface produces a longer slide distance.

c. *Tire chains*. An important factor. Tire chains tend to increase the coefficient of friction on mud, snow or ice. However, they tend to lessen the coefficient of friction on hard, paved surfaces.

d. *Studded tires*. Studded tires have a noticeable effect on stopping distance on most surfaces. On glare ice, studded tires on all wheels reduce stopping distance to about one-half of the distance required for studded tires on the rear wheels only. On dry or wet asphalt surfaces, studded tires make virtually no difference. On both dry and wet concrete surfaces, studded tires cause an important increase in stopping distance.

e.   *Tire tread.* The significance of tire tread for stopping distance is negligible on most ordinary dry, clean surfaces. Tire tread is important, however, on a surface having loose material, loose ice, or unpacked snow, where a good *grooved tread* will stop a vehicle more quickly than a tire with a smooth tread face. Tire tread is also important on icy surfaces, where a *smooth tread* will stop a vehicle more quickly than a good grooved tread because of its greater contact with the surface, providing better traction.

f.   *Tire type (e.g., radials, bias-ply, belted).* An insignificant factor.

g.   *Tire air pressure.* An insignificant factor. Tire air pressure makes very little difference in the stopping distance other than on ice, where a *low pressure* tire provides somewhat better traction because of the tire's wider than normal gripping surface or contact area with the roadway.

h.   *Wind direction and velocity.* Insignificant factors.

i.   *Oversize tires.* An insignificant factor.

j.   *Vehicle weight.* Vehicle weight is an important factor only *before* brake lockup. Heavy vehicles require only slightly longer for brakes to lock wheels. Nevertheless, there are tremendous retarding forces at play during this pre-lockup time. Once wheels lock up, the stopping distances of heavy and light-weight vehicles are about the same. Overall, stopping distances for heavy and light-weight vehicles, from the point at which the wheels lock up after the brakes are applied to the actual *stop point*, are approximately the same.

C6.022   The *coefficient of friction/drag factor* of a roadway may be determined by:

a.   Conducting test skids

b.   Pulling a tire and wheel, or other object, over the surface

c.   Using a drag sled

d.   Referring to a Coefficient of Friction Table (to get a range of values)

Under no circumstances should test skids, or any other tests, be made when there is a danger of causing another accident or causing injury or damage.

The prevailing conditions will often dictate how the coefficient of friction/drag factor will be determined; tests skids will usually not be carried out on icy surfaces, but a drag sled may be used.

353

C6.023 *Grade* is the change in elevation in unit distance in a specified direction along the center line of the roadway or the path of a vehicle. It is obtained by dividing the difference in elevation between two points along the roadway by the level distance between those two points. Grade is designated in feet (meters) of *rise* or *fall* per foot (meter) of level distance or of rise or fall as a percent of the level distance, where the rise or fall is in the same units as the level distance, not necessarily in feet (meters).

C6.024 Grade is positive (+) if the surface rises in the specified direction and negative (−) if it falls in that direction and should be measured every 100 feet (30 meters), that is, at intervals of 100 feet (30 meters) along the roadway, as the grade may change over a distance.

C6.025 *Superelevation (bank)* is the slope across the roadway at right angles to the center line from the inside to the outside edge on a curve and should be measured every 100 feet (30 meters).

C6.026 Grade and superelevation may be measured by using a *clinometer* or a *smart level*, which are instruments for determining angular inclination of surfaces.

C6.027 Other methods of measuring grade or superelevation are to use a 4-foot *carpenter's level* or a 4-foot section of string with a *line bubble*, as illustrated in Figures C6-9 and C6-10. If the length (run) of the carpenter's level is 48 inches (122 cm) and the rise or fall is 4 inches (10 cm), the percentage of grade (m) would be calculated as follows, using Formula C6-6. [Note: Formula C6-6 is presented ahead of Formula C6-5.]

United States

Metric

$$m = \frac{rise}{run}$$

$$m = \frac{rise}{run}$$

where   m = percent grade ±

rise = rise or fall

run = length or distance

$$m = \frac{4}{48}$$

$$m = \frac{10}{122}$$

m = .08 or 8%

m = .08 or 8%

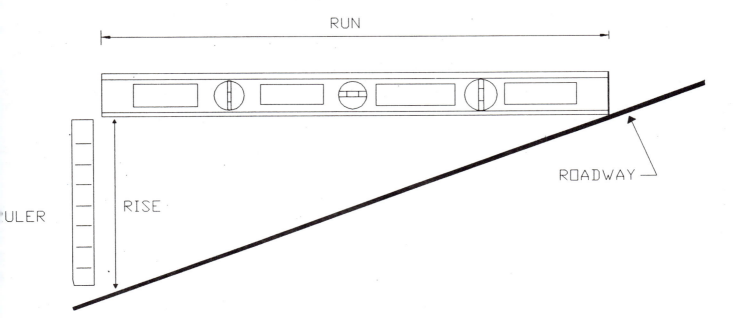

Figure C6-9 Measuring the grade or superelevation of a roadway using a carpenter's level

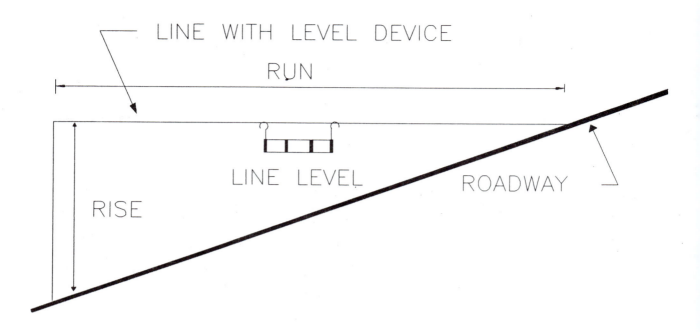

Figure C6-10 Measuring the grade or superelevation of a roadway using a line level

C6.028 When *tests skids* are carried out to determine the *drag factor*, the conditions under which such tests are conducted must be identical to or duplicate as closely as possible the conditions experienced or prevalent at the time of the accident. Duplication requires similarity of:

a. Vehicle (same vehicle if possible)
b. Type of roadway surface
c. Direction of travel
d. Vehicle load
e. Roadway temperature
f. Roadway surface conditions

356

C6.029 Buses, large trucks and motorcycles present special problems. Test skids and speed estimates for these types of vehicles are beyond the scope of this lesson.

C6.030 Procedures to follow when you conduct test skids:

a. Duplicate conditions as closely as possible.

b. Determine the accuracy of the speedometer. The true speed of the test vehicle must be known. The speedometer accuracy may be checked by radar.

c. If possible, use a test vehicle equipped with a *detonator*, which leaves a chalk mark on the roadway surface at the time and place of brake application.

d. For safety reasons, do not make test skids at a speed in excess of 35 mph (56 km/h).

e. Make test skids at the speed limit if the limit is 35 mph (56 km/h) or even substantially less. But do not make test skids at less than 15 mph (25 km/h) because there is a possibility of an excessively high resultant drag factor.

f. Travel in a straight path at a constant 3 to 5 mph (5 to 8 km/h) above the speed at which the test is to be made. Decelerate to the test speed. Apply the brakes quickly and hard and let the vehicle skid to a complete stop.

g.   Use one of two (2) methods of measuring test skid marks to determine the longest usable skid distance for calculating the drag factor.

METHOD 1

Conduct two test skids. If the *longest* skid mark of each test is within (±) 5% of the longest skid mark of the other test, use the longer of the two test skid marks as the test-skid distance. If the first two test skids fail to produce results that fall within the acceptable ±%, conduct a third and final test. If the longest test skid of the third test falls within the acceptable ±% of the longest test skid of either the first two tests, then disregard the unsuitable test skid from the first two tests and use the longer test-skid distance of the two test skids falling within (±) 5% of each other. If the third test does not produce a test skid that falls within the acceptable range, then use Method 2.

METHOD 2

Compare the longest skid mark from each of the three test skids that were conducted and select the longest two of these three skid marks. If the longest two skid marks are within (±) 10% of each other, use the longer of the two as the test-skid distance. If the two selected skid marks fail to be within (±) 10% of each other, compare the shorter of these two skid marks to the skid mark that was not selected from the original three skid marks. If the two skid marks now being compared are within (±) 10% of each other, use the longer of the two as the test-skid distance.

358

The principle involved in either of the two methods is to use as the test-skid distance always the longest skid mark available (from among the three test skids) that is within ($\pm$) 5%/($\pm$) 10% of a skid mark from one of the test skids other than the one from which the longest skid mark has been taken.

Once the longest usable skid distance has been determined by either Method 1 or Method 2, that distance can then be placed into the coefficient of friction/drag factor formula and the f value calculated.

Both methods are acceptable for determining the coefficient of friction. Method 1 favors the accident vehicle because it tends to result in a somewhat lower coefficient of friction than does Method 2.

For the purposes of this course, use Method 1 when the f value is being determined from test skids, unless otherwise advised.

To ensure a better understanding of measuring test skid marks, review C6.016 (f), (g), (h) and (j).

C6.031 Use the following formula to calculate the coefficient of friction/drag factor from test skids:

Formula C6-5

United States

$$f = \frac{S^2}{30D}$$

Metric

$$f = \frac{S^2}{254D}$$

where f = coefficient of friction/drag factor

          S = speed at which the test skids were made

          D = skid distance of the test skids

EXAMPLE 1 -- Longest skid distance (Using Method 1)

Two test skids were made at 30 mph (48 km/h). Their distances were not within ± 5% of each other. A third test was made, also at 30 mph (48 km/h), the longest skid mark falling within ± 5% of the longest skid mark of test 1. Therefore, the longest skid marks of tests 1 and 3 should be compared to determine the longest skid distance to be used to calculate the coefficient of friction.

	Test #1	Test #2	Test #3
LF	51 feet(15.54 m)	44 feet(13.41 m)	52 feet(15.84 m)
RF	50 feet(15.24 m)	45 feet(13.71 m)	51 feet(15.54 m)
LR	48 feet(14.63 m)	42 feet(12.80 m)	48 feet(14.63 m)
RR	49 feet(14.93 m)	40 feet(12.19 m)	49 feet(14.93 m)

(For the purposes of this course, go two places to the right of the decimal point, unless otherwise advised. This supports the practice of using always the minimum speed for the accident vehicles.)

The longer of the two longest test-skid distances obtained from the tests 1 and 3 is 52 feet (15.84 m). Place this value into the formula and solve for the coefficient of friction.

U.S.

$$f = \frac{S^2}{30D}$$

$$f = \frac{30^2}{30 \times 52}$$

$$f = \frac{900}{1560}$$

$$f = .57$$

Metric

$$f = \frac{S^2}{254D}$$

$$f = \frac{48^2}{254 \times 15.84}$$

$$f = \frac{2304}{4023.36}$$

$$f = .57$$

C6.032 The coefficient of friction/drag factor, as applicable to vehicle tires that are sliding on a highway surface, is the ratio of the force F in pounds (kilograms) required to move (slide) the vehicle at a constant speed over the surface divided by the weight W of the vehicle. The force (pull) required to keep the vehicle moving at a constant speed is the force that must be used in Formula C6-4 ($f = F/W$), not the initial static force required to start the vehicle moving from a position of rest.

C6.033 It is obviously not practical to weigh a vehicle and pull it along a roadway surface in order to determine the coefficient of friction/drag factor. It can be done more easily and just as accurately by using a much smaller, lighter object such as a drag sled, a tire and wheel, or a piece of metal, depending upon the facilities available and the circumstances or requirements involved.

C6.034 *Drag sled construction.* A drag sled can be constructed from part of a tire that is then filled with concrete, lead or any weighty material. The steps in the construction of a drag sled are:

1. Cut a section of tire to about the size of that shown in Figure C6-11, left unit.

2. Fill the tire section with water to the desired level of the material to be added later as weight. Mark this level on the tire with a line. This is the *original* level.

3. Remove the water and measure its volume, then pour half that volume back into the tire section. Mark the new water level on the tire. This line will pass through the *center of mass* of the drag sled when construction is completed.

4. Drill a hole through one end of the tire at the *center of mass* line, and then install an eye bolt by which the tire will be pulled (see Fig. C6-11, left unit).

5. Fill the tire section with *concrete, lead,* etc. to the *original* water level line. Once the material has set and hardened, the construction is completed.

C6.035 Procedures for *drag sled use*. Weigh the entire unit with a spring scale and use the same scale to pull the drag sled along the roadway surface each time the drag sled is used. During the pull, ensure that the scale, from which the force F is read, is held parallel to the roadway surface (see Fig. C6-12). Also, remember that the force required to keep the unit moving at a constant speed is the force that must be used in the formula. Heeding these precautions will save many arguments in court. The general procedures for the use of a drag sled are also valid for the use of a *tire and wheel* or a *piece of metal* when these objects are used to determine the coefficient of friction/drag factor. In some investigations the f value for metal might be needed if a metal object that was part of the load slid for a distance or if the vehicle itself slid on its top or side (see Fig. C6-11, right unit).

C6.036 It is necessary to pull the unit along the roadway approximately 2-3 feet (1 meter) to determine the amount of force required to move it at a constant speed. Several pulls should be made alongside the skid or yaw mark to ensure that the amount of force in pounds or kilograms registered on the scale is consistent. If the pavement consistency changes or there is worn or patched pavement over which the mark passes, the drag factor should be determined for each such expanse.

Figure C6-11 Drag sleds. Unit on left is a concrete-filled tire for obtaining the drag factor of rubber tires on a surface. Unit on right is of metal for obtaining the drag factor of metal parts on a surface. Note the scales for measuring the force *F*.

Figure C6-12 The scale must be pulled parallel to the surface in order to accurately measure the force *F* required to move the sled at a constant speed.

364

C6.037 Use Formula C6-4, presented earlier in C6.020, to calculate the coefficient of friction/drag factor when using a drag sled, tire and wheel, or piece of metal to obtain the force F.

Formula C6-4

$$f = \frac{F}{W}$$

where 　f 　= 　coefficient of friction/drag factor

F 　= 　force (pull) parallel to the surface, measured in pounds or kilograms, required to move the object at a constant speed

W 　= 　weight of the object being moved (e.g., a drag sled, tire and wheel, or piece of metal) measured in pounds or kilograms

EXAMPLE

A drag sled which weighed 50 lbs (22.7 kg) required a pull or force of 30 lbs (13.7 kg) to move it along a level roadway at a constant speed. The coefficient of friction is calculated as follows:

U.S.

$$f = \frac{F}{W}$$

$$f = \frac{30}{50}$$

$$f = .60$$

Metric

$$f = \frac{F}{W}$$

$$f = \frac{13.7}{22.7}$$

$$f = .60$$

C6.038 In the above example, if the drag sled had been pulled along a roadway that was not level but had a grade, the calculation performed would not have given a coefficient of friction value but rather a drag factor value f, since an adjustment for grade would have been automatically included in the force value F read from the drag sled scale.

C6.039 In cases where an accident occurs on a roadway that has a grade, the f value obtained from friction tests, including test skids conducted at the same location where the accident occurred and in the same direction as the accident vehicle was traveling, does not need to be adjusted for grade but can be placed directly into Formula C6-7, presented several pages further on.

C6.040 Often it is not possible to run test skids at the accident scene. When the grade varies from the accident scene to the test site, the investigator must adjust the f value obtained at the test site to reflect the difference in grade. To do this, the investigator must first find the percent grade of the test surface by using some instrument such as a smart level, carpenter's level, line level, clinometer or traffic template. If he does not already know the percent grade at the accident scene, he must find it also.

C6.041 If the accident vehicle skidded upgrade (+) and tests are conducted *on a level surface* or if a Coefficient of Friction Table is used, the grade percent must be added to the f value. If the accident vehicle skidded downgrade (–), the grade percent must be subtracted from the f value.

C6.042 Adjusting the f value for grade. There are two methods used to make a grade adjustment. The first is the *number line method*, which enables the investigator to count from the test side grade up or down to the accident-site grade. The second is the *crow's foot method*. The crow's foot method gives the investigator a visual idea of the relationship of the test-site grade to the accident-site grade. The diagrams for use with these two methods are shown below.

NOTE: Either method is acceptable and the governing rule for using either one is *always take the test site to the accident site*.

Number Line Method

.05 _____

.04 _____

.03 _____

.02 _____

.01 _____

_____ Level

-.01 _____

-.02 _____

-.03 _____

-.04 _____

-.05 _____

Crow's Foot Method

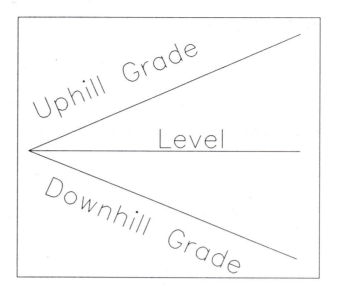

The investigator must remember the effect that gravity has on an object. It will be harder for a vehicle, whether an accident vehicle or a test vehicle, to slide uphill against gravity than to slide on a level surface or slide downhill. Conversely, it will be easier for a vehicle to slide downhill with gravity than to slide on a level surface or slide uphill.

Therefore, in using either the number line method or the crow's foot method, if the coefficient of friction tests are completed at a location other than the accident site, the coefficient of friction obtained from the tests will in most cases need to be adjusted either upward (by adding) or downward (by subtracting).

EXAMPLE 1 -- Downgrade adjustment using the number line method

A vehicle skidded on a roadway with a -04% (downhill) grade. Drag factor tests were conducted on a nearby surface of the same type with a +02% (uphill) grade and the *f* value of the test surface, was determined to be .75. Here the actual or adjusted drag factor at the location where the vehicle slid is determined by moving from the test site downward to the accident site, that is, from +.02 to −.04 for a total difference of .06 or 6 percent. Since the adjustment is downward, .06 will be *subtracted* from .75, giving an adjusted *f* value of .69 (f = .75 − .06 = .69).

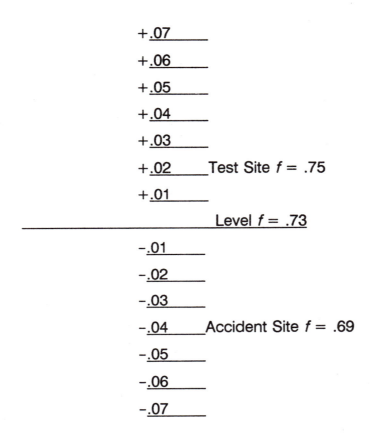

+.07 ____

+.06 ____

+.05 ____

+.04 ____

+.03 ____

+.02 ____ Test Site *f* = .75

+.01 ____

_____ Level *f* = .73

−.01 ____

−.02 ____

−.03 ____

−.04 ____ Accident Site *f* = .69

−.05 ____

−.06 ____

−.07 ____

EXAMPLE 2 -- Upgrade adjustment using the crow's foot method

A vehicle skidded on a roadway having a +.03 (uphill) grade. Drag factor tests were conducted on a nearby surface of the same type with a −.04 (downhill) grade and the *f* value of the test surface was

369

determined to be .68. Here the actual or adjusted drag factor at the accident location is determined by moving from the test site upward to the accident site, that is, from −.04 to +.03 for a total difference of .07 or 7 percent. Since the adjustment is *upward*, .07 will be *added* to .68, giving an adjusted of .75 ($f = .68 + .07 = .75$).

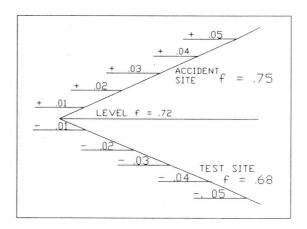

C6.043 *The Roadway Coefficient of Friction Table*. Table C6-2 represents the results of many tests conducted by different persons and organizations. There are many factors that have influenced the results. Resort to this table only when other testing capabilities are not available. When using this or any similar table, calculate a range of speeds based on the range of the coefficient of friction values listed for the given surface and conditions. Begin with the relevant lower-end coefficient of friction and proceed at selected intervals up through the upper end. Since the values given in the table are coefficient of friction values (for a level surface), they must be adjusted up or down from a level surface to any accident-site grade. The calculations using the adjusted values will give the investigator an indication of the lower-end and upper-end speeds at which a vehicle could have been traveling at the time of the accident.

370

TABLE C6-2

Possible Coefficients of Friction for Various Roadway Surfaces

NOTE: The values shown in this table are for information purposes only. They provide a starting point for the investigator to determine, through proper testing, the actual coefficient of friction for the surface(s) the investigator is concerned with.

Concrete

	Well-worn	Smoother from use	New, Fresh pavement	
Dry	.50 – .75	.60 – .75	.70 – 1.20	
Wet	.35 – .60	.45 – .70	.50 – .80	

Asphalt

	Excess tar, Bleeding	Well-worn	Smoothed from use	New, Fresh pavement
Dry	.35 – .60	.45 – .75	.55 – .80	.65 – 1.20
Wet	.25 – .55	.40 – .65	.40 – .65	.45 – .80

Gravel

		Loose	Packed, Well traveled	
		.40 – .70	.50 – .85	

Ice

	Cold, Frost	Warm, Wet		
	.10 – .25	.05 – .10		

Snow

	Loose	Packed		
Cold, Dry	.10 – .25	.25 – .55		
Wet	.30 – .50	.30 – .60		

C6.044 Speed from skid marks may be calculated by using Formula C6-7.

Formula C6-7

United States	**Metric**
$S = \sqrt{30Df}$	$S = \sqrt{254Df}$

where   S   =   minimum speed in mph (km/h) at the beginning of the skid marks

           D   =   skid distance based on skid-mark measurements

           f   =   coefficient of friction, adjusted for percent grade where required (see C6.041) to become drag factor.

NOTE: 30 (U.S.) and 254 (metric) are constants.

EXAMPLE

A vehicle skidded a distance of 69 feet (21.03 m) to a stop on a level roadway surface having a .75 coefficient of friction (*f* value). Its minimum speed at the beginning of the skid marks would have been?

U.S.	Metric
$S = \sqrt{30\ D\ f}$	$S = \sqrt{254\ D\ f}$
$S = \sqrt{30 \times 69 \times .75}$	$S = \sqrt{254 \times 21.03 \times .75}$
$S = \sqrt{1552.5}$	$S = \sqrt{4006.21}$
$S = 39.40$ mph	$S = 63.29$ km/h

Braking Capability or Efficiency

C6.045 Formula C6-7 is suitable for calculating speed from skid marks when all wheels have braking capability or when the accident vehicle is used for test skids to determine the coefficient of friction/drag factor. When the accident vehicle has less than 100 percent braking efficiency and the *f* value used assumes 100 percent braking efficiency, such as when test skids are performed with a four-wheel vehicle having braking capability on all wheels, or when the Coefficient of Friction Table is used, then modify the formula to allow for the percentage decrease in braking efficiency. If the vehicle in the example under C6.044 above had had rear-drive and had had braking capabilities on all wheels except the right-rear wheel, it would have had 80 percent braking capability (refer to Table C6-3) and its speed would have been calculated using Formula C6-8.

Formula C6-8

United States

$$S = \sqrt{30\ D\ f\ n}$$

Metric

$$S = \sqrt{254\ D\ f\ n}$$

where S = minimum speed in mph (km/h)
D = skid distance in feet (meters)
f = coefficient of friction (adjusted, if grade is involved, to become drag factor)
n = percent braking efficiency or capability

373

Using values from the C6.044 example:

U.S.	Metric
$S = \sqrt{30\ D\ f\ n}$	$S = \sqrt{254\ D\ f\ n}$
$S = \sqrt{30 \times 69 \times .75 \times .80}$	$S = \sqrt{254 \times 21 \times .75 \times .80}$
$S = \sqrt{1242}$	$S = \sqrt{3200.40}$
$S = 35.24$ mph	$S = 56.57$ km/h

C6.046 When a continuous skid mark traverses different kinds of roadway surfaces, the coefficient of friction and length of skid mark on each surface must be known in order to calculate the vehicle's minimum speed. In such a case, use Formula C6-9.

Formula C6-9

United States

$$S = \sqrt{30[(D_1 f_1) + (D_2 f_2)]}$$

Metric

$$S = \sqrt{254[(D_1 f_1) + (D_2 f_2)]}$$

where S = minimum speed at the beginning of the skid mark in mph (km/h)

D_1 = skid distance on the first surface

D_2 = skid distance on the second surface

f_1 = coefficient of friction on the first surface

f_2 = coefficient of friction on the second surface

NOTE: When there are additional surfaces involved, extend the formula with $(D_3 f_3)$, etc.

374

TABLE C6-3

Braking Percentages for Vehicles

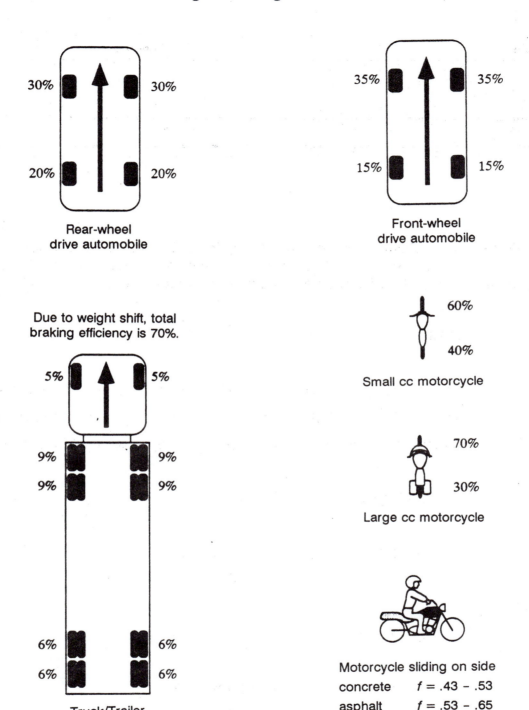

Rear-wheel
drive automobile

Front-wheel
drive automobile

Due to weight shift, total
braking efficiency is 70%.

Truck/Trailer

Small cc motorcycle

Large cc motorcycle

Motorcycle sliding on side
concrete $f = .43 - .53$
asphalt $f = .53 - .65$

Source: Gary L. Stephens, *Formula Workbook for Traffic Accident Investigation and Reconstruction*. Used with permission of author.

Asphalt   Concrete

Figure C6-13 Continuous skid marks on different surfaces. The length of skid marks on each surface must be measured separately and the coefficient of friction for each surface must be determined.

EXAMPLE

A vehicle skids to a stop over two different surfaces, e.g., a concrete bridge and an asphalt roadway. Use the data given below to calculate the vehicle's minimum speed at the beginning of the skid.

<u>Surface 1</u>

Concrete D_1 = 26 feet (8m)

                     f_1 = .82

<u>Surface 2</u>

Asphalt D_2 = 30 feet (9m)

                     f_2 = .75

Applying Formula C6-9:

U.S.	Metric
$S = \sqrt{30[(D_1f_1) + (D_2f_2)]}$	$S = \sqrt{254[(D_1f_1) + (D_2f_2)]}$
$S = \sqrt{30[(26 \times .82) + (30 \times .75)]}$	$S = \sqrt{254[(8 \times .82) + (9 \times .75)]}$
$S = \sqrt{30[21.32 + 22.50]}$	$S = \sqrt{254[6.56 + 6.75]}$
$S = \sqrt{30 \times 43.82}$	$S = \sqrt{254 \times 13.31}$
$S = \sqrt{1314.6}$	$S = \sqrt{3380.74}$
$S = 36.25 \text{ mph}$	$S = 58.14 \text{ km/h}$

C6.047 Speed calculations from skid marks when each side of the vehicle is on a different surface can be made using Formula C6-10.

Formula C6-10

United States	**Metric**
$S = \sqrt{30[(D_1f_1n_1) + (D_2f_2n_2)]}$	$S = \sqrt{254[(D_1f_1n_1) + (D_2f_2n_2)]}$

where   S = minimum speed in mph (km/h) at the beginning of the skid marks

D_1 = skid distance on first surface

D_2 = skid distance on the second surface

f_1 = coefficient of friction of the first surface

f_2 = coefficient of friction of the second surface

n_1 = braking percentage of vehicle on first surface

n_2 = braking percentage of vehicle on second surface

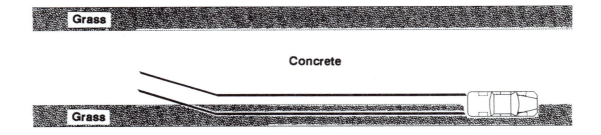

Figure C6-14   Each side of the vehicle may slide on a surface with a different coefficient of friction.

EXAMPLE

A vehicle skidded 51 feet (15 m) to a stop. During the skid, the left wheels were on pavement having a coefficient of friction of .72. The right wheels were on a grass shoulder having a coefficient of friction of .55. The vehicle's minimum speed was?

U.S.	Metric

$$S = \sqrt{30[(D_1f_1n_1) + (D_2f_2n_2)]}$$

$$S = \sqrt{254[(D_1f_1n_1) + (D_2f_2n_2)]}$$

$$S = \sqrt{30[51 \times .72 \times .50) + (51 \times .55 \times .50)]}$$

$$S = \sqrt{254[(15 \times .72 \times .50) + (15 \times .55 \times .50)]}$$

$$S = \sqrt{30[18.36 + 14.02]}$$

$$S = \sqrt{254[5.4 + 4.12]}$$

$$S = \sqrt{30 \times 32.38}$$

$$S = \sqrt{254 \times 9.52}$$

$$S = \sqrt{971.4}$$

$$S = \sqrt{2418.08}$$

$$S = 31.16 \text{ mph}$$

$$S = 49.17 \text{ km/h}$$

Note: When calculating the percentage of braking refer, to Table C6-3. There should always be at least 50 percent braking efficiency in this type of situation unless one or more brakes are not operational, in which case the investigator must adjust the braking percentage accordingly.

Combined Speeds

C6.048 When a vehicle skids a certain distance to a stop, the minimum speed of the vehicle at the beginning of its skid can be calculated using Formula C6-7. However, when a vehicle skids only partway to a stop and then the stopping distance is affected by another event, such as a critical speed yaw or the vehicle striking another object, at least two preliminary steps must be taken in order to calculate the initial minimum speed.

> Step 1 -- Calculate the speed based on the length of the skid marks (Formula C6-7) even though the vehicle has not yet stopped.

> Step 2 -- Calculate or determine the speed at the beginning of the second event.

C6.049 It must be remembered that when more than one speed enters into the calculation of initial speed at the beginning of the skid marks, the two or more speeds must not be added together in the usual sense. Rather the speeds must be placed into the combined speed formula and the initial speed then calculated as the square root of the sum of the squares of the speeds.

Formula C6-11 -- Combined Speed Formula

United States	*Metric*
$S_c = \sqrt{S_1^2 + S_2^2 \ldots + S_n^2}$	$S_c = \sqrt{S_1^2 + S_2^2 \ldots S_n^2}$

where S_c = speed combined

S_1 = initial speed, e.g., speed based on skid mark length

S_2 = calculated or estimated speed at the end of the skid or at the beginning of the second event

S_n = A variable which theoretically permits an unlimited number of speeds to be used in the equation.

EXAMPLE

A vehicle skidded 60 feet (18m) and then went into a critical speed yaw. Calculations indicated that the vehicle's speed at the start of the yaw was 40 mph (64 km/h). The roadway had a coefficient of friction of .80. The minimum speed at the beginning of the skid marks can be calculated using the combined speed formula.

Calculate first the speed based on the length of the skid marks, applying Formula C6-7.

U.S.	*Metric*
$S_1 = \sqrt{30 \times D \times f}$	$S_1 = \sqrt{254 \times D \times f}$
$S_1 = \sqrt{30 \times 60 \times .80}$	$S_1 = \sqrt{254 \times 18 \times .80}$
$S_1 = \sqrt{1440}$	$S_1 = \sqrt{3657.6}$
$S_1 = 37.94$ mph	$S_1 = 60.47$ km/h

381

The vehicle's speed for the first part of the speed calculation (S_1) was 37.94 mph (60.47 km/h). This speed is based on the length of the skid marks and obtained by using the slide-to-stop formula (Formula C6-7). We know from a second calculated speed, obtained from the critical speed yaw occurring at the end of the skid marks, that the vehicle's speed at the beginning of the yaw (S_2) was 40 mph (64 km/h). With this information, we can now use the combined speed formula (Formula C6-11) to calculate the vehicle's speed at the beginning of the skid marks (S_c).

Applying Formula C6-11:

U.S.	*Metric*
$S_c = \sqrt{S_1^2 + S_2^2}$	$S_c = \sqrt{S_1^2 + S_2^2}$
$S_c = \sqrt{37.94^2 + 40^2}$	$S_c = \sqrt{60.47^2 + 64^2}$
$S_c = \sqrt{1439.44 + 1600}$	$S_c = \sqrt{3656.62 + 4096}$
$S_c = \sqrt{3039.44}$	$S_c = \sqrt{7752.62}$
$S_c = 55.13 \text{ mph}$	$S_c = 88.04 \text{ km/h}$

Distance

C6.050 The skid distance required to stop when the speed and coefficient of friction are known can be calculated by using the Formula C6-12.

Formula C6-12

United States

$$D = \frac{S^2}{30f}$$

Metric

$$D = \frac{S^2}{254f}$$

where   D = skid distance

S = speed

f = coefficient of friction/drag factor

EXAMPLE

A vehicle traveling 69 mph (111 km/h) slides to a stop on a surface having a coefficient of friction of .85.   The distance the vehicle requires to stop is?

U.S.

$$D = \frac{S^2}{30f}$$

Metric

$$D = \frac{S^2}{254f}$$

$$D = \frac{69^2}{(30 \times .85)}$$

$$D = \frac{111^2}{(254 \times .85)}$$

D = 187 ft

D = 57 m

Time

C6.051 The time required to slide (skid) to a stop when the slide distance and coefficient of friction are known can be calculated using Formula C6-13.

383

Formula C6-13

United States

$$t = .249\sqrt{\frac{D}{f}}$$

Metric

$$t = 0.45\sqrt{\frac{D}{f}}$$

where   t = time in seconds

D = distance of slide or skid

f = coefficient of friction/drag factor

NOTE: .249 (U.S.) and 0.45 (metric) are constants.

EXAMPLE

A vehicle is traveling at 69 mph (111 km/h) and skids 187 feet (57 m) to a stop on a roadway having a coefficient of friction of .85. The time it takes the vehicle to skid to a stop is?

U.S.

$$t = .249\sqrt{\frac{D}{f}}$$

Metric

$$t = 0.45\sqrt{\frac{D}{f}}$$

$$t = .249\sqrt{\frac{187}{.85}}$$

$$t = 0.45\sqrt{\frac{57}{.85}}$$

$$t = .249\sqrt{220}$$

$$t = \sqrt{67.05}$$

$$t = .249 \times 14.83$$

$$t = 0.45 \times 8.18$$

$$t = 3.69 \text{ sec}$$

$$t = 3.68 \text{ sec}$$

Constant/Average Velocity Formulas

C6.052 Up to this point, the investigator has learned to find the distance, time and initial minimum speed in reference to a slide-to-a-stop. He will now learn to find the distance, time, and rate of travel using the *constant/average velocity formulas* for situations where the vehicle is neither skidding nor slowing or accelerating sharply or purposefully (as in braking to or departing from a stop).

Distance and time values appropriate for an accident are expressed in units of feet (meters) and seconds rather than miles (kilometers) and minutes or hours. In keeping with the practice in accident investigation of using in most instances feet per second (meters per second) to indicate *velocity* (rate and direction) rather than speed (rate only), the symbol *V* will appear in the constant/average velocity formulas although a direction may not always be specified in the given data.

The calculated velocity is either a *constant* (uniform) velocity or if there are fluctuations in the rate of travel over the given distance/time, as is frequently the case, an *average* velocity.

If any two of the three variables of distance, time, and velocity are known, the third, unknown variable can be calculated.

Formula C6-14

$$V = \frac{D}{t}$$

where   V = constant rate

D = known distance

t = known time

EXAMPLE

A vehicle travels 120 miles (193 kilometers) in 1 hour 33 minutes. What is its velocity in feet per second (meters per second)? See note below.

U.S.

$$V = \frac{D}{t}$$

$$V = \frac{633600}{5580}$$

V = 113.54 ft/sec

Metric

$$V = \frac{D}{t}$$

$$V = \frac{193080}{5580}$$

V = 34.58 m/s

NOTE: Miles (kilometers) must be converted into feet (meters):
1 mile = 5280 feet (1 km = 1000 m)
So 120 miles x 5280 feet = 633600 feet
(193 km x 1000 m = 193000 m).

Hours and minutes must be converted into seconds:
1 hour = 60 minutes
1 minute = 60 seconds
So 93 minutes x 60 seconds = 5580 seconds.

Formula C6-15

$$t = \frac{D}{V}$$

where   t   =   number of seconds

D   =   known distance

V   =   known constant velocity

EXAMPLE

If a vehicle is traveling 65 mph (104 km/h), how many seconds will the vehicle take to travel 127 miles (204 km)?

U.S.

$$t = \frac{D}{V}$$

$$t = \frac{670560}{95.29}$$

t = 7037.04 sec

Metric

$$t = \frac{D}{V}$$

$$t = \frac{204000}{28.91}$$

t = 7055.89 sec

NOTE: Remember to convert miles (kilometers) into feet (meters). For ease in converting miles per hour (kilometers per hour) to feet per second (meters per second), multiply mph by 1.466 (km/h by 0.278). The answers appearing in the calculations above and below, which were performed on a calculator, reflect use of these *conversion factors*.

Formula C6-16

$$D = V \times t$$

where   D = distance traveled

V = constant known velocity

t = known time

EXAMPLE

If a vehicle travels at a constant speed of 55 mph (88 km/h), how far in feet (meters) will the vehicle travel in 37 minutes?

U.S.   *Metric*

$D = V \times t$ $D = V \times t$

$D = 80.63 \times 2220$ $D = 24.46 \times 2220$

$D = 178998.6$ feet $D = 54310.08$ meters

Note: You must convert miles per hour (km/h) into feet per second (m/s) and minutes into seconds.

Curve Speeds

C6.053 When a vehicle travels around a curve, it is acted upon by two forces:

1.   *Centripetal force*, or adhesion of the tire to the road, which strives to keep the vehicle in its curved path.

2.   *Centrifugal force* or *inertia*, which attempts to make the vehicle escape from its curved path.

Inertia defined. According to *Newton*, "Every body continues in its state of uniform motion in a straight line" unless acted upon by external forces so applied to the body that the direction of motion may be changed. The *inertial tendency* of a body to continue in a straight line is a common observation. The occasional skidding of a motor vehicle when attempting to round a corner is an illustration of the effect of *inertia*.

C6.054 *Centrifugal force* or *inertia*. If a body is moving at a constant speed in one direction, a force is necessary to change either its speed or direction. However, when a vehicle is traveling around a curve, so that its direction is changing all the time, a force called *centrifugal force* acts on it, tending to maintain it at any point in a straight line tangent to the curve at that point.

C6.055 *Centripetal force.* An object being swung around at the end of a piece of string creates a tensional force on the string equal and opposite to the centrifugal force acting on the object. This *equal* and *opposite* force is called *centripetal force*. In a car traveling around a curve, this force is supplied by the *friction* or *adhesion* between the tires and the road surface and also by other forces brought into play by the superelevation. When a vehicle travels around a curve too fast, the centrifugal force may be greater than the centripetal force supplied by the road friction and superelevation and cause the vehicle to run off the road. When the road is icy or the superelevation is non-existent, a car may leave the road at a much lower speed and centrifugal force value. In the absence of centripetal force, a body does not travel in a curve but in a straight line. The centrifugal and centripetal forces must be in *equilibrium* for an object to travel in a curve.

C6.056 *Yaw.* Yaw is a term applied to a sideways movement of a vehicle, such as occurs when the rear of a vehicle rounding a corner sideslips and moves out from the curved path in which the vehicle has been moving. *Yaw*, which is the action of *revolving around the center of mass*, commences at the time the rear tires start to sideslip and depart from their *normal* tracking path. See Figures C6-15 and C6-16.

C6.057 At safe and reasonable speeds on curves, rear tires always track *inside* the front tires. At excessive speeds, causing the vehicle to go into yaw, the rear tires sideslip to a greater extent than the front tires and will eventually track *outside* the front tires.

C6.058 When a vehicle is traveling at a high speed on a curve, centrifugal force attempts to overcome centripetal force and if it succeeds, will cause the vehicle to break out of its path. As the vehicle is driven around a curve under these circumstances, it will sideslip (go into yaw) and possibly spin or overturn. See Figure C6-17.

C6.059 Centrifugal and centripetal forces work in the same manner on both the front and rear tires. The forces are particularly great on the *front lead tire*, however. This is the tire that leaves the most visible and distinguishable *yaw mark*. It is this front lead tire mark that is normally used to determine the *radius* of a yaw mark.

C6.060 Once a vehicle goes into yaw, the side thrust on the rotating front lead tire is great, causing it to sideslip as it travels around the curve. Before a vehicle goes into yaw, however, the front lead tire may leave a very narrow, dark mark as the result of weight being shifted onto that tire. This narrow mark, left *before* the vehicle goes into yaw, does not have sideslip striations and must not be confused with an actual yaw or sideslip mark, which has definite *sideslip striations*. *Yaw* can be considered definite at the point where the rear tire path crosses over the front tire path. See Figure

C6-16. This point can be used as the beginning of a yaw mark when determining its *radius*. See paragraph C6.062.

C6.061 A yaw mark commences as a narrow, dark mark with sideslip striations, and then gradually becomes wider as the vehicle begins to rotate and loses speed. The striations will have an angle to the mark in the direction of sideslip.

C6.062 To find the *radius* of a critical speed scuff or yaw mark:

a. Find the *crossover marks* where the rear tire has crossed over the path of the leading front tire after vehicle weight has been shifted onto the leading front tire. Beyond the crossover and within the first third of the yaw mark, measure a straight line from **a** to **b** as the *chord* **C**. See Figure C6-17 (yaw mark).

b. Divide the chord length in half. Label the mid-point as **c**. From **c**, measure at a right angle to the arc of the yaw mark and label this point **d** . The distance from **c** to **d** is the *middle ordinate* **M**.

c. Typically, the front lead tire will leave the heaviest mark. If possible use this mark to calculate the radius and the critical speed of the yaw. If this mark is not adequate for some reason, use whatever other yaw mark is visible and otherwise satisfactory.

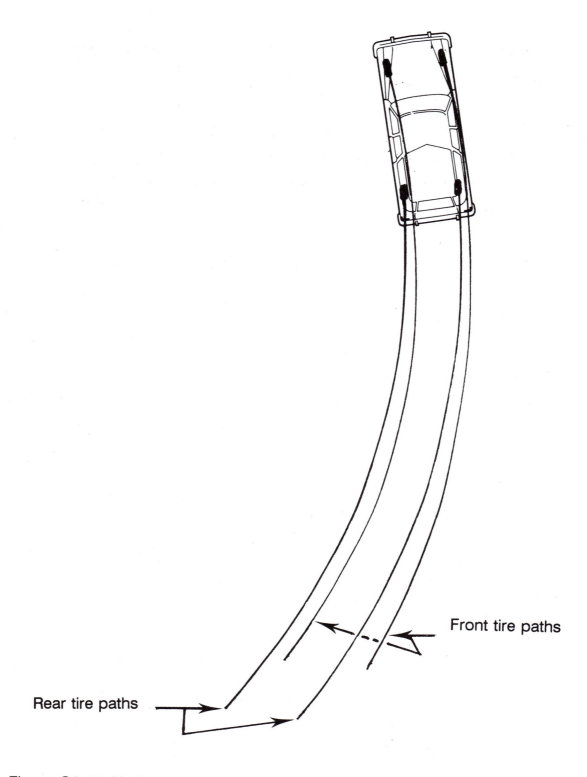

Front tire paths

Rear tire paths

Figure C6-15 Under normal conditions, the rear tires track *inside* the front tires on a curve.

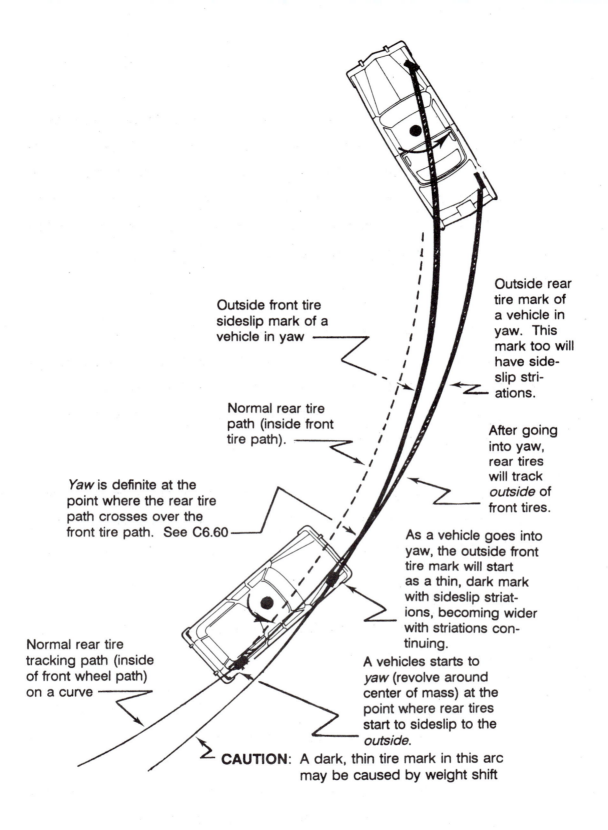

Outside front tire sideslip mark of a vehicle in yaw

Outside rear tire mark of a vehicle in yaw. This mark too will have side-slip striations.

Normal rear tire path (inside front tire path).

After going into yaw, rear tires will track *outside* of front tires.

Yaw is definite at the point where the rear tire path crosses over the front tire path. See C6.60

As a vehicle goes into yaw, the outside front tire mark will start as a thin, dark mark with sideslip striations, becoming wider with striations continuing.

Normal rear tire tracking path (inside of front wheel path) on a curve

A vehicles starts to *yaw* (revolve around center of mass) at the point where rear tires start to sideslip to the *outside*.

CAUTION: A dark, thin tire mark in this arc may be caused by weight shift

Figure C6-16 When a vehicle goes into *yaw*, the rear tires track outside the front tires.

393

C6.063 For estimating purposes, consider a car's *center of mass* (CM) to be located midway between its sides opposite the mid-point of the wheelbase and at one-third of the car's height above the ground. When plotting a vehicle's center-of-mass path on the roadway or on a scale diagram, take measurements between the vehicle's center-of-mass location and tire marks on the roadway in the manner described in Figures C6-18 and C6-19.

C6.064   The radius of the center-of-mass path can be estimated by calculating the radius of the outside yaw mark and subtracting one-half of the tracking width of the vehicle from the radius of that yaw mark.   The *tracking width* of a vehicle is measured from the outside of the left front tire to the outside of the right front tire.

C6.065 When there is severe yawing action evident, all tire marks should be accurately measured and then plotted on a scale diagram of sufficiently large size to permit use of a scale vehicle cut-out to plot the center-of-mass path.

C6.066 There are two speed calculations of particular importance to an investigator:

1.   *Critical vehicle speed*, or the speed at which a vehicle slides off the roadway in going around a curve.

2.   *Critical curve speed*, or the speed above which a vehicle slides out of its lane of travel in going around a curve.

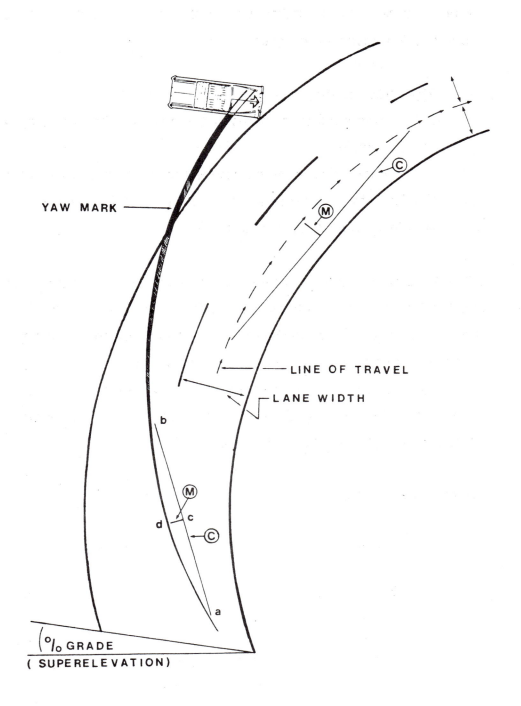

YAW MARK

LINE OF TRAVEL

LANE WIDTH

b

M

c

d

C

a

(°/o GRADE
(SUPERELEVATION)

Figure C6-17   Plotting the radius of a yaw mark and the radius of the roadway path of travel. Source: R. W. Rivers, *Traffic Accident Investigators' Handbook*, courtesy of Charles C. Thomas, Publisher.

395

C6.067 To calculate the critical speed of a vehicle or the critical speed of a curve, it is necessary to have:

1. The radius of the
    a. Yaw mark or center-of-mass path (for the critical speed of a vehicle)
    b. Lane of travel of the vehicle (for the critical speed of a curve)
2. Coefficient of friction (drag factor must be adjusted to level)
3. Roadway superelevation or bank

C6.068 To calculate the critical speed of a vehicle, use approximately the first third of the yaw mark as the arc from which to calculate the curve radius. To calculate the critical speed of a curve, use the center of the lane of travel (the vehicle's normal line of travel) as the arc. This may be done by first calculating the radius of the curve using the inner roadway edge as the arc and then adding one-half of the width of the travel lane to the radius. See Figure C6-17 at *A* (upper right).

C6.069 Formula C6-17 -- Critical speed formula

United States	*Metric*
$S = 3.86\sqrt{R(f \pm e)}$	$S = 11.27\sqrt{R(f \pm e)}$

where S = speed at the beginning of the yaw
       R = radius of the yaw mark
       f = coefficient of friction (drag factor adj. to level)
       e = superelevation or bank of roadway
       NOTE: 3.86 (U.S.) and 11.27 (metric) are constants.

An example will be given further below.

396

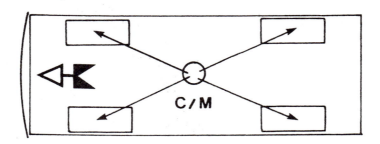

Figure C6-18 When a vehicle's center-of-mass path is used to determine a vehicle's speed in yaw, measurements must be made from the location of the center-of-mass on a vehicle to the roadway contact area of each tire as shown in this figure. All these measurements must in turn be related to the tire marks on the roadway by further measurements in order to plot the vehicle's center-of-mass path. See also Figure C6-19. These same procedures are used essentially to plot a vehicle's center-of-mass path on a scale diagram.

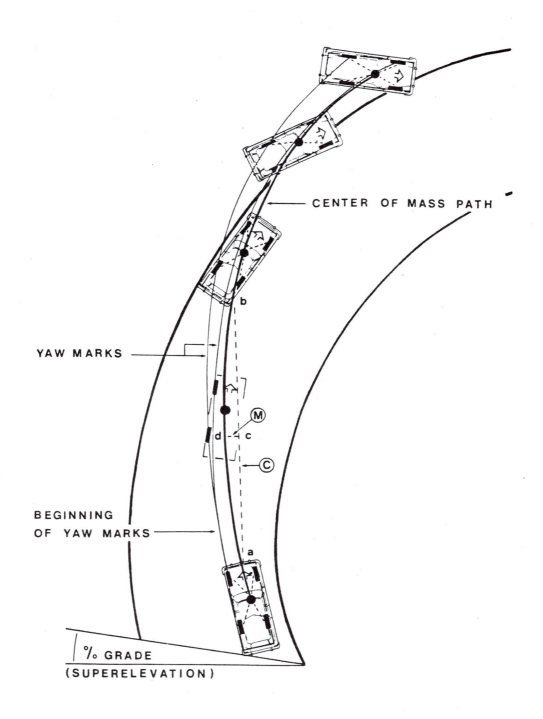

CENTER OF MASS PATH

YAW MARKS

BEGINNING
OF YAW MARKS

% GRADE
(SUPERELEVATION)

Figure C6-19 Plotting the radius of the center-of-mass path. Source: R. W. Rivers, *Traffic Accident Investigators' Handbook*, courtesy of Charles C. Thomas, Publisher.

C6.070 The radius of an arc (yaw mark, edge of roadway, center line of roadway) can be calculated using Formula C6-18.

Formula C6-18

United States

$$R = \frac{C^2}{8M} + \frac{M}{2}$$

Metric

$$R = \frac{C^2}{8M} + \frac{M}{2}$$

Where R = radius

C = chord

M = middle ordinate

NOTE: The numbers 8 and 2 are mathematical constants used in calculating the radius in both U.S. and metric.

EXAMPLE -- Radius of a yaw mark and critical speed of the vehicle

A vehicle traveled into a curve at a high rate of speed and skidded sideways, leaving a sideslip or yaw mark of 300 feet (100 meters) in length. With the first one-third or 100 feet (30 meters) of the yaw mark used as the arc, a chord was measured at 75 feet (23 meters), giving a middle ordinate of 3 feet (1 meter). The roadway superelevation was measured at + 05%. The coefficient of friction was determined to be .70. What is the critical speed of the vehicle for that curve?

Step 1 -- Calculate the radius of the yaw mark using Formula C6-18.

399

	U.S.		Metric

$$R = \frac{C^2}{8M} + \frac{M}{2} \qquad\qquad R = \frac{C^2}{8M} + \frac{M}{2}$$

$$R = \frac{75^2}{8 \times 3} + \frac{3}{2} \qquad\qquad R = \frac{23^2}{8 \times 1} + \frac{1}{2}$$

$$R = \frac{5625}{24} + 1.5 \qquad\qquad R = \frac{529}{8} + .5$$

$$R = 234.38 + 1.5 \qquad\qquad R = 66.12 + .5$$

$$R = 235.88 \text{ feet} \qquad\qquad R = 66.62 \text{ meters}$$

Step 2 -- Calculate the critical speed of the vehicle using Formula C6-17.

$$S = 3.86\sqrt{R(f \pm e)} \qquad\qquad S = 11.27\sqrt{R(f \pm e)}$$

$$S = 3.86\sqrt{235.88(.70 + .05)} \qquad\qquad S = 11.27\sqrt{66.62(.70 + .05)}$$

$$S = 3.86\sqrt{235.88 \times .75} \qquad\qquad S = 11.27\sqrt{66.62 \times .75}$$

$$S = 3.86\sqrt{176.91} \qquad\qquad S = 11.27\sqrt{49.96}$$

$$S = 3.86 \times 13.30 \qquad\qquad S = 11.27 \times 7.06$$

$$S = 51.33 \text{ mph} \qquad\qquad S = 79.66 \text{ km/h}$$

$$S = 51 \text{ mph} \qquad\qquad S = 79 \text{ km/h}$$

C6.071 To calculate the critical speed of a vehicle with the radius of the vehicle's center-of-mass path, subtract one-half of the vehicle's tracking width from the known radius of the yaw mark and use this adjusted radius in Formula C6-17.

EXAMPLE

Assume the same data as in the previous example.

Step 1 -- Determine the adjusted radius of the yaw mark.

Radius of yaw mark   = 235.88 ft (66.62 m)

Tracking width of vehicle = 6 ft (2 m)

One-half tracking width   = 3 ft (1 m)

Therefore, the adjusted radius will be

235.88 - 3 = 232.88 ft (66.62 - 1 = 65.62 m)

Step 2 -- Calculate the critical speed of the vehicle with the adjusted radius using Form C6-17.

U.S.	*Metric*
$S = 3.86\sqrt{R(f \pm e)}$	$S = 11.27\sqrt{R(f \pm e)}$
$S = \sqrt{232.88(.70 + .05)}$	$S = 11.27\sqrt{65.62(.70 + .05)}$
$S = 3.86\sqrt{232.88 \times .75}$	$S = 11.27\sqrt{65.62 \times .75}$
$S = 3.86\sqrt{174.66}$	$S = 11.27\sqrt{49.21}$
$S = 3.86 \times 13.21$	$S = 11.27 \times 7.01$
$S = 51.01$ mph	$S = 79.00$ km/h
$S = 51$ mph	$S = 79$ km/h

C6.072 *Critical curve speed*. It is not always possible to determine the radius of an actual yaw mark or to plot the center-of-mass path. In these instances, the radius of the roadway edge or roadway center line, to or from which half the width of the lane in which the vehicle was traveling would be added or subtracted, respectively, may be used to indirectly determine the radius of the vehicle's normal line or center-of-mass path of travel. The speed calculated from the determined radius would be the critical speed of the curve, that is, the minimum speed at which the vehicle would have had to be traveling in order for it to slide out of this path.

C6.073 DO NOT USE FORMULA C6-18 if :

1.   All wheels were not on at least similar type surfaces, or
2.   The vehicle was steered away from its yaw-curve path, or
3.   The brakes were applied, or
4.   The vehicle was a heavily loaded truck, particularly where there was a strong possibility of a load shift.

Lesson 6

SPEED ESTIMATES

Project A-1

Relate each symbol below to the correct explanatory statement on the following page. Enter the number of the statement in the blank space provided. (The first one has been done for you.)

S	=	7	M	=	_____
V	=	_____	F	=	_____
CM	=	_____	$\sqrt{}$	=	_____
R	=	_____	D_1	=	_____
D	=	_____	e	=	_____
f	=	_____	m	=	_____
n	=	_____	W	=	_____
C	=	_____	30	=	_____
f_2	=	_____	t	=	_____
a	=	_____	$\pm$	=	_____

Project A-1 cont'd

Explanatory Statements

1 = Distance

2 = Coefficient of friction for a *second* surface

3 = Coefficient of friction

4 = United States speed calculation constant

5 = Braking capability or efficiency

6 = Square root symbol

7 = Speed

8 = Weight

9 = Skid distance on the *first* surface

10 = Chord

11 = Grade

12 = Middle ordinate

13 = Radius

14 = Plus or minus

15 = Superelevation

16 = Time

17 = Velocity

18 = Acceleration

19 = Center of mass

20 = Force

Lesson 6
SPEED ESTIMATES
Project A-2

Coefficient of friction test skids were conducted at 30 mph (48 km/h) and resulted in the following skid mark distances:

LF	42 ft (13 m)	52 ft (16 m)	50 ft (15 m)
RF	46 ft (14 m)	48 ft (14 m)	47 ft (14 m)
LR	40 ft (12 m)	50 ft (15 m)	47 ft (14 m)
RR	42 ft (13 m)	47 ft (14 m)	49 ft (15 m)
	_____	_____	_____

1.   Name the methods that could be used under these circumstances to measure the test skid marks in order to obtain the distance to be used in calculating the coefficient of friction.

Answer

Project A-2 cont'd

2. Using one method, calculate the coefficient of friction based on the skid tests.

    a. Name the method used.

        Answer _____

        _____

    b. Show the formula and all calculations used, and briefly explain the purpose in making each calculation.

Answer

U.S.

f = _____

Answer

Metric

f = _____

Project A-2 cont'd

3. Using another method, calculate the coefficient of friction.

    a. Name the method used.

        Answer _____

        _____

    b. Show the formula and all calculations used, and briefly explain the purpose in making each calculation.

Answer

U.S.

f   =   _____

Answer

Metric

f   =   _____

Lesson 6
SPEED ESTIMATES
Project A-3

A drag sled (or a tire and wheel) weighs 62 lbs (28 kg) and requires a pull of 33 lbs (15 kg) to move it along a roadway surface.

Calculate the coefficient of friction. Show the formula and all calculations used.

Answer

U.S.

f = _____

Answer

Metric

f = _____

Lesson 6
SPEED ESTIMATES
Project A-4

A vehicle skids to a stop on a level roadway that has a coefficient of friction of .70. The skid distance is 56 ft (17 m).

1.   Calculate the vehicle's speed. Show the formula and all calculations used.

Answer

U.S.

S = _____ mph

Answer

Metric

S = _____ km/h

Project A-4 cont'd

2. This calculation was for the vehicle's speed at the beginning of the skid marks.

    True_____   False_____

3. The calculated speed is the:
    a. Maximum speed
    b. Fall speed
    c. Yaw speed
    d. Minimum speed
    e. Combined speed

Lesson 6
SPEED ESTIMATES
Project A-5

A vehicle skidded to a stop over a distance of 80 ft (24 m) on a downgrade of minus 5%. Test skids resulting in a coefficient of friction of .75 were conducted on a nearby level surface.

Calculate the vehicle's speed at the beginning of the skid. Show the formula and all calculations used.

Answer

U.S.

S = _____ mph

Answer

Metric

S = _____ km/h

Lesson 6
SPEED ESTIMATES
Project A-6

A vehicle traveled into a right-hand curve at an excessive rate of speed. It sideslipped, went into yaw, left the highway and overturned. A close examination of the tire marks revealed a definite yaw mark from the lead (left-front) tire. Measurements of this mark and the roadway are shown in the following diagram.

Project A-6 cont'd

1. Calculate the radius of the yaw mark. Show the formula and all calculations used.

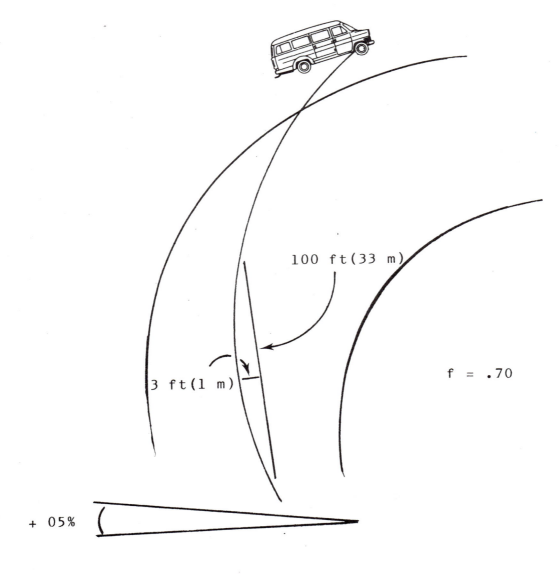

100 ft(33 m)

3 ft(1 m)

f = .70

+ 05%

Answer

U.S.

R = _____ ft

Answer

Metric

R = _____ m

413

2.   Calculate the vehicle's speed at the beginning of the yaw mark. Show the formula and all calculations used.

Answer

U.S.

S = _____ mph

Answer

Metric

S = _____ km/h

INTRODUCTION

Lesson 7

SUBJECT: Traffic Template

At-scene traffic accident investigators are required to prepare field sketches and scale diagrams of traffic accident scenes. The objects and features found at the scene are represented in these drawings by symbols.

This lesson will familiarize the student with the use of the IPTM Traffic Template to draw the symbols needed for accident field sketches, maps, reconstruction diagrams and scale diagrams.

Lesson Contents

This lesson will cover the following topics:

- a.   Purposes of the traffic template
- b.   Accuracy of the template
- c.   Template scales
- d.   Protractor
- e.   Curves, circles and arcs
- f.   Angles
- g.   Drawing of vehicles
- h.   Skid marks
- i.   Maps and symbols
- j.   Bodies and cycles
- k.   Slope measurements
- l.   Speed calculations

Lesson Objectives

Upon completion of this lesson, the student will be able to do the following to the satisfaction of the instructor:

1.   Given a hypothetical at-scene traffic accident situation:

    a.   Use the template symbols in preparing a field sketch and scale diagram.

    b.   Use the template to prepare a scale diagram of trafficways, curves, angles, circles and arcs from field sketch measurements.

    c.   Demonstrate an understanding of the capabilities and limitations of template use.

Lesson 7

IPTM TRAFFIC TEMPLATE

C7.001 This lesson consists basically of a reproduction of the Instruction Manual for the IPTM Traffic Template using the U.S. measurement system.

C7.002 The Instruction Manual is followed by six projects requiring the use of an IPTM Traffic Template. Persons who wish to complete the projects, but do not have this template, may purchase one from IPTM.

C7.003 Since procedures for using a metric template are essentially the same as for using a U.S. template, a separate section for metric has not been provided in this lesson. However, users of metric measure who wish to acquire, for their professional use, a metric version of the template illustrated here may purchase from IPTM an IPTM Metric Traffic Template with a metric Instruction Manual.

IPTM

TRAFFIC TEMPLATE

Instruction
Manual

R.W. RIVERS

Institute of Police
Technology and Management

University of North Florida
4567 St. Johns Bluff Road, South
Jacksonville, Florida 32224-2645
Telephone (904) 646-2722

Copyright 1985 (rev. 1994)

418

Contents

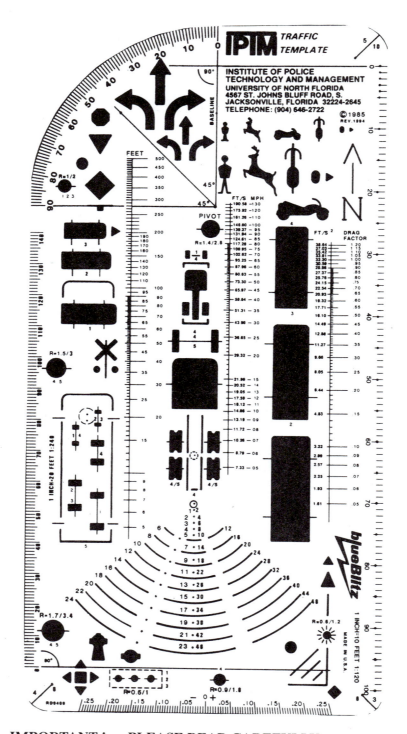

IMPORTANT ! PLEASE READ CAREFULLY

The IPTM blueBlitz Traffic Template is a precision instrument. Unlike less accurate instruments, it requires a **sharp pencil** or **fine tip ball point pen.** Used with proper accessories, the *blueBlitz* should enable you to produce diagrams to exact scale.

The IPTM Traffic Template

Introduction

The IPTM Traffic Template is an instrument designed especially to meet the requirements of traffic accident investigators in preparing field sketches, scale diagrams and maps of traffic accident scenes. The instrument is of value, however, not only to traffic accident investigators but also to engineers, architects, attorneys, insurance investigators, claims adjustors and others who wish to prepare sketches and diagrams of traffic-related scenes.

The IPTM Traffic Template is constructed with edges. corners, cutouts and scales so that standard-size motor vehicles, trailers, motorcycles and pedestrians as well as commonly used arcs, curves and circles can be drawn quickly and accurately. In addition, the template is provided with a nomograph (a set of scales for distance in feet, speed in miles per hour, velocity in feet per second, drag factor and deceleration rate in feet per second per second) making it easy to determine any of these variables from relevant known data. Finally, a clinometer, used in conjunction with a specially prepared clipboard, enables the investigator to measure the grade or superelevation of a roadway with reasonable accuracy.

Template cutouts are constructed to allow for the width of pencil and pen points. However, a thin, sharp point should always be used. A mechanical pencil must have a 0.5 mm point to fit into the small holes in the template. A pencil/pen point should always be held firmly against the straightedge, arc or edge of a cutout to ensure an evenly drawn line or outline.

If the template lacks a convenient feature, such as a cutout of a vehicle, a body or other item of evidence that must be drawn to scale, then straightedge measurements should be used for the drawing. Similarly, if an arc must be drawn to a scale not provided for on the template, a compass should be used.

Vehicles, pedestrians and straightedges, as well as the slots, corners and holes used for drawing arcs, curves and circles of given radii, are prepared in two scales:

    1 inch = 10 feet, also shown as 1:120
    1 inch = 20 feet, also shown as 1:240

Light, thin numbers designate a scale of 1 inch = 10 feet (1:120). Dark, bold numbers indicate a scale of 1 inch = 20 feet (1:240).

The larger scale (1:120) should be used in preference to the smaller scale (1:240) because larger scale drawings can be made more quickly and accurately and in greater detail than smaller scale drawings.

1

Protractor

The top left corner of the IPTM Traffic Template has a protractor graduated in degrees from 0 - 90. The protractor is divided into two equal sections by a 45 degree line originating at the vertex, or center hole, where the baseline and 90 degree line come together. A guide hole along the baseline and along the 45 degree line, and a slot along the 90 degree line, can be used in conjunction with the vertex to draw 45 and 90 degree angles.

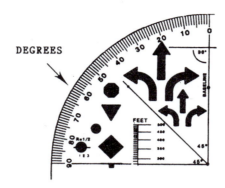

Figure 1. The protractor is particularly useful for drawing or measuring the departure angle at which a vehicle has left a collision point, the angle formed by a baseline (at some identified point) with an item of evidence, or the angle at which roadways intersect.

Any angle **BAC** *(see Fig. 2A)* can be measured in the following manner *(see Fig. 2B):*

a. Place the vertex of the protractor over the vertex of the angle **BAC** so that the baseline of the protractor is aligned with the base arm **AC** of the angle.

b. Read the number of degrees in the angle from the protractor scale where line **AB** crosses the scale.

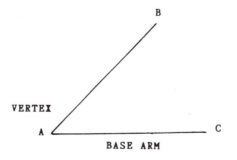

Figure 2A. Angle **BAC** with vertex at **A** and base arm **AC**

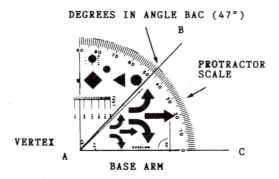

DEGREES IN ANGLE BAC (47°)

B

PROTRACTOR
SCALE

VERTEX

A

BASE ARM

C

Figure 2B. Vertex of the protractor placed over the vertex of angle **BAC** with the baseline of the protractor aligned with the base arm of the angle; degrees in the angle read where line **AB** crosses the protractor scale.

The protractor can be used to draw an angle of less than 90 degrees. To draw an angle of 60 degrees, for example, proceed as follows *(see Fig. 3):*

a. Draw a straight line to form the base arm of the intended angle.

b. Place a dot on the base arm to indicate the vertex of the intended angle.

c. Place the vertex of the protractor on the dot indicating the vertex of the intended angle and align the baseline of the protractor with the base arm of the intended angle.

d. Place a dot on the paper opposite the 60 degree mark on the protractor scale.

e. Draw a straight line from the vertex indicated on the base arm to the dot opposite the 60 degree mark on the protractor scale to complete the 60 degree angle.

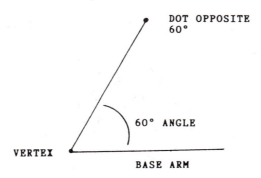

DOT OPPOSITE
60°

60° ANGLE

VERTEX

BASE ARM

Figure 3. An angle of less than 90 degrees

The protractor can also be used to draw an angle of more than 90 degrees. To draw an angle of 130 degrees, for example, proceed as follows *(see Fig's. 4A, B & C):*

a. Draw a straight line to form the base arm of the intended angle.

b. Place a dot on the base arm to denote the vertex of the intended angle.

c. Place the vertex of the protractor over the dot indicating the vertex of the intended angle and align the baseline of the protractor with the base arm of the intended angle *(see Fig. 4A).*

d. Place a dot on the paper opposite the 90 degree mark on the protractor scale *(see Fig. 4A).*

3

e.   Rotate the template around its vertex until the baseline of the protractor passes through the dot placed opposite the 90 degree mark *(see Fig. 4B)*.

f.   Place a dot on the paper opposite the 40 degree mark on the protractor scale *(see Fig. 4B)*.

g.   Remove the template.

h.   Draw a straight line from the vertex indicated on the base arm to the dot placed opposite the 40 degree mark on the protractor scale to complete the 130 degree angle (90 degrees + 40 degrees = 130 degrees).

i.   Erase all unnecessary construction lines and marks, leaving only the completed 130 degree angle *(see Fig. 4C)*.

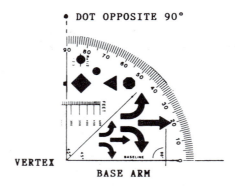

Figure 4A. Vertex of the protractor placed over the vertex indicated on the base arm; the baseline on the protractor aligned with the base arm; a dot placed on the paper opposite the 90 degree mark on the protractor scale.

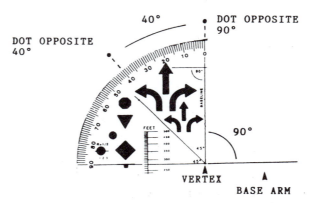

Figure 4B. Protractor rotated so that the baseline now passes through the dot at 90 degrees to the base arm; another dot placed on the paper opposite the 40 degree mark on the protractor scale.

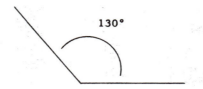

Figure 4C. Template removed; line drawn from the vertex on the base arm to the dot opposite the 40 degree mark; construction lines and marks erased, leaving completed 130 degree angle.

Arcs and Curves

The IPTM Traffic Template is designed so that arcs, curves and circles of various radii can be drawn to either the 1:120 or 1:240 scale.

Table 1

Radii		Location of curve/hole on template	Method of Use
1:120	**1:240**		
3 ft	6 ft	Lower right corner	To make arcs or curves of these radii, use the appropriate curved corner of the template.
4 ft	8 ft	Lower left corner	
5 ft	10 ft	Upper right corner	
1 ft to 24 ft	2 ft to 48 ft	Holes running from the center hole (below dual wheels) toward bottom and located among curved slots.	These radii require the use of a pair of holes. Place a pencil point in the center hole and press the point firmly against the paper. Place another pencil point in the hole representing the required radius. Rotate the template around the center hole (pivot hole) to draw the arc. (Fig. 5 shows how to draw an arc having a radius of 17 ft on a scale of 1:120 or 34 ft on a scale of 1:240.)
1 ft to 100 ft	2 ft to 200 ft	Holes located in the straight-edge, right side.	Use the zero hole of the right-side scale as the pivot hole and the holes at intervals of 5 from 5 to 100 as holes for the radii. If a radius is required that falls between two radii for which holes have been provided, use as the pivot hole the hole between 1 and 4 whose number, when subtracted from the higher of these two radii, will give the required radius. (On the 1:240 scale, this number must be doubled before being subtracted.)

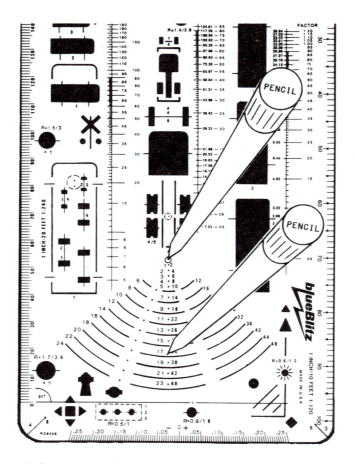

Figure 5. Two pencil points used to prepare arcs, curves and circles; one placed in the center hole and the other in the required radius hole located toward the bottom of the template among the curved slots.

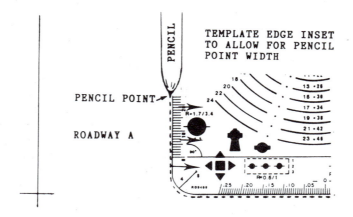

Figure 6. Two intersecting lines, such as those representing curb lines, can be joined by an arc having a specific radius. When a template corner is used to draw such an arc, the corner must be slightly inset to allow for pencil-point width so that when the arc is drawn, the pencil-point mark will be superimposed on the intersecting lines.

6

426

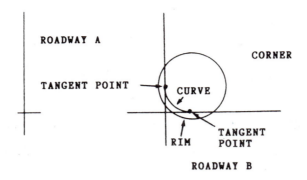

Figure 7. A procedure similar to that explained in Figure 6 should be followed when a hole is used to draw an arc. In such a case, position the rim of the hole outside the tangent points sufficiently to allow for pencil-point width when making the drawing.

Signs, Signals and Fire Hydrants

There are cutouts in the template for directional arrows, a railway crossing sign and top and face views of traffic signal lights, stop signs, warning signs, cautionary signs and fire hydrants. These items are of a larger scale than either of the template scales but may be drawn as illustrated in Figure 8 and explained in a legend incorporated into the sketch.

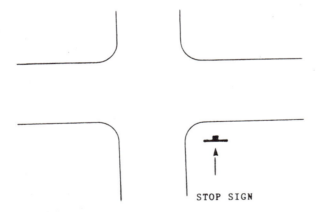

Figure 8. A stop sign explained in a legend

Holes and Their Uses

The template has holes of various sizes that are suitable for drawing the wheels of cars, trucks, trailers and buses to both scales. These holes can also be used to draw arcs, curves and circles. Each hole is labeled with R (radius) values in feet, for example, R = 1.4/2.8. The value to the left of the slash is for use with the 1:120 scale; the value to the right of the slash is for use with the 1:240 scale. Thus, 1.4 would indicate a radius of 1.4 feet on the 1:120 scale and 2.8 a radius of 2.8 feet on the 1:240 scale.

7

Table 2

Hole Radius	Location on Template and Use
PIVOT R=1.4/2.8	**Center, 31/2" from top.** Serves as pivot point in measuring grades on the scale at the bottom of the template. Can also be used to draw the wheels of trucks, trailers, buses, or vehicles 4 and 5 to a scale of 1 in = 10 ft.
R=1/2 1 2 3	**Upper left corner.** Can be used to draw the wheels of vehicles 1, 2 and 3 to a scale of 1 in = 10 ft.
R=1.5/3 4 5	**Left center.** Can be used to draw the wheels of truck tractors and trailers, buses, or vehicles 4 and 5 to a scale of 1 in = 10 ft.
R=1.7/3.4 4 5	**Lower left.** Can be used to draw the wheels of truck tractors and trailers, buses, or vehicles 4 and 5 to a scale of 1 in = 10 ft.
4 R=0.9/1.8	**Bottom center.** Can be used to draw the wheels of a truck tractor or vehicle 4 to a scale of 1 in = 20 ft.
R=0.5/1 1 2 3	**Bottom left.** Can be used to draw wheels of vehicles 1, 2 and 3 to a scale of 1 in = 20 ft.
R=0.6/1.2	**Bottom right.** Can be used to indicate a street lamp. The shaft immediately above or below can be used as the lamp post.

Vehicles and Wheels

The template has cutouts for small, medium and large cars and for motorcycles, truck tractors, commercial trailers, and buses — drawn to scales of 1:120 and 1:240. Wheels can be related to these vehicles (except motorcycles) by numbers. Dark, bold numbers designate vehicles and their wheels for use on the scale of 1:240. Other numbers designate vehicles and their wheels for use on the scale of 1:120. One vehicle body has two numbers, a bold 4 and a light 3, since that body can be used with either scale. Some wheels have more than one number because they can be used with more than one vehicle body size. Investigators will find the locations of the cutouts readily enough on their own once they begin to work with the template.

Table 3 illustrates some combinations of vehicle body cutouts and wheel cutouts for vehicle drawings. The left-hand column shows the vehicle body positioned vertically as it appears on the template; the center column shows the corresponding wheels; the right-hand column shows the completed drawing with a side-view contour sketched in.

8

Table 3

Vehicle Body	Corresponding Wheels	Completed Drawing

Speed, Drag Factor, Velocity, and Deceleration Rate Calculations

The IPTM Traffic Template can be used to determine the minimum speed of a vehicle at the beginning of a skid-to-a-stop. Two values, however, must first be known:

1. Total skid-to-a-stop distance.
2. Drag factor (f value), i.e., the friction, drag, traction or adhesion created by the tires against the roadway surface. (The terms drag factor and coefficient of friction are synonymous for the purposes of this manual.)

The drag factor can best be determined from a test skid. Another satisfactory method of determining the drag factor is by use of a drag sled or tire and wheel. For a very rough drag-factor estimate (usually not suitable for courtroom testimony), a drag-factor guide table may be consulted. The investigator should refer to a reliable textbook on traffic accident investigation for the procedures to be followed in determining the drag factor by these methods. Space in this instruction manual does not allow for adequate coverage of this crucial topic.*

* *The author of this instruction manual, R.W. Rivers, covers procedures for determining the drag factor in his* **Technical Traffic Accident Investigators' Handbook** *(1995) and* **Traffic Accident Investigators' Manual** *(1995) published by Charles C. Thomas, Publisher; Springfield, Illinois.*

The following example illustrates the use of the template in determining the **drag factor** and **deceleration rate** from a test skid.

Example

A test-skid vehicle traveling at 30 mph skids a distance of 50 ft to a stop. The drag factor can be calculated as follows:

Place a straightedge on the template so that the straightedge passes through the 50 ft mark on the **FEET** scale and the 30 mph mark on the **MPH** scale. Read the drag factor where the straightedge crosses the **DRAG FACTOR** scale — in this example at .60. As indicated on the corresponding **FT/S²** scale, this drag factor equals a deceleration rate of 19.32 ft/s². *(See Fig. 9.)*

9

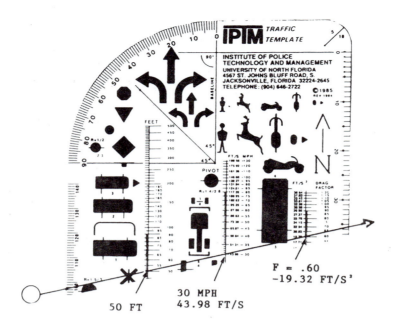

F = .60
-19.32 FT/S²

30 MPH
43.98 FT/S

50 FT

Figure 9. The IPTM Traffic Template has a nomograph with scales that represent five separate values: (1) FEET, (2) FT/S, (3) MPH, (4) FT/S² [deceleration rate] and (5) DRAG FACTOR. If among the variables of distance (FEET), speed (FT/S or MPH) and drag factor any two are known, by drawing a line through these two, the third variable can be read from the template.

Once the drag factor of the roadway and the skid distance of the accident vehicle are known, the minimum speed in mph and velocity in ft/s at the beginning of the skid can be read from the template.

Example

An accident vehicle skids 50 ft to a stop. The drag factor is determined to be .60.

Place a straightedge on the template so that the straightedge passes through the 50 ft mark on the **FEET** scale and the .60 mark on the **DRAG FACTOR** scale. Read the minimum speed where the straightedge crosses the **MPH** scale — in this example at 30 mph, which corresponds to a velocity of 43.98 ft/s. *(See Fig. 9.)*

Grade and Superelevation

A specially prepared clipboard can be used with the template as a clinometer to measure the grade or superelevation of a roadway or the slope of any other incline .

To prepare the clipboard, proceed as follows:

a. Drill midway between the short edges of the clipboard a 5/16 inch hole approximately 1/4 inch in from the long edge of the clipboard that will be used as the line-of-sight edge. (With the clipboard turned so that the clip is at the side, the line-of-sight edge will be the top edge.) Ensure that the distance from the template pivot hole to the bottom edge of the template does not exceed the distance from the drilled hole to the bottom edge of the clipboard *(see Fig. 10).*

10

b. Draw a line from the line-of-sight edge of the clipboard to the bottom edge (roadway edge) of the clipboard so that the line passes over the center of the drilled hole and forms a 90 degree angle with either of these edges.

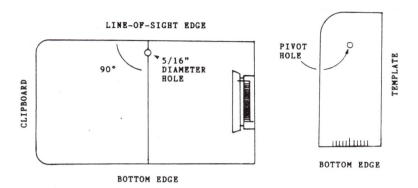

Figure 10. Location of the 5/16 inch diameter hole drilled in the clipboard. Distance from the pivot hole to the bottom edge of the template must not exceed the distance from the hole drilled in the clipboard to the bottom edge of the clipboard.

To measure the grade or superelevation of a roadway, proceed as follows *(see Fig. 11)*:

a. Insert a round pencil or pen through the hole in the clipboard so that the pencil or pen protrudes approximately one inch beyond the side of the clipboard on which the line has been drawn.

b. Slide the pivot hole of the template over the pencil or pen so that the template is suspended and can swing freely across the line drawn on the clipboard.

c. Place the roadway edge of the clipboard onto the roadway.

d. Let the template swing freely and come to rest.

e. Press the template against the clipboard.

f. Read the percent grade where the line drawn on the clipboard crosses the grade scale at the bottom of the template.

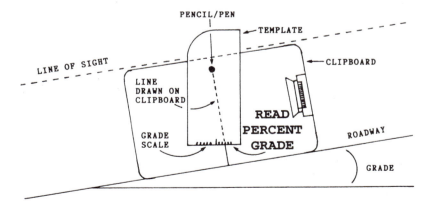

Figure 11. Template suspended from the round pencil/pen inserted through the hole in the clipboard and able to swing freely; roadway edge of the clipboard placed onto the roadway; grade scale at the bottom of the template giving the percent grade reading where the line drawn on the clipboard crosses the grade scale.

11

431

If the roadway is rough or uneven, proceed as follows:
a.   (i)   Place the roadway edge of the clipboard against a straight, even
          board (such as a 2 by 4) of 4 - 6 feet in length laid on its edge, or
     (ii)   With an object such as a vehicle or an assistant in the line of sight at
          a distance of some 30 feet along the grade, sight with the line-of-
          sight edge of the clipboard at a spot on the object or assistant known
          to be at the same height above the roadway as your eye level *(see
          Fig. 12).*
b. Let the template swing freely and come to rest.
c. Press the template against the clipboard and read the percent grade.

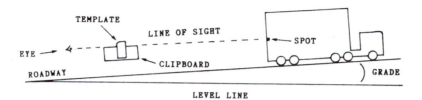

Figure 12. A spot on a vehicle in line of sight of the investigator and at
the same height above the roadway as his eye level; investigator sighting the spot; percent grade read from the template as in Figure 11.

*Source for Grade and Superelevation: R.W. Rivers, **Traffic Accident Field Measurements and Scale Diagrams Manual,** Charles C. Thomas, Publisher;
Springfield, Illinois, 1983, pp. 38 and 48.*

Appendix A

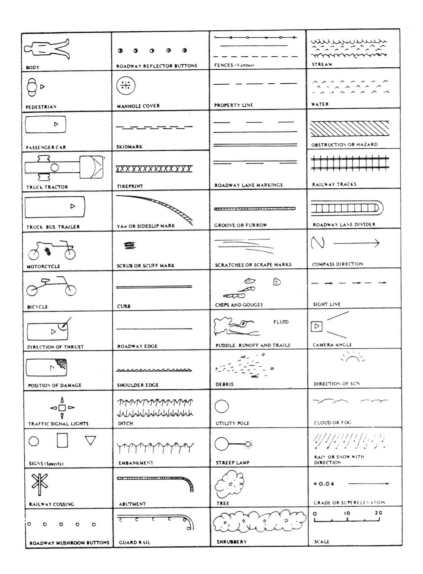

Symbols that are useful in preparing freehand drawings for field sketches. **Source:** R.W. Rivers, **Traffic Accident Investigators' Manual,** 1995, p. 127. Courtesy of Charles C. Thomas, Publisher; Springfield, Illinois. Most of these symbols can also be drawn with the IPTM Traffic Template. *(See also Appendix B.)*

Appendix B

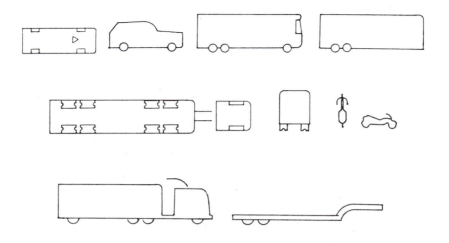

CARS, TRUCKS, VANS, BUSES, TRAILERS AND MOTORCYCLES

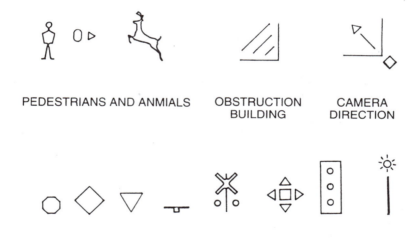

PEDESTRIANS AND ANMIALS   OBSTRUCTION BUILDING   CAMERA DIRECTION

SIGNS, SIGNALS AND LIGHTS

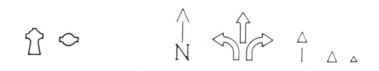

FIRE HYDRANTS   DIRECTIONAL ARROWS

Symbols drawn with the IPTM Traffic Template

Lesson 7
IPTM TRAFFIC TEMPLATE
Project A - 1

Use the **IPTM Traffic Template** to draw the following items in the spaces provided. The first one has been done for you.

1. Draw the compass direction **North**.

2. Draw the top view of a small car to a scale of 1 in = 10 ft.

3. Draw to a scale of 1 in = 10 ft a medium-size station wagon that has come to rest on its side.

4. Draw the prone body of a large person appropriate for a scale of 1 in = 10 ft.

5. Draw the body of a small person appropriate for a scale of 1 in = 10 ft.

6. Draw the prone body of a large person appropriate for a scale of 1 in = 20 ft.

7. Draw a standing pedestrian facing to **your** right (for 1:120 scale).

8. Draw a large motorcycle appropriate for a scale of 1:120.

   a. Top view

   b. Side view

9.   Draw to a scale of 1:120 a pair of vehicle skid marks 28 feet long.

10.   Draw an obstruction (building).

11.   Draw a bicycle appropriate for a scale of 1:240.

       a.   Top view

       b.   Side view

12.   Draw a circle using the template **pivot** hole.

13.   Draw to a scale of 1:120 a curve with a radius of 17 feet.

14. Draw an arrowhead that indicates **forward** direction of a vehicle.

15. Draw to a scale of 1:240 a curve with radius of 26 feet.

16. Draw dual wheels for a truck or trailer to a scale of 1:120.

17. Draw a medium-size car to a scale of 1 in = 10 ft.

18. Draw an angle of 30 degrees to the vertex of the base arm.

Vertex ●━━━━━━━━━━━━━

BASE ARM

19. Draw a curve with a radius of 5 feet on a 1:120 scale or a radius of 10 feet on a 1:240 scale.

20. Draw a circle with a radius of 1 foot on a 1:120 scale or a radius of 2 feet on a 1:240 scale.

21. Draw a large car to the 1:240 scale.

22. Draw the outline of a large trailer to a scale of 1 in = 10 ft.

23. Draw to a scale of 1 in = 10 ft the outline of a large trailer, the length of which includes the trailer extension provided on the template.

24. Draw a face view of a traffic control sign, e.g., stop sign.

25. Draw a circle with a radius of 1.5 feet on a 1:120 scale or a radius of 3 feet on a 1:240 scale.

26. Draw a curve with a radius of 4 feet on a 1:120 scale or a radius of 8 feet on a 1:240 scale.

27. Draw a truck-tractor to a 1:240 scale. Include the cab, front wheels, fifth wheel and rear dual wheels in the outline.

28. Draw a curve with a radius of 3 feet on a 1:120 scale or a radius of 6 feet on a 1:240 scale.

29.   Draw a large car to a scale of 1 in = 20 ft.

30.   Draw a truck-tractor to a 1:120 scale. Include the cab and front and rear wheels in the outline.

IPTM TRAFFIC TEMPLATE

Project A - 2

Connect curb lines *A* and *B* by drawing a curve with a radius of 40 feet on a scale of 1:240.

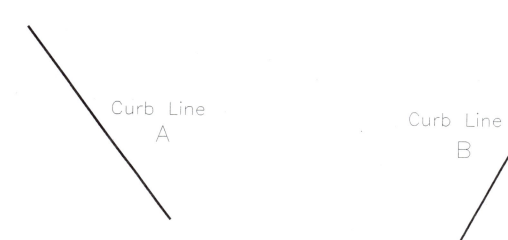

Curb Line
A

Curb Line
B

Lesson 7
IPTM TRAFFIC TEMPLATE
Project A - 3

Connect lines *A* and *B* by drawing an arc that has a radius of 60 feet on a scale of 1:120. Use the vertex shown at the bottom of this sheet.

A   B

● Vertex

Lesson 7
IPTM TRAFFIC TEMPLATE
Project A - 4

In the boxes provided, draw the indicated **freehand** symbols suitable for field sketches.

FENCE	WATER
SIGHT LINE	SHRUBBERY/TREE
SCRUB OR SCUFF MARK	TIRE PRINT
STREAM	YAW OR SIDESLIP MARK

Lesson 7
IPTM TRAFFIC TEMPLATE
Project A - 5

A driver was traveling along a highway. In an attempt to avoid striking a pedestrian who was crossing the roadway, he applied the brakes. All wheels locked up. The vehicle skidded 150 feet to a stop on the roadway, which had a drag factor of .75.

With the limited information available, use the **IPTM Traffic Template Instruction Manual** and the **Template** to determine the vehicle's minimum speed at the beginning of the skid marks.

ANSWER

_____ mph

Lesson 7

IPTM TRAFFIC TEMPLATE

Project A - 6

The drawing on the following page represents a field sketch of a traffic accident scene.

    a.   Draw a scale diagram from the sketch. Use a scale of 1 in = 10 ft.

    b.   At a convenient location on your diagram, identify your work by including your name and the date on which it was done. Draw a frame around this information.

Project A-6 (CONT'D)

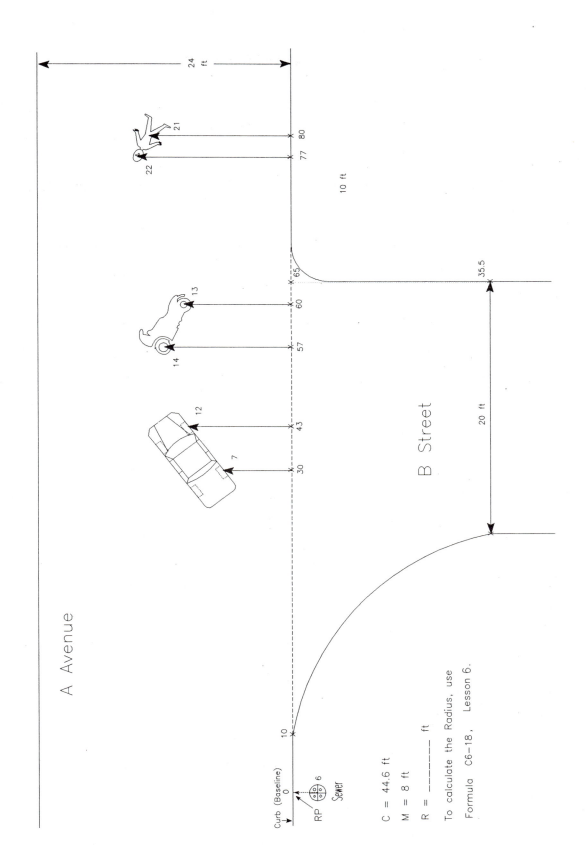

A Avenue

B Street

24 ft

10 ft

35.5

20 ft

21
22
80
77
65
13
60
14
57
12
43
7
30
10

Curb (Baseline)
0

RP 6

Sewer

C = 44.6 ft

M = 8 ft

R = _____ ft

To calculate the Radius, use
Formula C6–18, Lesson 6.

447

INTRODUCTION

Lesson 8

SUBJECT: Field Measurements and Scale Diagrams

At-scene traffic accident investigators take field measurements and prepare field sketches and scale diagrams.

This lesson will provide the student with the knowledge necessary to perform these tasks.

Lesson Contents

This lesson covers the following topics:

a.   Purpose of measurements

b.   What to measure

c.   Scale diagrams

d.   Evidence

e.   Trafficway definitions

f.   Investigator's inventory

g.   Sketch

h.   Field sketch

i.   Preparing a field sketch

j.   Contents of a field sketch

k.   Reference points

l.   Methods of measuring

m.   Methods of recording measurements

n.   Coordinate method

o.   Triangulation method

p.   Straight line method

q.   Preparing a scale diagram

r.   Grade and superelevation

s.   Curves

t.   Angles at intersections

u.   Offset streets

v.   Inaccessible areas

Lesson Objectives

Upon completion of this lesson, the student will be able to do the following to the satisfaction of the instructor:

1.   Given a hypothetical at-scene traffic-accident situation using an indoor or outdoor plan:

    a.   Identify all applicable items of evidence requiring measurements.

    b.   Use the coordinate method to measure the accident scene.

    c.   Use the triangulation method to measure the accident scene.

    d.   Use the straight-line method to measure distances between items of evidence at or near the accident scene.

    e.   Prepare a table and a legend of measurements taken.

    f.   Record measurements directly on the field sketch (other than by the use of a table).

    g.   Prepare a scale diagram of the accident scene.

Lesson 8

FIELD MEASUREMENTS AND SCALE DIAGRAMS

Purpose

C8.001   One of the most important aspects of the entire traffic accident investigation process is the taking and recording of accurate and adequate measurements during the at-scene investigation. Good measurements and records serve to:

- a.   Assist in determining *where, how* and *why* an accident occurred and *what* happened (the results).
- b.   Refresh an investigator's memory of his investigation.
- c.   Enable an investigator to testify, perhaps at a much later time, with accuracy and confidence regarding the location of objects and events at an accident scene.
- d.   Assist in reconstructing an accident.
- e.   Enable an investigator or someone else to prepare a scale diagram or map of an accident scene.
- f.   Assist in determining the truthfulness of statements given by drivers and witnesses.

What to Measure

C8.002 Upon arriving at an accident scene, the investigator must -- along with attending to many other urgent requirements -- decide what to measure and how best to complete the measurements. The positions of vehicles and other objects that are not likely to be moved immediately from their final positions can be measured after he attends to immediate concerns such as caring for the injured, ensuring safety at the scene, and taking measurements of short-lived evidence.

C8.003   There are basically five kinds of accident results that the investigator should look for. They are:

1.   Locations of vehicles
2.   Locations of dead or injured persons
3.   Tire marks, including skid marks, yaw marks, scrub marks, ruts and furrows
4.   Damages to the roadway surface and roadside objects
5.   Debris, such as patches of glass, liquids and dirt; personal belongings; broken and detached vehicle parts and load spillage

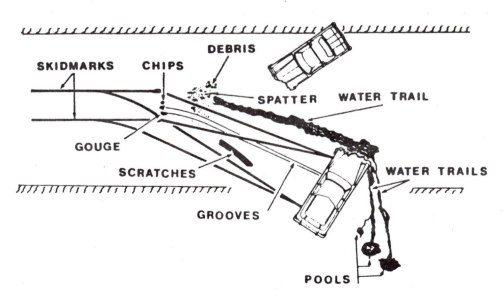

Figure C8-1 Collision evidence

C8.004   In a typical fatal or other serious type accident, measurements should be taken of but not limited to the following:

    a.   Final positions of vehicles

    b.   Locations of dead or injured persons

    c.   Tire marks

    d.   Marks on the roadway such as scratches, gouges, and chips

    e.   Objects on or near the roadway that are broken, damaged or marked

    f.   Permanent and temporary view obstructions

    g.   Drivers' and witnesses' sight distances

    h.   Debris that shows pre- and post-collision vehicle paths

    i.   Actual or believed point of impact

    j.   Camera positions when photographs are taken

    k.   Any evidence that points to or suggests where a vehicle was at any given time, particularly during the series of events

C8.005   The seriousness of an accident will usually dictate the extent to which measurements should be taken.

    a.   Take comprehensive measurements in all fatal and personal injury accidents.

    b.   Take sufficient measurements to satisfy both criminal and civil court proceedings.

    c.   Take measurements where a view obstruction is present, particularly if it is believed to be a contributing factor.

    d.   Take measurements in those cases where there seems to be no logical explanation for an accident to have occurred.

    e.   Take measurements where there are marks or other evidence that you cannot explain.

f.   Take measurements at all boundary-line accidents where jurisdiction might be disputed.

C8.006 The investigator must decide what measurements he should take to meet the objectives of the investigation. He should bear in mind that measurements that might suffice for preparing a scale diagram may not by themselves meet court requirements. For example, measurements that will fix the location of a yaw mark may meet the requirements for preparing a scale diagram but additional measurements may be required for speed calculation purposes. As a further example, while the measurements in Figure C8-2 are sufficient to fix the positions of the vehicles and body at the accident scene, for court evidence purposes, measurements of the skid marks as shown in Figure C8-3 would also be needed. It is important to remember that field measurements must satisfy the requirements for both scale diagrams and court evidence.

C8.007 Some measurements should be taken at all accident scenes. They can be made quickly and easily and it is better to have measurements that are not needed later than to need measurements that are not available and can no longer be obtained.

C8.008 In most cases, an investigator is able to adequately measure an accident scene. In serious or complicated cases, however, a surveyor or civil engineer may be used to take measurements at the scene and to prepare a scale diagram. When this is done, it is important that the investigator accompany the surveyor or engineer at the scene and explain to him precisely what measurements are required. Measurements so taken must be in addition to and not in place of measurements taken by an investigator as part of his investigation.

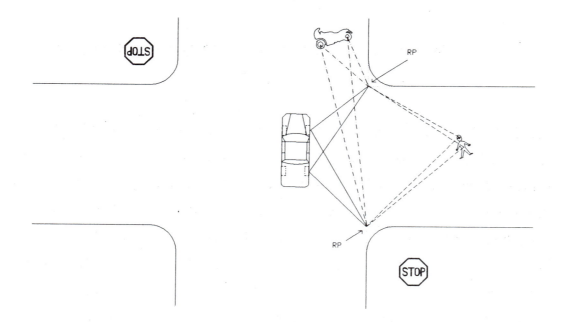

Figure C8-2   Measurements should be taken to fix the positions of the vehicles and body at the accident scene. In this example, the triangulation method is used.

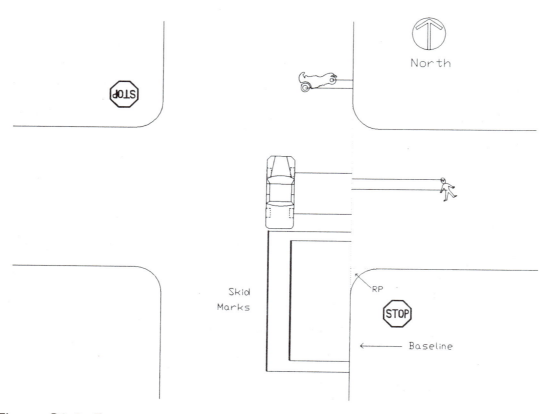

Figure C8-3   For court purposes, measurements should also be taken to show the relationships among the items of evidence. Here the coordinate method is used (note measurements are at 90 degrees to the baseline).

Scale Diagrams

C8.009 Provided that proper and sufficient measurements are taken at an accident scene, it is quite easy to reconstruct the scene on a *scale diagram*. The investigator must choose the *scale* he wishes to use. He may choose one inch (millimeter or centimeter) or any part thereof to represent one foot (meter) or any number of feet (meters).   For example: ¼ inch = 1 foot, 1 inch = 10 feet, 1 inch = 20 feet (1 millimeter = 1 meter, 1 centimeter = 1 meter, 1 centimeter = 10 meters, 1 centimeter = 20 meters) and so forth.

C8.010 A sharp-pointed pencil or pen must be used to prepare a scale diagram.   A broad-pointed instrument, if used, could make a mark representing several inches (centimeters) or even feet (meters) in width, depending upon the scale used. Other items should include (see Figure C8-4):

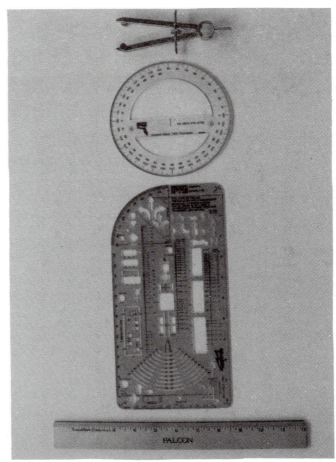

a.   Compass

b.   Protractor

c.   Traffic template
      (*U.S. or metric*)

d.   Ruler

e.   Flex curve
      (not shown)

Figure C8-4

A *traffic template* is very beneficial to the investigator in preparing a scale diagram. Many templates have *cutouts* for vehicles, traffic lights, traffic-control devices, and scale curves and also have a protractor. A good template can save many hours' labor in preparing scale diagrams.

Evidence

C8.011 Evidence at the scene may be divided into one of two categories, depending upon its probable length of existence where it is located (see Fig. C8-1).

1. *Short-lived evidence* is evidence that should be photographed and measured as soon as possible, and includes the following:

    a. Gasoline spills
    b. Water stains, puddles, and their trails or spatter
    c. Tire prints made in snow, mud, or other soft material
    d. Tire tread deposits such as burned-off tire particles, dust and dirt that adhere to pavement
    e. Skid mark shadows and impending skid marks
    f. Light debris or rubbish that has fallen from a vehicle and can be blown or swept away by passing vehicles
    g. Positions of persons who have been injured or killed and who will be moved or removed
    h. Positions of vehicles on the roadway, particularly those which are blocking or impeding the traffic flow (in jurisdictions requiring immediate removal of accident vehicles from the roadway)

i. Tire prints made on a dry pavement surface by a tire wet from nonpetroleum fluids

j. Blood and blood stains

k. Squeegee marks

l. Damage to fixed objects that are likely to be repaired with urgency, e.g., a traffic signal, power pole, telephone pole

m. Damage to removable property that is on the roadway and is obstructing traffic, e.g., large vehicle parts, vehicles, spilled cargo

2. *Long-term evidence* is evidence that will last for several days, a month, or longer, e.g., chips, gouges, grooves and other damage or marks to or on the roadway or roadside objects.

C8.012   Some evidence normally considered *long-term evidence* may become *short-lived evidence*, depending upon the degree of impression or damage caused and also upon the weather conditions and the amount and kind of traffic at the time.

C8.013   When circumstances are such that photographs and measurements cannot be taken before an item of evidence is moved or removed, its position may be marked with crayon, spray paint, spray chalk, or tape for later measurement and recording (see Fig. C8-5). Whenever possible, however, photographs should be taken before the position of the item to be moved or removed is marked. This precaution may facilitate acceptance of the photographs in court, as the photographs will then not represent anything other than what was initially found at the scene.

Figure C8-5 Tape can sometimes be used to mark the location of a tire on the roadway before the vehicle is moved. Use of crayon is more common.

Field Sketches

C8.014 A *field sketch* is a rough drawing made quickly and as soon as possible after the investigator arrives at the accident scene. A prime purpose of a field sketch is to record the positions and measurements of items that will soon be moved, lost, destroyed, altered, or mutilated. Accordingly, the first items to be drawn onto the field sketch in their approximate positions should be those that are classified as short-lived

458

evidence (see Fig. C8-6). Accurate after-accident measurements taken at the scene will be added to the field sketch later.

C8.015   Field sketches must also clearly show the distances and relationships between items at an accident scene. These items include bodies, debris, marks on the roadway, objects on or beside the roadway, roadway markings, ditches, obstructions and any other type of physical evidence that has or might have bearing on the accident.

C8.016   An important requirement of a field sketch is to provide the investigator with adequate data to complete an accurate scale diagram. To meet this requirement, the sketch must include the dimensions of items of evidence as well as the distance measurements that fix the locations of the items of evidence and relevant scene features. This information may be placed in a *legend* instead of directly in the sketch. (A legend is a boxed area on the drawing which includes symbols representing certain features of the drawing.)

C8.017   A field sketch in its completed state should contain all features, roadway configurations, and measurements of the accident scene as witnessed by the at-scene investigator.

C8.018. The field sketch should be handled as evidence similarly to notes made at the scene and retained in the investigator's case file. The sketch, like the notes, is an *original* document and subject to a discovery motion filed in court cases.

Preparing a Field Sketch

C8.019 When preparing a field sketch (see Fig. C8-6):

a. Include only that which is seen at the time the sketch is made.

b. Do not include objects and features from other situations.

c. Indicate an area or approximate point of impact based on scene evidence and/or the statements of witnesses. In the absence of scene evidence and/or witnesses, do not indicate such an area or point.

d. Draw objects so that they are relative in size and distance. It is not necessary, however, to prepare the sketch to scale.

e. Decide on the method of taking measurements, i.e., triangulation, coordinate, or a combination of both, and at the same time decide on the reference point or points that will be used for the measurements. (Refer to sample Measurements Record forms at the end of this lesson.)

f. Record measurements as they are made. The person who records measurements to be placed on a field sketch should be the person who reads the measurements from the measuring device.

g.   Take accurate and sufficient measurements to satisfy the investigation.

h.   Use *symbols* such as those found in Figure C8-7.

i.   Do not erase errors. Neatly cross out an error and write in the correction. Initial the correction (e.g., street names swapped or north arrow redirected) to forestall any question being raised in court as to the propriety of the change.

j.   Complete a field sketch as neatly as possible. Once it is completed, however, do not remake it for the sake of neatness as this could affect its validity or admissibility in court.

k.   Do not include anyone's opinions or witnesses' statements.

l.   Extend the sketch onto an additional sheet of paper when a single sheet is not large enough to accommodate the sketch.

m.   Include the north arrow.

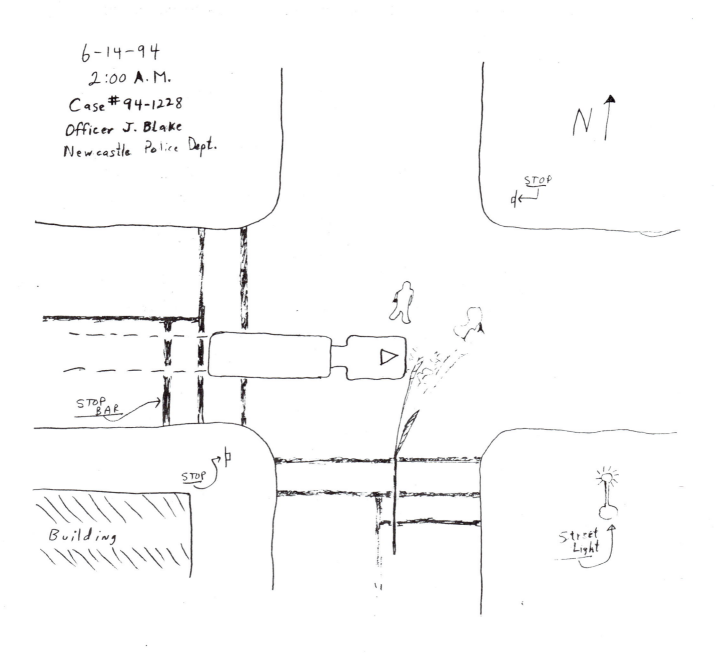

Figure C8-6 A field sketch showing the relative positions of tire scuff marks, a body, a blood spot and vehicles -- short-lived evidence that may soon be moved, lost or destroyed. Measurements fixing the positions of these items and of scene features and giving their dimensions should be noted in a legend or placed on the sketch itself.

SYMBOLS

BODY	ROADWAY REFLECTOR BUTTONS	FENCES (Various)	STREAM
PEDESTRIAN	MANHOLE COVER	PROPERTY LINE	WATER
PASSENGER CAR	SKIDMARK		OBSTRUCTION OR HAZARD
TRUCK TRACTOR	TIREPRINT	ROADWAY LANE MARKINGS	RAILWAY TRACKS
TRUCK BUS TRAILER	YAW OR SIDESLIP MARK	GROOVE OR FURROW	ROADWAY LANE DIVIDER
MOTORCYCLE	SCRUB OR SCUFF MARK	SCRATCHES OR SCRAPE MARKS	COMPASS DIRECTION
BICYCLE	CURB	CHIPS AND GOUGES	SIGHT LINE
DIRECTION OF THRUST	ROADWAY EDGE	PUDDLE, RUNOFF AND TRAILS	CAMERA ANGLE
POSITION OF DAMAGE	SHOULDER EDGE	DEBRIS	DIRECTION OF SUN
TRAFFIC SIGNAL LIGHTS	DITCH	UTILITY POLE	CLOUD OR FOG
SIGNS (Specify)	EMBANKMENT	STREEP LAMP	RAIN OR SNOW WITH DIRECTION
RAILWAY COSSING	ABUTMENT	TREE	GRADE OR SUPERELEVATION
ROADWAY MUSHROOM BUTTONS	GUARD RAIL	SHRUBBERY	SCALE

Figure C8-7   Symbols useful in preparing field sketches, diagrams and maps.   Source: R. W. Rivers, *Traffic Accident Investigators' Manual*. Reproduced with permission of Charles C. Thomas, Publisher.

463

Contents of a Field Sketch

C8.020 A field sketch should show the following (see Fig. C8-6):

a.   An *arrow* pointing to the direction of *north*. If precise compass directions are not known, use approximate directions.

b.   An outline of roadways and roadway markings.

c.   Reference point or points.

d.   Precise points on items to which measurements are made.

e.   Baseline (reference line) from which measurements are made.

f.   Distance and direction to the nearest well-known landmark, when the accident is not at an intersection.

g.   Highways, including right-of-ways, ditches, shoulders, roadways, driveways, sidewalks, crosswalks, center lines, lane lines, banks, railroad tracks, railings and bridges -- for later use in making a scale diagram.

h.   Names of roadways, lanes, paths, and other trafficways.

i.   Highway measurements.

j.   Special measurements of curves and angles of intersections.

k. Vehicles, bodies and other evidence showing relative sizes, configurations and locations or positions.

l. Traffic control devices, e.g., signal lights and signs.

m. Roadway defects and damage, such as potholes and construction work.

n. Drain outlets, culverts, headwalls, etc.

o. Fences, hedges, trees, poles, billboards, buildings, and all possible view obstructions. These types of things should be crosshatched. See the crosshatched building and tree in Figure C8-6.

p. An arrow indicating the vehicle heading.

q. Parked vehicles, with an arrow showing their heading parked.

r. Debris, e.g., dirt, glass, metal parts or fragments, parts of vehicles, load spillage. Particular attention should be given to debris and other evidence such as skid marks, gouges, and scrape marks, from which an assumption might be drawn regarding the point or area of impact.

s. Weather, road and light conditions. (Alternatively, this information may be placed in field notes.)

t. Date and approximate time the accident occurred, and date and time the measurements were taken and the field sketch was prepared.

u. Name of assistant in taking measurements.

v. Printed name and signature of the person who made the field sketch. Some jurisdictions may require that an assistant also sign or initial the sketch.

Reference Points

C8.021 A *reference point* (RP) is a point *from* which measurements are made to establish or fix points on items of evidence (see Fig. C8-8). Reference points may be *tangible* (permanent) or *intangible* (either temporary or constructed).

Note: The practice in this text, insofar as the coordinate method is concerned (but not triangulation), is to label as RP only the original or zero reference point (from which measurements to other points, including other reference points, are made.)

1. *Tangible reference points* include such permanent items as posts, buildings, bridges, signs, trees, fire hydrants, roadway damages and other permanent objects or conditions.

2. *Intangible reference points* include such temporary points as crayon or spray paint marks placed on the roadway, constructed or temporarily marked curb extension lines, or other temporary

identification marked, placed, or indicated on a surface. An intangible reference point should always be related to or in some way identified with a tangible reference point.

C8.022 A *spot* on an item of evidence *to* which a measurement is taken *from* either a tangible or intangible reference point is known as a *point* (P). The difference between a *reference point* (RP) and a *point* (P) must be well established in the mind of the student or investigator (see Fig.'s C8-8 and C8-9).

C8.023 Two or more tangible reference points, or one tangible reference point and one or more intangible reference points, may be used for the base of triangles when the investigator uses the triangulation method of measuring. When there is a tangible reference point nearby, such as a fire hydrant, but it is not in a suitable location to be used as the base corner for a triangle, an intangible reference point may be fixed by connecting it to the tangible reference point through measurement as shown in Figure C8-8. This established reference point replaces the tangible reference point as the zero reference point and is labeled RP.

C8.024 One of the very first steps in measuring an accident scene is to decide on the *baseline* (reference line) that will be used (see C8.037). Preferably, the baseline should be straight, although this is not absolutely essential. For example, a roadway edge around a slight curve can be used as a baseline. Preferred baselines include such items as a curb, guard rail, fence, roadway edge, center line or marked center line.

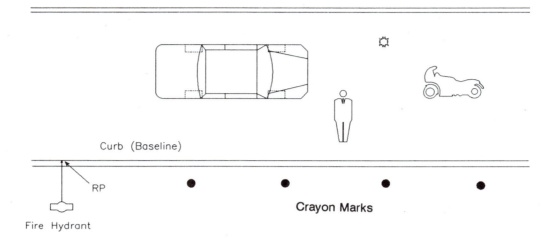

Figure C8-8 A curb has been selected as a baseline. The fire hydrant is a tangible reference point (RP). The crayon marks are intangible reference points tied to the fire hydrant by measurements. From these points measurements can be made to the points marked on the items of evidence.

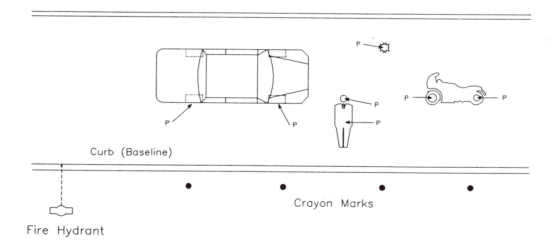

Figure C8-9 Points have been selected on items of evidence to which measurements can be made from a tangible reference point (RP) or from intangible reference points tied to a tangible reference point.

468

C8.025 Once a baseline is decided upon, the investigator must decide on how many points he will establish along the baseline or connect in some way to the baseline in order to fix the positions of the various items of evidence to which measurements must be taken. These points must include at least one tangible point (see Fig. C8-8).

C8.026 After the baseline and the reference point have been decided upon, the investigator should then decide where to establish *points* on the items of evidence in order to fix the positions of the evidence in relation to the points on the baseline (see Fig. C8-9).

1. *One* point is usually sufficient on small items (see Fig. C8-10).

    a. A small part of a body.

    b. Broken and separated vehicle parts, e.g., wheels, tires, and fenders.

    c. Short gouges, grooves, chips, and other roadway damages which are less than 2 feet (0.6 meters) in length or width, unless the mark is circular, showing vehicle rotation, or the mark has peculiarities or indicates evidence so as to warrant more than one point being established.

    d. Small contact damage areas on guard rails, trees, posts, etc.

    e. Small areas of debris that are of less than 2 feet (0.6 meters) in width, except in the case of a *fan-out* pattern resulting from impact and indicating a vehicle's direction of travel, when more than one point might be required.

f.   Small puddles and spatter areas having a width of less than 2 feet (0.6 meters).

g.   Posts. Generally, only one point is required on a post and that point should be near the base.

2.   Use at least *two* points on larger items (see Fig. C8-11).

a.   Vehicles. Most often, the tires of a vehicle suffice as points. On each tire the point should be placed where a line drawn from the center of the wheel perpendicular to the road surface would intersect the road surface.

b.   Tire marks. Skid and other tire marks should be measured for length and for purposes of fixing their locations. On a straight mark, a point is required at least on each end. A curved mark requires a series of points along the mark to which to take measurements, these points being at intervals of 5 feet (1.5 meters), 10 feet (3 meters), 15 feet (4.5 meters), 20 feet (6 meters) and so on, depending upon the sharpness of the curve and the reference point locations.

c.   Debris. A patch of debris that is in excess of 3 feet (1 meter) in width usually requires at least four points around its boundary in order to fix its location. If there is a concentration of material within the patch, this concentration can be delineated by using a number of points around its boundary as well (see Fig. C8-11).

d.   Sections of curbs, guard rails, roadway edges, roadway damages, lane markings and other items of evidence that are in excess of 2 feet (0.6 meters) in length require at least two points.

e.   Bodies. Usually two points can locate a body properly. A point at the forehead and one at the navel/belt-buckle area will locate the body and orient it properly when you make a scale diagram.

A point which is marked on an item of evidence and to which measurements are made is called an *evidence point*.

C8.027 When deciding upon the number of points to use on an item of evidence, always remember that by using only one point, the item can revolve around that point when an attempt is made to reposition it on the roadway or place it on a scale diagram.

C8.028 The *reference point* and each *evidence point* must be identified and described either on the face of the sketch or in a legend included in or attached to the sketch.

Measurements

C8.029 Measurements should be taken and recorded as soon as possible after the investigator's arrival at the accident scene. Any delay may result in measurements being made of objects that have been moved from their original positions at the scene.

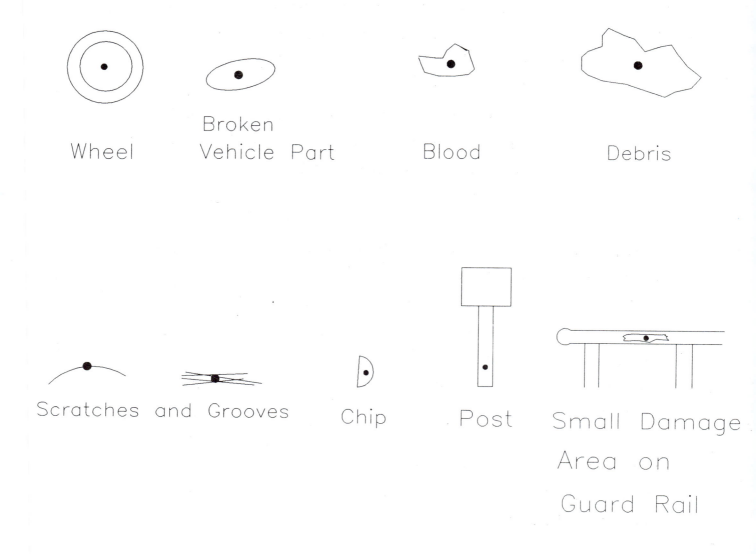

Wheel

Broken
Vehicle Part

Blood

Debris

Scratches and Grooves

Chip

Post

Small Damage
Area on
Guard Rail

Figure C8-10 One point placed as shown on these small items of evidence
suffices to fix their positions in relation to the reference point (see C8.026-1).

472

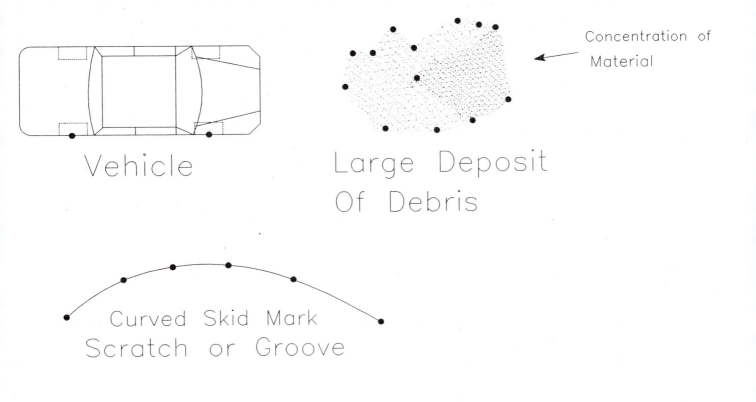

Vehicle

Large Deposit
Of Debris

Concentration of
Material

Curved Skid Mark
Scratch or Groove

Guard Rail

Figure C8-11 Most larger items of evidence require more than one point
to fix their positions in relation to the reference point (see C8.026-2).

C8.030   There are various ways to take accident scene measurements. Very short distances may be measured with a pocket measuring tape, ruler or yard (meter) stick. Long distances may require a 300-foot (100-meter) measuring tape. (Longer distances may be measured adequately by using a vehicle odometer.) Procedures for taking measurements:

1.   For reasons of safety, use the inside edge of a curve or side of the roadway as a baseline whenever possible.

2.   Take measurements to the nearest inch (centimeter).

3.   For other than short distances, get an assistant.

4.   The person who records the measurements should hold the measurement end of the tape and should, in all cases, read the measurements from the device being used. Switching positions with the assistant so that both persons always read the measurements is recommended for court purposes.

Methods of Measuring

C8.031 The following methods can be used to measure distances:

1.   Measuring tape

        a.   Use a pocket measuring tape to measure distances of less than 12 feet (3 meters).

        b.   Always keep the tape taut when measurements are being read.

c. When measuring distances between two points greater than the tape measure length, make a crayon mark on the pavement or sidewalk at the end of each measurement and mark the number of feet (meters). Allow the assistant to come to this point and observe him put the *zero* end of the tape at the markings. Then complete the distance to be measured, using the same procedure.

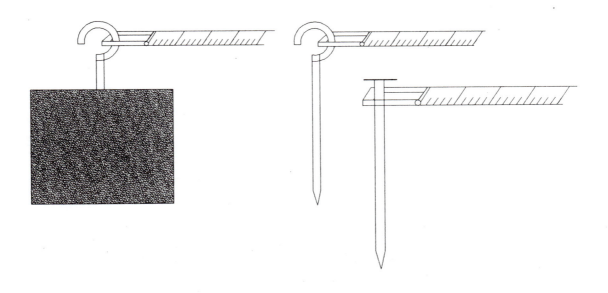

Figure C8-12 A lead weight, steel pin or spike, or a case-hardened nail can be used to secure the zero end of a measuring tape when an assistant is not available.

2.   Rolling wheel

A surveyor-type rolling wheel (12 inches or larger diameter) is a particularly useful device for measuring long distances. Caution should be taken, however, when measurements are made on rough or slippery surfaces. Under these conditions, the wheel may skip, bounce, or slide and the recorded distance may be shorter than the actual distance.

3.   Heel-to-toe

The heel-to-toe method can be used for short distances. When using this method, determine the length of shoes worn and multiply this length by the number of heel-to-toe steps required over the distance measured. Use only as a last resort.

4.   Pacing

a.   The pacing method should not be used unless the distance to be measured is in excess of 20 ft (6 m). When using this method, first determine what the person's average natural pace length is and then multiply that length by the number of paces required over the distance measured.

b.   The pacing method, as well as the heel-to-toe method, should be used only as a last resort because either one denotes a lack of professionalism and the results can be strongly objected to in court.

5.   Odometer

Greater distances, those, say, in excess of ¼ mile (0.4 kilometers), may be suitably measured using a vehicle odometer. The odometer readout may later be converted to feet (meters) if necessary.

6. Electronic measuring devices using laser and infrared technology allow for precise measurements of distances and increased officer safety during measurement of an accident scene.

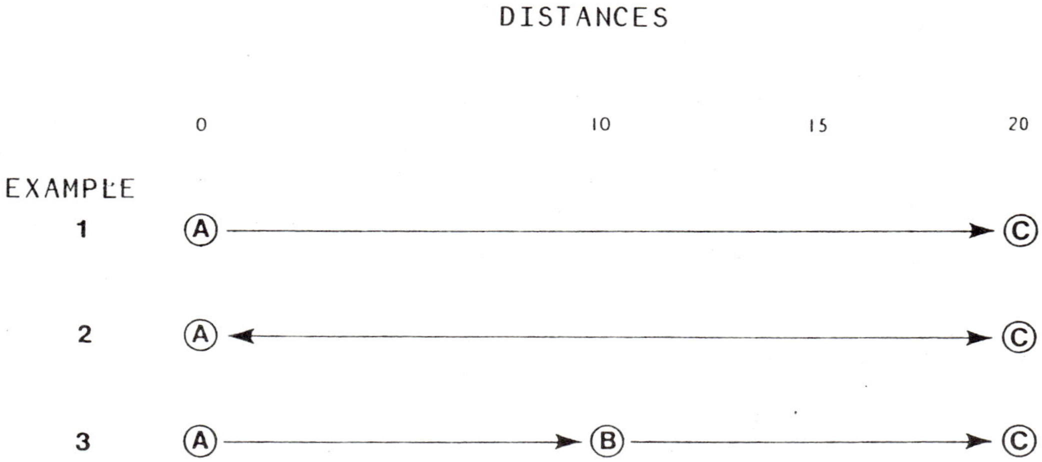

DISTANCES

Figure C8-13 Lines and directional arrows may be used to indicate the distance from a zero point to any point being measured to, or the distance between two points. In Example 1 the measurement is from zero point *A* to point *C*, a distance of 20. Note the arrow on the right end of the line at point *C*. In Example 2 the measurement is between points *A* and *C*, a distance of 20. However, there is an arrow on either end of the line, indicating that the measurement could have been taken from either point *A* or point *C*. In Example 3 the measurement is first from zero point *A* to point *B*, a distance of 10, and then continues from mid-point *B* on to point *C*, a total distance of 20 from zero point *A*.

Conventions for Recording Measurements

C8.032 When recording measurements, do not use the apostrophe (') and quotation marks (") to indicate feet and inches because these symbols can be mistaken for the numbers 1 and 11.

C8.033 Record feet and inches as illustrated in the following examples:

    a.   Record thirteen feet and three inches as $13^{\underline{3}}$

    b.   Record eleven feet as $11^{\underline{0}}$

    c.   Record ten inches as $0^{\underline{10}}$

When using a measuring device marked in feet and tenths of a foot, place a decimal point in front of the digit indicating tenths of a foot.

    a.   Record seven feet as 7.0

    b.   Record seven feet and five tenths as 7.5

    c.   Record five tenths of one foot as 0.5

C8.034 When using the metric system, indicate whether measurements are in centimeters (cm), meters (m), or kilometers (km).

    a.   Record 7.55 centimeters as 7.55 cm

    b.   Record 7.55 meters as 7.55 m

    c.   Record 7.55 kilometers as 7.55 km

C8.035 Most measurements using the metric system are in meters or parts of a meter. Therefore, it is acceptable to show all measurements in meters or parts of a meter without their being followed by the meter designation *m*, provided that any measurement in any other unit, such as a centimeter, taken at the scene or otherwise recorded in the investigation, is properly designated.

Measurement Recording Methods

C8.036 Data should always be placed on a field sketch or a scale diagram in a manner that is easily understood and useful to the investigator. In the case of a minor motor vehicle accident requiring only a few measurements, these can quite easily be recorded on the face of the sketch as shown in Figure C8-14. However, when there are a great number of measurements, they should be recorded in a table on a separate sheet of paper that is then attached to the sketch. Also, when there are several reference points and items of evidence that need to be described, it is often easier to identify them with a number and/or letter appearing on both the sketch and in the table (see Fig. C8-15 and Fig. C8-16) and then give their descriptions in a legend accompanying the table (see Fig. C8-17).

Coordinate Measuring Method and the Baseline

C8.037 *Coordinates* are distances measured at right angles from the baseline to a point on an item of evidence. When the edge of a roadway is straight or it has only a very slight curve, the edge may be used as the baseline. See Figures C8-19, C8-20 and C8-21. For the purposes of location and future reference, the baseline must be related by measurement to a reference point. The RP should be a point on the baseline or roadway either at or related to a permanent, recognizable landmark or object. The RP is the *zero point* from which to measure the distance to other points along the baseline. If a permanent object does not lie directly on the baseline, an intangible point that is close to and easily related by measurement to such an object may be labeled RP and used as the zero point (see Fig. C8-18). Sometimes curb lines or road edges can be extended to intersect at such an intangible point (see Fig. C8-22).

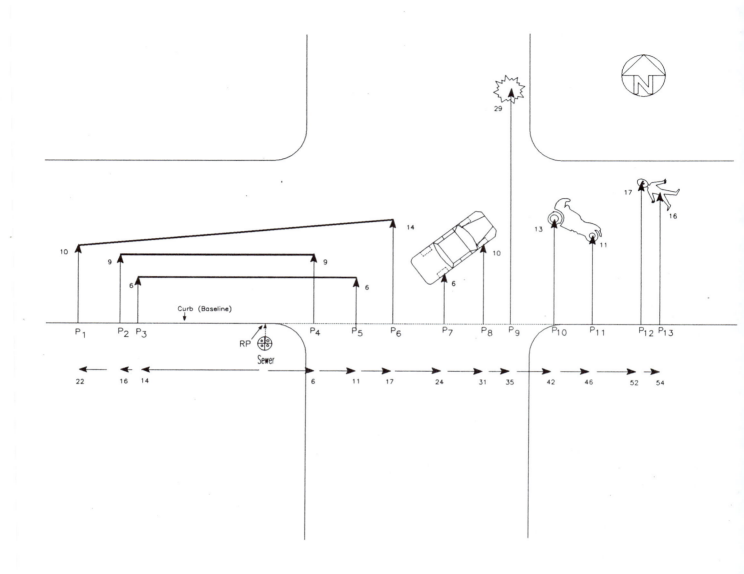

Figure C8-14 Measurements may be recorded directly on a field sketch or scale diagram. Whenever possible, the measurements should be recorded as closely as possible to the points being measured to. In this sketch, for example, a measurement is taken *from* P_8 to the right front wheel of the car. The measurement is therefore recorded near the wheel.

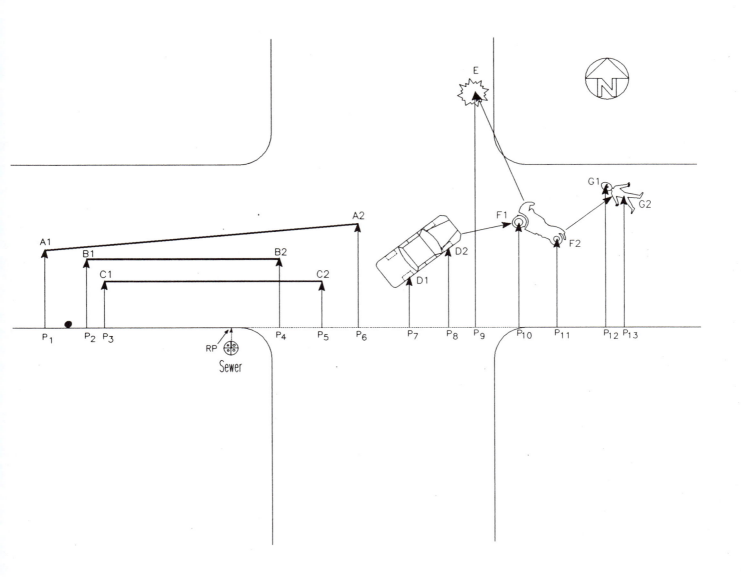

Figure C8-15 Letters and numbers may be used to identify items on a sketch or a scale diagram, with the measurements recorded in a table containing the same letters and numbers (see Fig. C8-16).

MEASUREMENT TABLE

FROM	DIST.E-W	TO/FROM	DIST.N-S	TO	COMMENTS
RP	W22	P_1	N10	A1	Begin LF skidmark (car)
RP	W16	P_2	N9	B1	Begin LR skidmark (car)
RP	W14	P_3	N6	C1	Begin RR skidmar (car)
RP	E6	P_4	N9	B2	End LR skidmark (car)
RP	E11	P_5	N6	C2	End RR skidmark (car)
RP	E17	P_6	N14	A2	End LF skidmark (car)
RP	E24	P_7	N6	D1	RR wheel, car at final rest
RP	E31	P_8	N10	D2	RF wheel, car at final rest
RP	E35	P_9	N29	E	Blood spot
RP	E42	P_{10}	N13	F1	Front wheel, MC at final rest
RP	E46	P_{11}	N11	F2	Rear wheel, MC at final rest
RP	E52	P_{12}	N17	G1	Head of MC rider body at final rest
RP	E54	P_{13}	N16	G2	Torso of MC rider body at final rest
A1	NE48	A2			
B1	E22	B2			
C1	E25	C2			
Car	E9	MC			
MC	NW16	Blood Spot			
MC	E8	Body			

Directly measured shortest distances

Figure C8-16 A table can be developed to record measurements using letters and numbers that appear on a sketch or diagram (see Fig. C8-15). Additional explanatory detail in respect to items of evidence shown in the sketch can be given in a *legend* accompanying the table (see Fig. C8-17).

LEGEND

RP	=	Point on baseline directly opposite sewer cover
Baseline	=	South curb and curb extension
A1 – A2	=	Length of skidmark LF (car)
B1 – B2	=	Length of skidmark LR (car)
C1 – C2	=	Length of skidmark RR (car)
Car – MC	=	Shortest distance from car to motorcycle
MC – Blood Spot	=	Shortest distance from motorcycle to blood spot
MC – Body	=	Shortest distance from motorcycle to body

Figure C8-17 A *legend* can be developed for a measurement table (see Fig. C8-16) in order that the items of evidence shown in the table can be more extensively described.

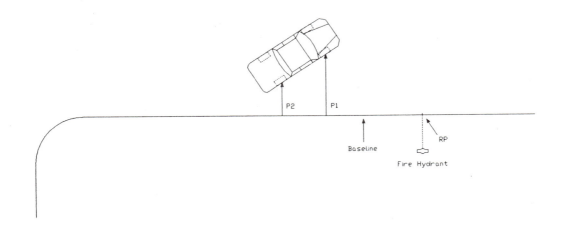

Figure C8-18 A curb used as a baseline. The reference point (RP) is located on the baseline directly opposite a permanent object, a fire hydrant. The RP is the *zero point* from which all measurements to other points on the baseline are made.

483

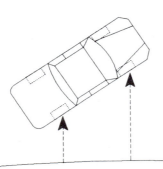

Edge of Roadway

Figure C8-19 The edge of a roadway with a *very slight* curve may be used as a baseline from which to measure coordinates, and the coordinates can be measured at *right angles* directly from the roadway edge. If the curve is other than slight, however, an alternate baseline must be established. See Figure C8-20.

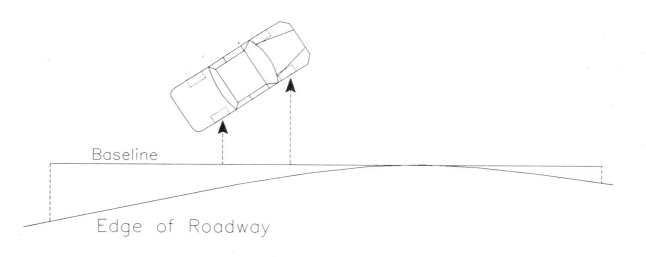

Baseline

Edge of Roadway

Figure C8-20 Establishing a baseline on a curve. Note that all coordinate measurements are taken at right angles from the *baseline* -- not from the roadway edge.

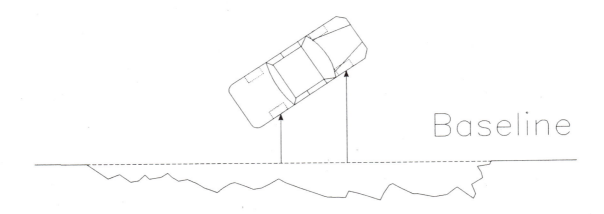

Figure C8-21 When the edge of a roadway is irregular or uneven, use an imaginary line -- or mark a line -- to serve as an *average edge*. This average edge can then be used as a baseline.

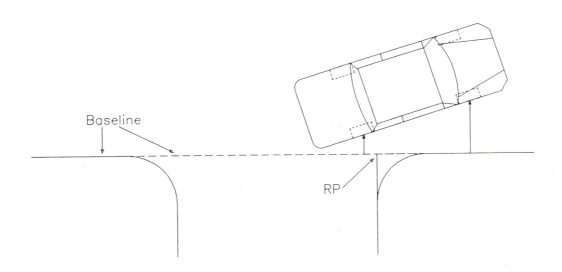

Figure C8-22 *Imaginary* or *marked* curb line extensions can also be used as a baseline. At right, intersecting curb line extensions establish an RP.

Triangulation Measuring Method

C8.038 *Triangulation* is a method of locating a *point* or a *spot* on an item of evidence or within an area by measurements taken from two or more reference points (tangible or intangible). The locations and types of reference points used must be identified for future use.

C8.039 There are three basic steps in measuring by triangulation:

1. Locate one or two tangible (permanent) reference points or one tangible and one intangible reference point on or near the roadway edge, constructed baseline, or feature that is being used as a baseline. (In triangulation all reference points are labeled RP.)
2. Measure from each reference point to one point on the object or item of evidence being measured to.
3. Measure in a direct line between the reference points to form a triangle.

See Figures C8-23 to C8-25 inclusive.

C8.040 When using the triangulation method, one should observe certain rules.

   a. Always attempt to select reference points that are a sufficient distance apart to give a reasonably wide triangle base. Do not use long, thin triangles.
   b. Fix small objects by measuring to their centers. This procedure is usually satisfactory for small patches of blood or other liquids and small areas of evidence that are not more than 2 feet (0.6 meters) in width.

c. Except for small items of evidence, fix all items with a least two triangles.

d. Use one triangle for each point on an item of evidence to which a measurement is made.

e. Whenever possible, use the same baseline from which to form triangles when fixing points on the same side of an item of evidence.

f. Yaw or other curved tire marks should be fixed by triangles at intervals of 10 to 20 feet (3 to 6 meters), depending on the length and radius of the curve.

g. Irregular angles and marks should be fixed with sufficient numbers of triangles to enable the investigator or some other person to reposition the evidence at its precise location both at the scene and on a scale diagram.

C8.041 Triangulation may be a better method of measuring than the coordinate method in areas where it is difficult to locate or establish a good, reasonably straight baseline. Examples of such areas are where a roadway

a. does not have an adequate curb line;

b. has an uneven edge as sometimes found on dirt, snow, or gravel surfaces;

c. has a sharp curve;

d. forms a part of and is within a complicated intersection; or

e. has places to which it is difficult to make measurements from the roadway edge.

C8.042 Sometimes it is advisable to use both triangulation and coordinates to fix items of evidence at the scene of an accident. For example, while coordinates may fix the location of a skid mark readily enough, it may be easier to fix the location of a small item of evidence such as a motorcycle helmet by triangulation. See Figures C8-23 and C8-26.

C8.043 The coordinate and triangulation methods satisfy most measurement requirements for measuring an accident scene. However, it is often necessary to take additional measurements in order to satisfy court requirements. These additional measurements most frequently involve the distances between items of evidence. These distances can be measured using the *straight-line* measuring method. It is conventional to use the shortest possible distance for each such measurement. See Figure C8-27.

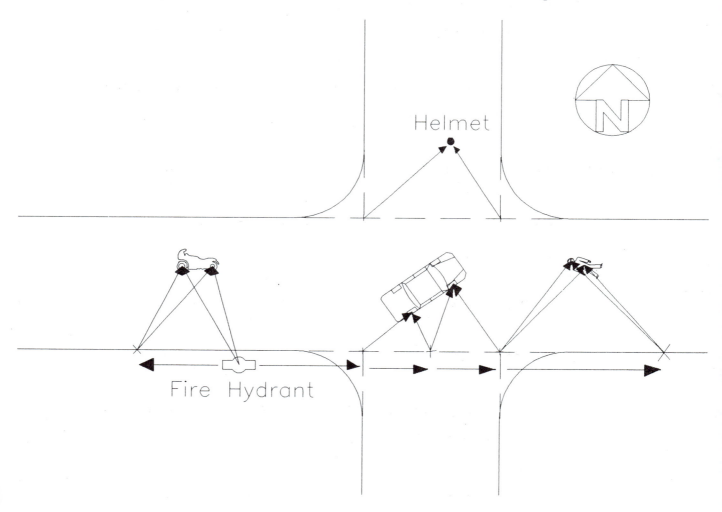

Figure C8-23 Use of *triangulation* to fix the positions of items of evidence on a sketch

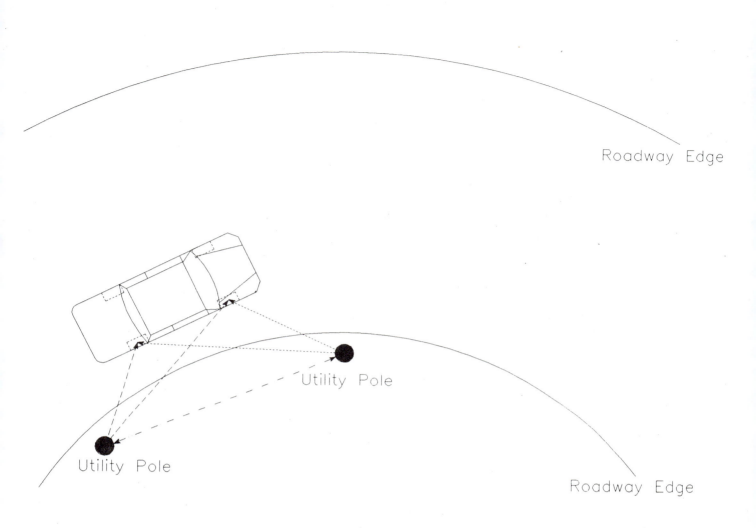

Figure C8-24 Use of triangulation to fix the position of a vehicle on a curve by utilizing utility poles as *tangible reference points*

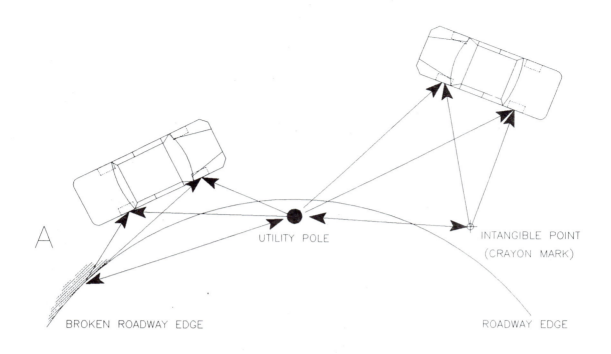

A

UTILITY POLE

INTANGIBLE POINT
(CRAYON MARK)

BROKEN ROADWAY EDGE

ROADWAY EDGE

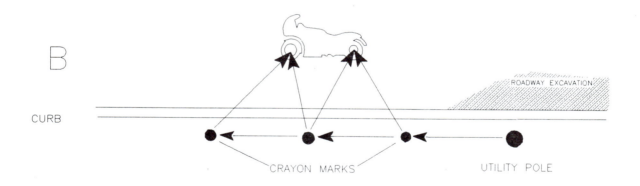

B

CURB

ROADWAY EXCAVATION

CRAYON MARKS

UTILITY POLE

Figures C8-25A and B Both diagrams use of a combination of *tangible* and *intangible* reference points to fix positions from which to make measurements. The utility poles and the broken roadway edge are *tangible* reference points; the crayon marks on the roadway and along the curb are *intangible* reference points. Here the triangulation method is then used to fix the positions of items of evidence.

490

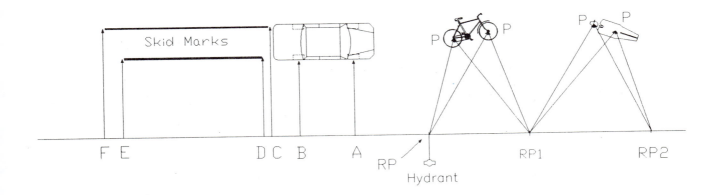

Figure C8-26 Coordinates (on left) and triangulation (on right) may both be used to fix the positions of items of evidence, but see also Figure C8-27.

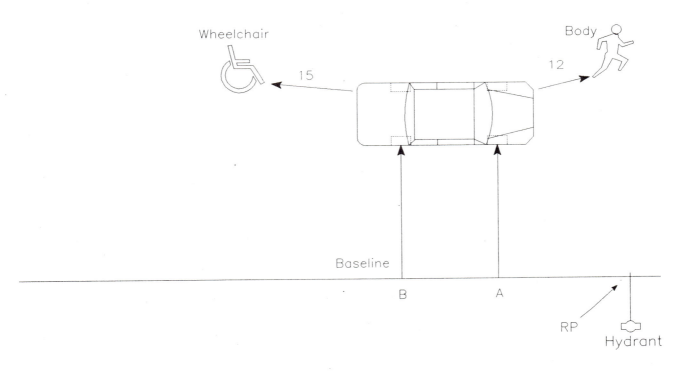

Figure C8-27 Accident investigations generally require the distances separating items of evidence to be obtained for court testimony purpose. Here shortest distance measurements have been made from the car directly to the wheelchair and to the body without immediate reference to the baseline.

491

Preparing a Scale Diagram

C8.044 To prepare a scale diagram from the field sketch measurements shown in Figure C8-28, complete the roadways to their correct measurements. Then use a compass in the following manner to position the blood spot:

1.   Set the compass point to scale [here 1 in = 10 ft (1 cm = 1 m)] for the distance of 20 feet (6 meters) measured from *A* to the item of evidence (blood spot). See Figure C8-29.

2.   Place the compass pinpoint at *A* and scribe an arc *a* so that the arc passes through the general area where the item of evidence is to be positioned. See Figure C8-30.

3.   Set the compass point to a scale for the distance of 14 feet (4.2 meters) measured from *B* to the item of evidence.

4.   Place the compass pinpoint at *B* and scribe an arc *b* intersecting with arc *a*.

5.   The point where the two arcs *a* and *b*, intersect is the exact, scale-diagram position of the blood spot described in the field sketch.

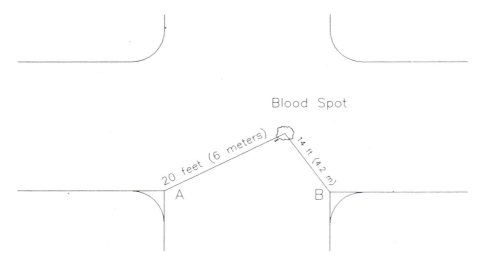

Figure C8-28 Field sketch containing measurements

492

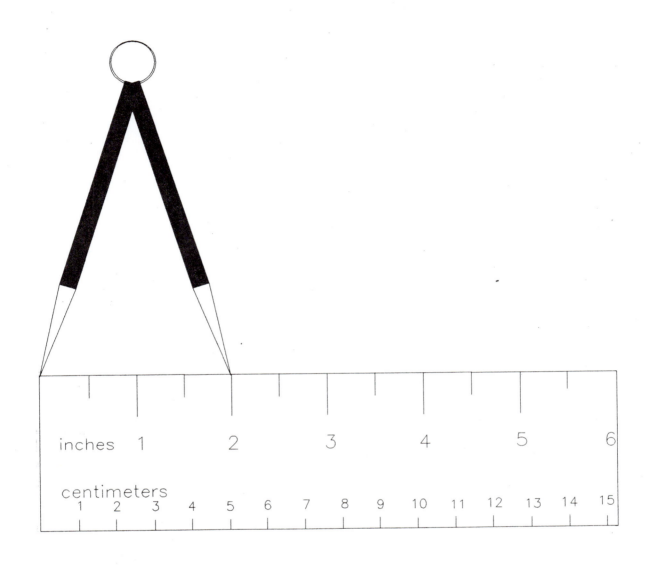

inches 1 2 3 4 5 6

centimeters 1 2 3 4 5 6 7 8 9 10 11 12 13 14 15

Figures C8-29 Setting a compass for a distance of 20 feet on a scale of 1 in = 10 ft. A similar procedure would be used for a distance in metric measure, where 1 centimeter might equal 1 meter.

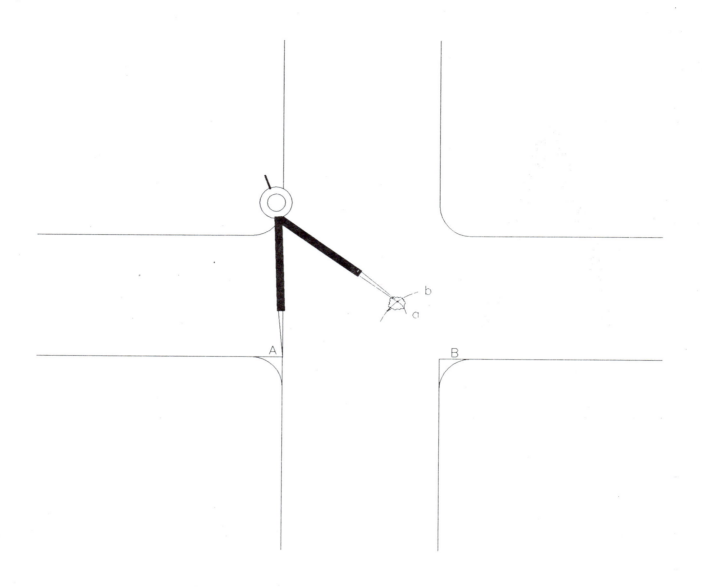

Figure C8-30 A compass is used to scribe intersecting arcs *a* and *b* at the set distances from reference points *A* and *B*. Here the compass is positioned for drawing arc *a* .

Grade and Superelevation

C8.045 *Grade* is the inclination of the center line of a roadway to the horizontal. Grade is positive (+) if the roadway is rising and negative (–) if it is falling. Grade is calculated as the percent of rise or fall from the horizontal, or level, over a given distance. An arrow should be used to indicate the direction of the plus (+) grade. See Figure C8-31.

C8.046 *Superelevation* or *bank* is the grade across the roadway. Formula C8-1 below is used to calculate either a grade, as defined in C8.045, or a superelevation, superelevation being a kind of grade. To calculate the superelevation of a roadway at a place where the roadway curves, you would measure the width of the roadway at the curve from the inside edge of the roadway to the outside edge, as is the usual practice. You would also measure the rise or fall of the roadway over the measured width (see Fig. C8-31).

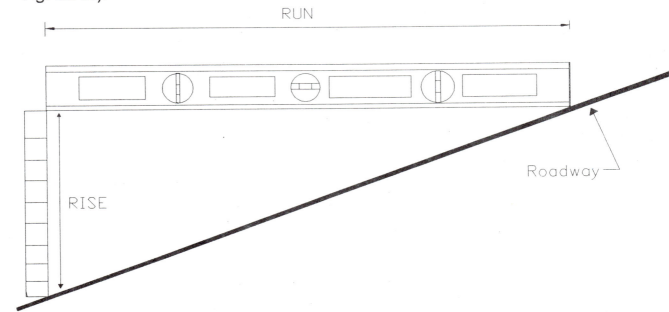

Figure C8-31 In the absence of a more modern instrument such as a smart level, which gives you the slope directly as a decimal percent, a *carpenter's level* can be used to measure the rise or fall over a short span of roadway in order to calculate the grade or superelevation.

Formula C8-1

United States   **Metric**

$$e = \frac{rise}{run} \qquad\qquad\qquad e = \frac{rise}{run}$$

where   e   =   superelevation

rise   =   vertical distance in ft

run   =   horizontal distance in ft

Note: When this formula is used to calculate the grade, the letter m (grade) would be used in place of e.

EXAMPLE (superelevation)

Let us assume that the roadway has a rise of 6 inches, or 0.50 feet (0.152 meters), over a measured 28 feet (8.5 meters) width. You would calculate the percent superelevation as follows:

U.S.   *Metric*

$$e = \frac{rise}{run} \qquad\qquad\qquad e = \frac{rise}{run}$$

$$e = \frac{.50}{28} \qquad\qquad\qquad e = \frac{.152}{8.5}$$

$$e = .0178 \qquad\qquad\qquad e = .0178$$

To express e as a percent, multiply .0178 by 100.

e = 1.7 percent   e = 1.7 percent

Curves

C8.047 A *curve* is a part of a circle. As with a circle, in order to determine its size, it is necessary to calculate its radius. The *radius* R may be calculated using this formula:

Formula C8-2

United States	*Metric*
$R = \dfrac{C^2}{8M} + \dfrac{M}{2}$	$R = \dfrac{C^2}{8M} + \dfrac{M}{2}$

where
R   =   radius

C   =   chord

M   =   middle ordinate

See the figure below.

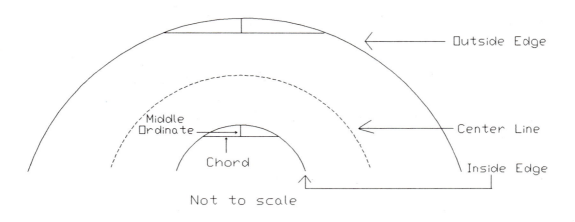

Figure C8-32 Parts of a curve

497

C8.048 To measure a curve such as the one shown in Figure C8-33 for the purpose of finding its *radius*, locate a point at each end of the outside edge of the curve just before the curve straightens out. Mark these points *a* and *b* and measure the straight-line distance between them. This distance is the *chord C*. Divide the *chord C* in half to find its midpoint and mark the midpoint *c*. Then at a 90 degree angle, measure the distance from *c* to the opposite point on the outside edge of the curve and mark it *d*. The distance from *c* to *d* is the *middle ordinate M*.

Figure C8-33 A rounded curb at one end of a traffic island is measured like any curve.

EXAMPLE

In Figure C8-33, we will assume the length of chord C to be 24 feet (7.32 meters) and the length of middle ordinate M to be 4 feet (1.22 meters). The radius R can be calculated as follows using Formula C8-2:

U.S.	*Metric*

$$R = \frac{C^2}{8M} + \frac{M}{2} \qquad\qquad R = \frac{C^2}{8M} + \frac{M}{2}$$

$$R = \frac{24^2}{8 \times 4} + \frac{4}{2} \qquad\qquad R = \frac{7.32^2}{8 \times 1.22} + \frac{1.22}{2}$$

$$R = \frac{576}{32} + \frac{4}{2} \qquad\qquad R = \frac{53.58}{9.76} + \frac{1.22}{2}$$

$$R = 18 + 2 \qquad\qquad R = 5.49 + 0.61$$

$$R = 20 \text{ ft} \qquad\qquad R = 6.1 \text{ m}$$

C8.049 When the radius of a curve is known, the curve may be plotted on a scale diagram. We will assume that the radius of the curve of the west corner of Florida Avenue and Gulf Boulevard in Figure C8-34 is 10 feet (3 meters). This curve can be plotted using the *parallel line method*:

1. Draw in extended street edges. Show the streets where the curve is to be completed as intersecting at a right angle at point *x*.

2. Measure to scale from point *x* a distance of 10 feet (3 meters) -- the length of the radius -- along *curb line B* and mark the point at that

distance *Ba*. From *Ba* draw *construction line a* (broken) parallel to curb line *A*.

3. Measure a similar distance from point *x* along *curb line A* and mark point *Ab*. From *Ab* draw *construction line b* parallel to *curb line B*.

4. Mark the point *o* where the two construction lines intersect.

5. Set the compass to scale for the radius distance of 10 feet (3 meters). Place the compass pinpoint at *o* and scribe an arc from *Ab* to *Ba* to draw in the curve.

This same procedure may be used to construct other types of curves, i.e., those having acute or obtuse angles.

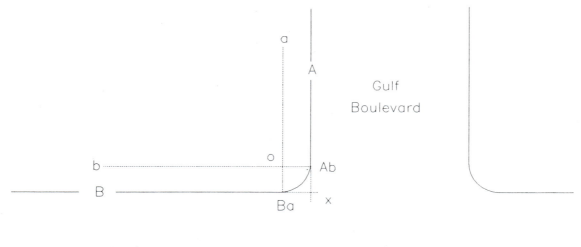

Figure C8-34 Plotting a curve of known radius on a scale diagram by the *parallel line method*.

C8.050 Following are the steps for use of the *compass method* of drawing in the radius for 90 degree corners:

a. Set the compass to scale for the radius being used. From the vertex x of the 90 degree corner strike an arc across each street edge--the north edge of Florida Avenue and the west edge of Gulf Boulevard in Figure C8-35. Label as a and b, respectively, the points where the arcs intersect the street edges.

b. Place the compass at point a, still set to the same scale for a radius of 10 feet (3 meters), and strike an arc inside the area of the corner (see Fig. C8-35). Repeat this at point b and allow this second arc to cross the arc struck from point a. Call the point at which the arcs intersect point c.

c. Set the point of the compass at point c and strike a large arc. This step should connect the two street edges with a curve of the required radius.

This method works only for 90 degree corners or for corners that are very close to 90 degrees.

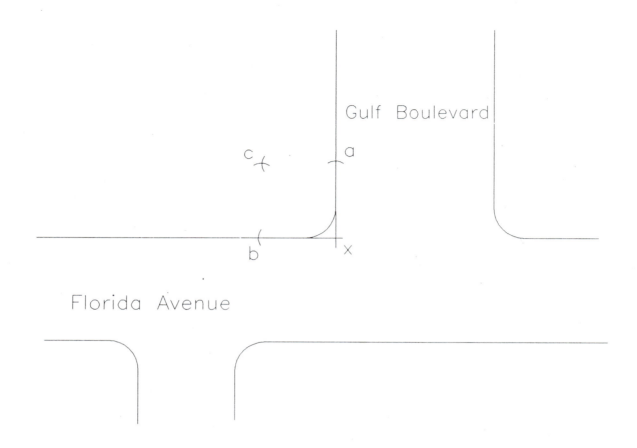

Figure C8-35 For 90 degree corners, the *compass method* can be used to draw in a curve of known radius.

C8.051 The radius at any desired point on a curved roadway can be found indirectly. Using Formula C8-2, you first calculate the radius at some convenient location, such as one of the arcs formed by the inside edge, center line, or outside edge of the roadway. (For safety reasons, the inside edge should be selected if possible.) You then measure the shortest distance separating the desired point (*P* in Fig. C8-36) from the arc whose radius you have calculated and add/subtract this distance, as the situation requires, to/from that radius to give you the radius at the desired point.

502

EXAMPLE

The radius of the inside edge of the curve shown in Figure C8-36 has been determined to be 100 ft (30 m). The shortest distance from the inside edge to point *P* measures 6 ft (2 m). To calculate the radius of the curve at point *P*, you would add this distance to the radius of the inside edge:

U.S.	*Metric*
100 + 6 = 106 ft	30 + 2 = 32 m

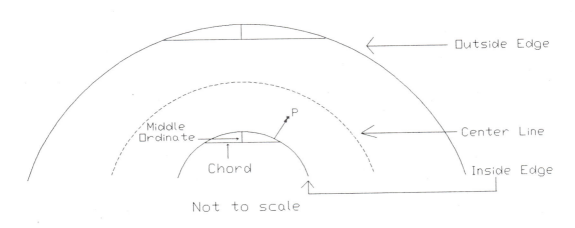

Figure C8-36   Indirect method of finding the radius at any point on a roadway

Angles at Intersections

C8.052 When a street intersects another street at an angle other than 90 degrees, special field measurements are required in order for you to plot the intersection on a scale diagram. Keep in mind that you must make these field measurements at the scene and indicate them on your field sketch. Figure C8-37 is a field sketch showing two roadways that intersect at an acute angle. The distances that you would measure and indicate are

503

shown with dotted lines. The points that you would establish and label are shown with small letters. (Those letters are not italicized that will later be duplicated to form a second triangle identical to the triangle created in Figure C8-37. When used for the second triangle, the letters will appear italicized.) Points *a* and *b* on the corner of St. Johns Street and Florida Avenue mark where the curved portion of the intersection begins on St. Johns Street and Florida Avenue, respectively. (These points will be needed to establish the radius of the curve.) The steps for making the field measurements required for Figure C8-37 are listed after the figure.

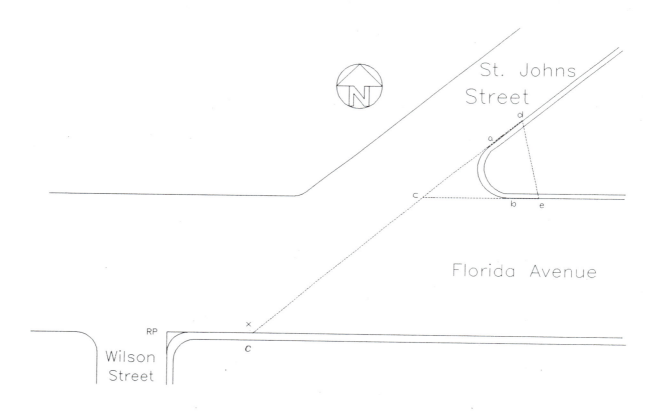

Figure C8-37 Field sketch showing two roadways that intersect at an acute angle

Steps to be performed at the scene:

a. Establish an apex at the corner of St. Johns Street and Florida Avenue by extending tape measures from along the straight edges of St. Johns Street and Florida Avenue out into the intersection until the two tape measures cross at point c.

b. Measure from the apex point *a* at this corner a convenient distance along the edge of St. Johns Street to establish point d and along the edge of Florida Avenue to establish point e.

c. Measure the distance de to complete the measurements required for triangle cde. This last measurement is needed to establish the angle at which St. Johns Street intersects Florida Avenue.

d. Sight along the line dc to a point on the south edge of Florida Avenue. (This point will become point *c* in the scale diagram.)

e. Measure the distance along the south edge of Florida Avenue from this point to the east edge of Wilson Street. The point where this measurement intersects Wilson Street will become the RP.

f. Measure the middle ordinates and chords at the curves of both corners of St. Johns Street and Florida Avenue and both corners at Wilson Street and Florida Avenue. See C8.048.

g. Measure street widths for Florida Avenue, St. Johns Street and Wilson Street.

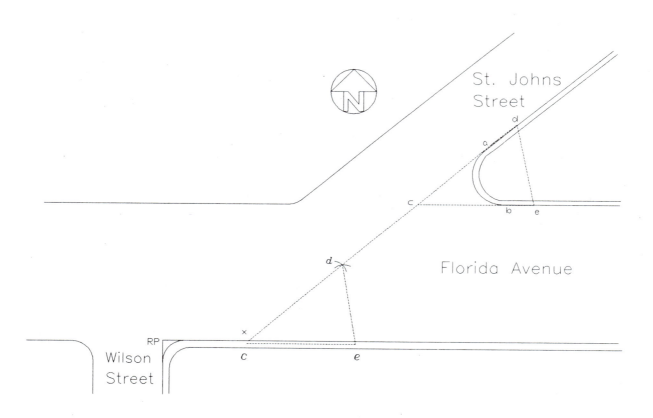

Figure C8-38 Scale diagram in the process of being drawn from measurements taken at the accident scene and placed on the field sketch (see Fig. C8-37). When the diagram is finished, the dotted lines and labeled points will be removed.

C8.053 To plot on a scale diagram the angle at which roadways intersect, you work with the measurements indicated on the field sketch of Figure C8-37 (measured distances shown by dotted lines). The two sides of each roadway are known to be parallel. Following are the steps to be performed in drawing the scale diagram of Figure C8-38:

506

a. Draw a baseline to become the south edge of Florida Avenue.

b. Select a point on the baseline and label it *c*. (This is the point sighted in step d at the scene.)

c. Draw to scale the measured distance from point *c* to the east edge of Wilson Street.

d. Set a compass to scale for the measured distance ce. Then set the needle at point *c* and at the scale distance east along the baseline mark point *e*.

e. Set the compass to scale for the measured distance de. Then set the needle at *e* and draw a long arc at that distance north of the baseline.

f. Set the compass to scale for the measured distance cd. Then set the needle at *c* and draw an arc at that distance to intersect with the first arc.

g. Label the point at which the arcs intersect as point *d*. Lines *cd* and *de* (it is not necessary to draw them) form a triangle *cde* similar to triangle cde measured at the scene and being recreated in the scale diagram. Angle *dce* is therefore the same as angle dce, the angle at which St. Johns Street intersects Florida Avenue.

h. From point *c* extend a line through point *d* toward the upper right edge of the paper. Part of this extended line will become the southeast edge of St. Johns Street.

i.   Using the measured street width, draw the opposite edge of St. Johns Street parallel to the edge established in the previous step.

j.   Draw at the measured street width the opposite side of each of the other streets parallel to the established side.

k.   Set in the curve for each corner to scale using the parallel line method (see C8.049) or the compass method (see C8.050).

l.   Once all corners and streets have been drawn to scale, erase all construction lines and labels that are no longer needed.

Offset Streets

C8.054   To plot an offset street on a scale diagram, you also work with measurements indicated on the field sketch. Following are the steps to be performed with reference to the sketch in Figure C8-39 (part of the same location as in Figure C8-37 but showing an offset street not included in that figure):

a.   Draw in the north arrow pointing directly toward the top of the diagram.

b.   Draw to scale Florida Avenue and Wilson Street, with corners *A* and *B*. (Duval Street, the offset street, does not yet appear in the diagram.)

c.   Measure on your diagram from the RP at Wilson Street due east to point *a*, which is the point on the south edge of Florida Avenue in direct line with what will become the west edge of Duval Street.

d.   Imagine that you are sighting due north from point *a* on the south edge of Florida Avenue. Draw line *b* as an extension of your line of sight to form the west edge of Duval Street just before Duval Street intersects Florida Avenue.

e.   Plot the width of Duval Street (what will become the distance from point *c* to point *d* when these points are plotted) and draw a line through point *d* parallel to line *b* to form the east edge of Duval Street.

f. Complete the edges of Duval Street with permanent lines, construct corners *C* and *D* to scale (labeling points *c* and *d* where the curves end) and erase unnecessary construction lines. Your scale drawing will look similar to the field sketch but will be to scale.

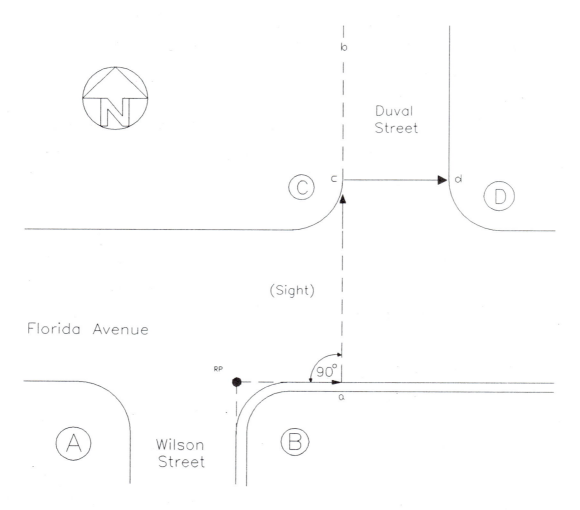

Figure C8-39 Field sketch showing an offset street (Duval Street)

Inaccessible Areas

C8.055 *Congruent triangles* are triangles that are equal in all their corresponding sides and angles and can be used to measure indirectly to the position of a vehicle in a lake, river, pond or other area that is difficult to reach. You first establish a baseline -- along a shoreline, for example -- then sight through the midpoint on the baseline and construct two such triangles.

EXAMPLE (see Figure C8-40)

a. Lay a baseline *BD* of any convenient length. The *B* end of the baseline must be at a right angle (90°) to a convenient point *A* on the vehicle.

b. Find the midpoint of the baseline and label it *C*. The lines *BC* and *CD* are made equal in length.

c. Proceed at an angle of 90° (south in this example) from the baseline at *D* to a point where *C* may be sighted in direct line with *A*. Mark this location point *E*. The triangles *ABC* and *CDE* thus formed will be *congruent triangles*.

d. Measure the distance from *D* to *E*. This distance is the same as the distance from point *A* on the vehicle out in the river to point *B* on the shore, since side *DE* of triangle *CDE* corresponds to side *AB* of triangle *ABC* and is therefore equal to side *AB*.

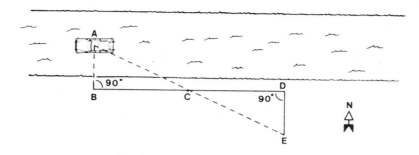

Figure C8-40 Measuring indirectly to a vehicle in a river

Measurement Records

C8.056 Following are three forms that may be useful in recording measurements from an accident scene:

Traffic Accident Investigation
Coordinate Measurements Record

Case # _____ Date _____ Page _____ of _____

Location _____

Base Line _____

Reference Point _____

Distance from Reference Point to Base Line _____

Officer(s) _____

Point	Description	Distance From Point 0/RP	Distance 90° to Object

Traffic Accident Investigation
Triangulation Measurements Records

Case # _____   Date _____   Page _____ of _____

Location _____

Base Line _____

Reference Point #1 _____

Reference Point #2 _____

Distance from Ref. Pt. #1 to Ref. Pt. #2 _____

Distance from Base Line to Ref. Pt. #1 _____; to Ref. Pt. #2 _____

Officer(s) _____

Point	Description	From Reference Point #1	From Reference Point #2

Traffic Accident Investigation
Supplemental Measurements Record

Case # _____   Date _____   Page _____ of _____

Location _____

Officer(s) _____

From a Point (Description)	To a Point (Description)	Distance

515

INTRODUCTION

Lesson 9

SUBJECT: Accident Photography and Video Recording

At-scene traffic accident investigators use photography and video recording to process and record the evidence of an accident scene.

This lesson will provide the student with the knowledge necessary to record evidence from an accident scene by use of photography and/or video recording.

Lesson Contents

This lesson covers the following topics:

  a.   Introduction to accident photography
  b.   Credibility of accident photography
  c.   Who should take accident photographs
  d.   When to take accident photographs
  e.   What to photograph at an accident scene
  f.   Planning the photography of an accident scene
  g.   Photographic equipment
  h.   Techniques in photographing an accident scene
  i.   Identification of photographs
  j.   Video recording of the accident scene

Lesson Objectives

Upon completion of this lesson, the student will be able to do the following to the satisfaction of the instructor:

1. State the best method for taking photographs and/or video taping of an accident scene.

    a. Planning the photography and/or video taping of an accident scene
    b. Items to photograph or video tape
    c. Camera or video camera positions
    d. Photographing and/or video taping techniques

2. State the best method of identifying photographs or video tape taken of an accident scene.

ACKNOWLEDGEMENT

IPTM wishes to thank Cpl. B. J. Turner of the Alabama Highway Patrol for his extensive contributions to the writing of this lesson on photography.

517

LESSON 9

ACCIDENT PHOTOGRAPHY

Considerations

Introduction

C9.001 The at-scene investigator collects evidence from the accident scene that may be presented later to a court, to insurance adjustors, or to reconstruction experts.

C9.002 Photography is a means by which such evidence can be collected and preserved. Although photography should be regarded as a supplement to rather than a substitute for the standard procedures for gathering evidence, a photograph may sometimes reveal a mark on the road, damage to a vehicle, or some other detail the investigator did not observe at the scene.

C9.003 After investigating several hundred accidents, the investigator may come to mix up the details of one accident with those of another. Since photographs make it unnecessary for the investigator to recall the details of a particular accident from memory, they help prevent such confusion.

C9.004 Photographs also help the investigator explain to someone else what was observed at the scene. *A picture is worth a thousand words.*

Credibility of Photography Evidence

C9.005   People tend to believe that *photos don't lie*.   Yet in reality, photographs may not represent the accident scene exactly as it appeared at the time it was photographed.   The photograph may show the scene in a different lighting.   If black and white film was used, the colors present will not be visible, and even if color film was used, the colors appearing in the photo may not always reflect the colors that were actually present.   When viewing a photograph of the scene, the investigator should keep such factors in mind.

C9.006   The accident investigator must take care to photograph the evidence in its undisturbed state and avoid photographing recreated evidence, that is, evidence that has been altered and/or moved and then restored to its approximate post-impact state and/or returned to its approximate post-impact location.

C9.007 The accident investigator must follow the established procedure for taking measurements at the scene.   These measurements are more accurate than those obtained by measuring objects and distances from photographs of the scene.   However, a color photograph taken through a polarizing filter can show an incipient skidmark to advantage and help verify where the skid actually began.

Who Should Take Photographs

C9.008 The at-scene accident investigator would be the primary person to take photographs at the accident scene.   The investigator knows what evidence needs to be collected and documented.   If the investigator is not the person operating the camera, the investigator needs to direct that person as to what evidence needs to be photographed and recorded. Circumstances where such direction might be required:

a. Investigating officer requests crime scene personnel to take photographs.

b. Investigating officer requests photographer from another police department or another organization.

c. Professional photographer is contracted by police agency.

d. Free-lance photographer, newspaper photographer, or lay photographer takes the photographs.

C9.009 Courts have ruled that the person taking the photographs need not be an expert. There is the example of the famed Zapruder film taken of the Kennedy assassination. Mr. Zapruder had a basic understanding of the operation of the equipment he was using but was not an expert in photographic techniques.

When to Take Photographs

C9.010 Photographs need to be taken as soon as possible after the occurrence of the incident and/or completion of the rescue.

C9.011 The investigator needs to set priorities for collecting and preserving the evidence from the accident scene. Evidence that will be very short-lived should be photographed and measured first. Evidence not considered short-lived can be photographed and measured later in the investigation. However, the accident scene should be photographed prior to any marking at the scene, as the scene needs to be viewed as it appeared when the accident took place. Additional photos can be taken of evidence after it has been marked and removed. These photos can assist the investigator later with testimony and/or in identifying items on the scale drawing.

C9.012 A reason for a delay in the taking of photographs might be the need to clear the road surface of debris first. Sometimes marks on the road may be obscured by debris, water, snow, and other foreign objects. After clean-up of the accident area, these marks become visible.

C9.013 Some photography may be postponed. Postponement might be caused by light or weather conditions. The investigator should make a practice of also taking daylight photographs to supplement limited light photographs, if the accident occurred during times other than daylight. And sometimes vegetation on shoulders may die several days later showing evidence of the path of the vehicles involved.

What to Photograph

C9.014 The investigator should begin with overall accident scene photographs. This could require the investigator to begin at the final rest positions of the evidence and work backwards to the suspected beginning of the accident.

Figure C9-1 A photo should be taken to capture the view presented to the driver or passenger of an accident vehicle as it was approaching the scene. Such a photo is especially important in recording the series of events.

C9.015 The views from the approach paths of vehicles and/or pedestrians leading to the accident scene should be photographed from the eye level of the drivers, passengers or pedestrians and should reflect what they would have seen prior to impact (see Fig. C9-1).

C9.016 The final rest positions of vehicles and bodies will be needed. If a particular landmark is used to complete measurements, this landmark should be included in the photograph. Having the landmark appear in the photograph will assist in placing the evidence in relationship to this object and ultimately within the accident scene.

C9.017 Before being moved from their final rest position, all vehicles should be photographed from several different perspectives to assure capturing views from 360 degrees. Refer to the diagram at the end of this chapter showing the minimum number of camera positions needed to document a vehicle. Treat final positions of bodies the same way as final positions of vehicles. Also treat detached parts of vehicles exactly the same as whole vehicles.

C9.018 The investigator also needs to photograph the results of the accident. This would include all evidence on the roadway, for example, all tire marks and irregularities in or caused by these tire marks. These irregularities require individual views. Some examples of such irregularities would be offsets, scrub marks, striations in yaw marks, tire prints, and pavement texture.

C9.019 Other evidence important to photograph would be, but is not limited to, debris and rubbish from vehicles, gas and water puddles, any other liquid evidence, gouges or scratch marks, ruts and furrows.

C9.020 The investigator needs to take damage photographs that will be used in reconstructing the accident, giving testimony, evaluating contact versus induced damage, and evaluating repair of the vehicle.

C9.021 A minimum of four photographs should be taken of the exterior damage of each vehicle, each taken at a right angle to the vehicle. The entire side, front or rear being photographed must appear in the photograph. Additional close-up photographs should be taken of damage areas at a right angle to the direction of contact to further show depth of penetration or collapse. These photographs also need to show details of damage, including imprints or paint from one vehicle to another, friction or abrasion marks, damage to lamps, damage to cargo, sources of injury to pedestrians, and tire damage.

C9.022   In conjunction with the exterior damage photographs, interior damage photographs need to be taken of any component part of the passenger compartment damaged by occupant contact, deformation of vehicle structure, overturn, etc.

C9.023   The damage photographs, both exterior and interior, will assist in matching the evidence to the damage incurred.

C9.024   An example would be the matching of a scored underpart of a vehicle to a gouge in the pavement, or a tire print to the tread of the tire causing the print, or a broken engine block or transmission case to a corresponding oil splatter, or the imprint of the brake or accelerator pedal on the shoe soles of the driver to the ribs of the pedal that made the imprint, or a mark on the vehicle to the object that made it.

C9.025   Also to be photographed at the accident scene are roadway situations that would cause view obstructions, especially if they involve something that may change at a later date, e.g., road construction areas, removable vegetation, vehicle cargo. Remember to photograph the scene views from the eye level of the drivers!

C9.026   Photographs also need to be taken of the nonchanging items in the accident scene, e.g., a hillcrest, curves.

C9.027   Visibility conditions such as smoke, fog, rain, snow, etc. may change quickly and need to be photographed.

C9.028 Photographs are needed of positions and conditions of traffic control devices. These photographs can depict confusing backgrounds, parked vehicles and any other objects obstructing the traffic control devices.

C9.029 Likewise, road surface conditions need to be photographed. These conditions include, but are not limited to snow, water, pot holes and significant surface irregularities.

Planning the Photographs

C9.030 Planning the management of the accident scene includes planning for the taking of photographs. As you know, "The best laid plans of mice and men often go astray." This is also true of accident scene photography, but you should nevertheless plan how to take the photographs.

C9.031 First, decide what you want the picture to show. Does the camera see all you want it to see? Ensure that the entire view is in the camera view finder. Move in or out to accomplish this. Ask people to move from the view. Also, have the Fire and Rescue equipment removed before taking the photographs.

C9.032 The investigator may need to take a series of photographs to obtain a view of the entire accident scene. Or the investigator may need to take only one general overview photograph. Either way, the investigator should follow up with close-up photographs. This technique will provide more information than unrelated single photographs. Close-up photographs can assist in explaining an unfamiliar subject, such as vehicle parts, evidence inside a vehicle, etc.

C9.033 This procedure is particularly helpful in photographing long marks on the roadway or shoulder. Start with a general view showing an object anyone can easily recognize. A closer view showing a recognizable area from the previous picture will then lead up to the vehicle part or other item of special interest that can be captured in a close-up photograph.

C9.034 When photographing the approach views of vehicle paths and/or pedestrian paths prior to the accident, be sure the camera height is the same as the view of approaching persons. Finally, consider aerial photos if aviation assistance is available.

Photographic Equipment

C9.035 Equipment has changed from the days of the Kodak Brownies and size 126 film. The investigator needs to use suitable modern equipment but it must also be affordable to the department's budget and available. If a photograph needs to be taken of a piece of short-lived evidence and all that is available is an "instamatic" type camera, better to take the photograph with it than to wait for a fancy camera and miss the evidence. Following are suggestions as to the type of equipment to be used, but these are not etched in stone.

C9.036 Cameras come in all shapes and sizes. Almost any camera can be used, but obviously some are better than others. A 35 mm SLR (single lens reflex) is generally the best type of camera for accident photography.

Advantages of the SLR camera:

    a.   Has interchangeable lenses.

    b.   Has macro or extension-bellows capability for close-ups.

    c.   Can produce usable negatives with flash under almost all conditions.

    d.   Allows good enlargements to be made from negatives.

    e.   Is capable of totally manual operation.

C9.037 Another type of camera is the 2 1/4 x 2 1/4 roll film camera. This camera has the same characteristics as the SLR type camera, but is more expensive to purchase and to operate.

C9.038 The *instant picture* camera offers the most readily available photos.

Advantages of the instant picture camera:

    a.   Permits the inexperienced photographer to see the results and try again if the photograph is unsatisfactory.

    b.   The picture requires no separate processing.

Disadvantages of the instant picture camera:

    a.   The cost of film tends to discourage picture taking.

    b.   Not as flexible as SLR cameras.

    c.   Negatives not available for reprints or enlargements.

C9.039 Along with the camera, the photographer needs to be familiar with the flash equipment available. An electronic flash must have a guide number of 100 (be rated at ISO 100) or higher in order to be powerful enough to work outdoors at night. The features available on flashes vary greatly. If the flash is an after-market brand, make sure it is compatible with your particular brand of camera. (Or buy a flash that is manufactured by the same company that built your camera.)

C9.040 There is a wide range of camera lenses to select from. Used with an SLR 35mm camera, the lenses are generally interchangeable. The most prescribed lens in accident photography is the normal 50mm lens. This lens has the closest view and depth to that of the human eye. The lens should be at least f 2.8 because night pictures require maximum light. Macro lenses or close-up attachments are desirable for detailed evidence.

C9.041 The investigator now has the camera, flash and lens. What is still needed is the film. Film is available in all speeds (ISO). Generally, for daylight photography, ISO's of 100, 125, and 200 are good. For nighttime photographs, ISO of 400 or higher is needed. Caution should be exercised if enlargements are to be made from the negatives. When ISO is higher than 400, the photographs may become grainy and difficult to view.

C9.042 The question now arises, do I use color or black and white film? Color film gives better representation of the accident scene than black and white film and is no more costly to process. However, color film requires more precise exposure.

C9.043 Black and white film can be used for traffic accident photography. While the cost of processing black and white film is similar to the cost of color processing, black and white film takes longer than color film to process because most of the processing centers are set up for color film and not black and white film.

Photographic Techniques

C9.044   The most difficult type of photograph to take is a nighttime photograph. Getting the right focus and exposure is more challenging than daylight.

C9.045 You can use a flashlight to illuminate the object on which you wish to focus the camera.

C9.046   Three factors must be considered in determining the flash exposure:

    a.   Distance from flash to principal object

    b.   Strength of flash source

    c.   Speed of film

C9.047   When using a flash at night, flareback is a common problem. Flareback is caused by the flash reflecting off shiny surfaces. Sometimes it cannot be avoided, but a change in the camera angle will help.

C9.048 Another problem with nighttime photography is caused by falling rain or snow. The falling rain or snow will show up as spots of light in the photograph.

C9.049   When photographing great distances or wide areas at night, multiple flash may be necessary. The camera must be mounted on a tripod to ensure it will not move. The flash must be fired independently of the camera shutter release.   To complete the photograph follow these suggested steps:

    a.   Focus the camera on the subject.

    b.   Cover the lens opening.

c.   Set the lens opening (f stop) to the correct exposure for flash to subject, not camera to subject.

d.   Open the camera shutter and hold it open.

e.   Remove lens cover, have an assistant fire the flash, then cover the lens.

f.   Repeat the flash at space intervals necessary to illuminate the entire subject or area.

C9.050 Taking daylight photographs also requires special attention. A lens shade is useful to prevent lens flare. When taking photographs that have a shadow, use the flash to fill in the dark areas of the shadow.

C9.051 Again, when photographs are taken of views that drivers and/or pedestrians had of an accident scene, the camera must be placed at the eye level of the drivers or pedestrians in order to best represent the accident scene as they would have viewed it. A camera placed too high makes nearby objects look too low and a camera placed too low makes nearby objects look too high and exaggerates view obstructions.

C9.052 The investigator also needs to ensure that the camera is set up or held level. Aiming the camera up or down will misrepresent perspective. Photographs taken parallel to uphill or downhill terrain will cause the terrain to look level. On the other hand, a level road photographed with the camera tilted up or down will appear to have a grade.

C9.053 The camera position is also very important. To show distances between objects, more than one picture will have to be taken. Distances in the direction in which the camera is aimed are difficult to judge. If the camera is positioned at a right angle to the distances to be shown, the distances can be approximated.

Identification of Photographs

C9.054   The last task for the investigator is to identify the photographs taken of the accident scene.   A numbering system is desirable for this purpose.   The following information should be noted on the back of each photograph:

    a.   Where taken

    b.   Date taken

    c.   Who took the photograph

    d.   Accident number or case number

    e.   Who has custody of the negatives

C9.055   The investigator may be required to present certain technical data in regard to the photographs taken.   The investigator should note and be able to explain the following:

    a.   Camera and lens used

    b.   Filters used, if any

    c.   Kind of film

    d.   How the film was processed

    e.   Whether the print is an enlargement

    f.   Whether the print shows all that appears on the negative

    g.   Whether a flash was used and, if so, how many times

    h.   Height of the camera from the ground

    i.   Distance from the camera to the principal object in the photograph

C9.056   This information can be provided by the photographer if the investigator did not personally take the photographs and can be included in the narrative of the accident investigation report.

Use of a Video Camera

C9.057   The advent of the video camera has provided the accident investigator with another means of collecting and preserving evidence. Video camera recordings, however, should be used as a supplement to photographs and *not as a substitute*.

C9.058   The video camera can provide a live, on-site view of the accident scene during the investigation. The advantage of this procedure is that it makes it hard to dispute what was taking place. The infamous video recording in the speeding arrest case involving Mr. Rodney King and several officers of the Los Angeles Police Department captured, to the dismay of some, what occurred that evening.

C9.059   But sights and sounds can be recorded by use of the video camera. One disadvantage is the unwelcome remarks that are sometimes made by persons at the accident scene. The video camera records all sights and sounds.

C9.060   To eliminate unwanted sounds, a blank mike plug can be placed in the microphone jack of the video camera. Most courts have allowed video evidence where the sound has been turned down or removed from the video. The investigator must authenticate the video during the court proceeding.

C9.061 Video camera equipment is as varied as camera equipment. Video camera equipment has fallen in price in recent years, bringing its cost down to the level of moderately priced cameras. Still, cost can be a major consideration, as video camera equipment must be purchased in addition to, not instead of, camera equipment.

C9.062 The planning and procedures used with a still camera apply also to a video camera. The accident scene, including all evidence, must be recorded. Following are guidelines for use of the video camera:

a.   Follow a logical sequence when filming the accident scene. Take the court or jury on guided tour of the accident scene.

b.   Do not use the zoom control excessively. Overuse often confuses a viewer and can cause the court or jury to lose concentration. If the zoom function is required to focus in on a piece of evidence, stabilize the shot, zoom in, pause, then zoom back out, pause again, then continue with the accident scene.

c.   Use the fader control to fade in/fade out when starting/stopping the video recording. This results in a more polished presentation of the video evidence.

d.   Use a tripod after completing the walk through the accident scene. This allows the video camera to record the investigation, clean-up, and other activities at the accident scene. The video camera should be placed in such a position to record the entire scene.

e.   Practice walking with the video camera in the record mode to learn to eliminate the bumping motion caused by walking.

f.   Do not record audio at the accident scene.

g. Remember to use all the rules that apply to still photography when recording the accident scene. Orient the viewers by showing landmarks, and walk the viewers through the accident scene. Walk the viewers into the close-up views when using the zoom control. When changing views, reorient the viewers before continuing.

GLOSSARY OF TERMS FOR PHOTOGRAPHY

Aperture   The adjustable lens opening through which light enters the camera. Aperture size is expressed as an f/number.

Aperture Priority   An automatic exposure system where the aperture is selected manually and the camera automatically sets the appropriate shutter speed for the amount of light present.

ASA   The American Standards Association, who provided us with the numerical system for rating the speed or light sensitivity of film.

Balance   A term used to describe the pleasing arrangement (i.e. visual balance) of subject matter in a composition.

Bellows   An accordion like attachment used between the camera and the lens for closeup photography. Sometimes called extension bellows.

Bracketing   When *bracketing* you shoot a slightly overexposed frame as well as a slightly underexposed frame in addition to the normal exposure. This ensures that even with slight variations you will have one photograph that is properly exposed.

Cable Release   A long flexible cable that is used to release the shutter without touching the camera body. Used with a tripod for long exposures. (Newer electronic cameras may be equipped with **dedicated** electronic cable releases that are available only from the manufacturer of that particular camera.)

Close-Up Photography This is the shooting of objects at very close focusing distances that results in image magnification. Close up work can vary from the closest possible focusing distance of a normal lens to the magnifications that are possible only with accessories such as bellows and extension tubes.

Color Imbalance Unnatural colors that result from using a color film with incorrect lighting. For example, daylight balanced film shot indoors under fluorescent lighting will produce green hued pictures.

Color Negative Films like KODACOLOR (tm) and FUJICOLOR (tm) are color negative films that yield a color *negative* image from which color prints are made.

Color Positive Films such as FUJICHROME (tm) and EKTACHROME (tm) are color positive films that yield a color positive (slide) after processing.

Color Temperature The KELVIN temperature rating of a light source or film. For example, daylight color film is balanced for the KELVIN temperature of 5500K (noonday sun). Warm colors in photos taken at dawn or dusk are due to the different color temperatures of sunlight at those times.

Composition The arrangement of visual elements such as people, horizon and trees when *framing* a photograph in your viewfinder.

Dedicated A term that means a particular piece of equipment is designed for use on a particular camera or lens (to the exclusion of all others -- sometimes including cameras made by the same manufacturer). For example, a dedicated flash for a CANON camera cannot be used on a NIKON.

Depth of Field The zone of sharp focus in a photo from in front of and to the rear of the main subject which was the primary focus point. This is the dimension in a photograph that can be seen but can't be measured when viewing a photograph. It can be used by the photographer either creatively or to intentionally make the viewer look at a certain object in the photograph.

Developing The chemical processing of exposed film. It takes several chemical steps to reveal the latent image and fix it so that light will not cause any further exposure.

Din Deutsche Industrie Normen (German Standards Association) is the organization that gave Europe and other parts of the world outside the U.S.A. their numerical system for the sensitivity rating or speed of film.

Distortion Curving, stretching or other changes seen in photographs that are caused by the particular lens used to make the photograph. The resulting photo is different from what you would normally see with a standard lens.

Enlargement A print that is larger than original negative or slide from which it was made.

Exposure The effect of light striking light sensitive film. Exposure creates a latent photographic image that materializes after chemical processing. (The correct exposure for the available light -- or lack of it -- is a subject all to itself.)

Exposure Meter A device (called a *lightmeter*) to set exposure by measuring a scene's light intensity in relation to the film speed being used.

Extension Tubes Interlocking hollow tubes connected between the camera and the lens to increase magnification for closeup photography.

Film Speed The measure of a film's sensitivity to light. Film that is more sensitive to light has a higher numerical rating and is said to be "faster."

Filter A piece of optical quality glass or plastic (sometimes known as *gelatin*) usually used in front of the lens to affect the light entering the camera. They have many functions, such as color correction, increase contrast and reducing glare or reflections.

Fisheye Lens A lens with the widest possible angle of view. A fisheye lens has a full 180 degree angle of view. A circular fisheye lens creates a round picture and a full-frame fisheye lens causes strong curving distortion in the image.

Fixed Focal Length A lens with one set focal length. For example, a 100mm lens is fixed at 100mm and cannot be shifted or zoomed. Also known as a *prime* lens.

Flash An electronic flash used to provide artificial lighting, usually powered by batteries.

Focal Length The distance from the optical tip of a lens to the camera's focal plane. Commonly used to identify the size and type of lens -- a 28mm wide-angle lens has a focal length of 28mm measured from the tip of the lens to the focal plane in the back of the camera.

Focus Adjustment of the lens focusing ring to get the main subject in sharp, clear relief.

Format The size, usually referring to the size of film cameras and prints.

Framing Composing a picture within the boundary of the camera's viewfinder.

f/Stop A fixed-size opening in a lens aperture. f/stops are standard numerical measurements obtained from the ratio of aperture diameter to the lens focal length.

Grain Light sensitive silver in the form of grains is used in film. H i g h speed film requires larger silver grains which can be seen as a grainy pattern in large prints.

ISO International Standards Organization is the newest system for rating film speeds. ISO combines ASA and DIN ratings.

Light Meter (see exposure meter)

Light Sensitivity The measure of a film's reaction to light expressed as film speed. The light sensitive film emulsion reacts when light strikes it.

Macrophotography (see close-up photography)

Matting Surrounding the print with a paper board to protect the print. The mat also acts as a neutral border to enhance the photographic image.

Motor Drive A camera accessory for automatic power film advance with each shot. Speed up to 5 frames per second. Also features power rewind.

Normal Lens (see standard lens)

Open Up Adjusting the aperture to allow more light to enter the lens. For example, going from f/16 to f/11 is opening up one stop.

Overexposure Allowing excess light to strike the film. Overexposure results in bright, washed out prints and slides.

Panning Tracking a moving subject with the camera. Swing the camera smoothly as the subject passes by.

Perspective The point of view chosen when taking a picture.

Photomacrography (see close-up photography)

Power Winder An auto film advance accessory that allows for shooting up to 2 frames per second.

Printing The process of making a paper print from a negative or slide.

Processing The chemical development of exposed film. Prints also must be processed to get the final photograph.

Proportion The ratio of major areas within a picture composition. For example, the proportion of sky in relation to the horizon in a landscape.

Reciprocity Failure Reciprocity is a predictable relationship between light intensity and the exposure of light sensitive film -- doubling the light doubles the exposure. However, extreme exposure times such as 10 seconds require extra exposure because the Law of Reciprocity begins to fail (reciprocity failure).

Rhythm Visual rhythm is produced by the repetition of shapes, lines, or colors in a composition.

Standard Lens The 50mm lens sold with most new 35mm SLR cameras. A standard lens has a viewing perspective similar to the angle of human eyesight.

Stop Down Adjusting the aperture to decrease the amount of light entering the lens. Changing from f/5.6 to f/8 is stopping down one full stop.

Symmetry Equal visual weight on either side of a central axis.

Shutter The mechanical control for the time interval of an exposure.

Shutter Priority The exposure system that automatically selects an aperture to match the shutter speed manually set by the photographer.

SLR A single lens reflex camera allows the photographer to focus directly through the shooting lens.

Telephoto Lens The long lens that yields a larger image magnification than that produced by a normal lens.

35MM The film size using sprocketed film with a diagonal measure of 36 millimeters.

Tripod A stable three-legged support for a camera.

TTL An abbreviation for *through the lens* meaning that any light reading taken, whether for available light or flash photography, is made off the film plane after the light passes through the lens.

Underexposure An exposure made without a sufficient amount of light. Underexposure results in dark prints and slides.

Viewfinder The camera's viewing system that shows what will appear in the final picture.

Wide-Angle Lens A lens with a wider than normal angle of coverage.

Zooming A technique with a zoom lens where the lens is zoomed, shifted through its focal lengths, during the exposure.

Zoom Lens A lens with variable focal lengths that can be shifted to obtain different angles of view.

This glossary is taken from *The ABC's of Picture Taking Ease* by Canon, USA and is for use in IPTM training programs.

PHOTOGRAPHS TO BE TAKEN OF CASE VEHICLE BY FIELD INVESTIGATOR

Photo records are essential because if data interest shifts to other areas not listed on the form, photo interpretation can update the report. They also verify the reported data. It is recommended that you use at least one 24-exposure roll of film (slides preferred) on the vehicle.

1. For a complete photographic record of the case vehicle, it is recommended that descriptive photographs of the inside and outside of the vehicle be taken from the camera positions shown and explained below:

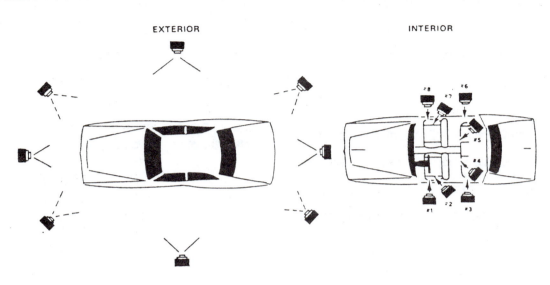

EXTERIOR   INTERIOR

2. Take the 8 overall exterior photos as indicated above left; all views should show the entire vehicle as seen from each position.

3. Take the 8 interior photos from the positions indicated above right. These views should show the interior components listed below:

#1,8	Opposite Side: Door or interior panels Side roof rail Seat	#4	Right Side: Windshield header A-pillar Instrument panel
#2	Left Side: Instrument Panel Steering wheel Windshield	#5	Left Side: Windshield header A-pillar Steering wheel
#3,6	Opposite Side: Door or interior panels Side roof rail Seat	#7	Right Side: Instrument panel Windshield

4. Take a close-up view of the steering-assembly energy-absorbing device and/or shear capsules from the right front side of the passenger compartment, if possible.

5. Extra photos should be taken of each damaged area and all occupant contact areas at angles different from those in the above photos.

6. If the vehicle was rear impacted, the fuel tank should be photographed whether damaged or not.

7. Photographic coverage of other items you consider important or interesting is encouraged.

EXPOSURE CONTROLS AND GUIDELINES

There are two primary exposure settings on adjustable cameras that control the amount of light that reaches the film and exposes it. These are shutter speed and lens opening.

■ The shutter speed controls the *length of time* the film is exposed to light and is expressed in numbers such as 30, 60, 125, etc. These numbers represent *fractions* of a second (e.g., 125 = 1/125 of a second).

■ The B setting on the shutter speed scale means the shutter will stay open as long as you press the shutter release. Use the B setting for time exposures.

■ The *size* of the lens opening on your camera (indicated by f-numbers) is the other factor that controls the amount of light that reaches the film.

■ The smallest f-number on a lens refers to the biggest lens opening and the largest f-number refers to the smallest lens opening.

■ When you change from one lens opening to the next nearest number, you're adjusting the lens by 1 stop (except from the maximum lens opening to the next smaller opening on some lenses).

Lens Opening f-Number	Shutter Speed	
4	1/30	MORE
5.6	1/60	LIGHT
8	1/125	OR
11	1/250	EXPO-
16	1/500	SURE

"Equivalent Exposures" are many combinations of shutter speed and lens opening that allow the same amount of light to reach the film for proper exposure. This lets you use a smaller lens opening to increase depth of field or a higher shutter to stop action; e.g., as the setting in one column is increased, the setting in the other column must be decreased to maintain the same exposure for the lighting conditions in the scene you want to photograph.

GUIDELINES FOR SELECTING THE f-NUMBER

Lens Opening	Guidelines	Example-- 50 mm f/2 Lens Normal Focal Length
Maximum for lens	Good for obtaining enough exposure in poor lighting conditions, such as existing light. Minimum depth of field--very shallow. Poorest image quality for specific lens	f/2
One stop smaller than maximum lens opening	Good for obtaining enough exposure in poor lighting. Shallow depth of field. Helpful to throw background out of focus to concentrate attention on subject. Good image quality.	f/2.8
Two and three stops smaller than maximum lens opening	Best image quality for specific lens. Better depth of field than with larger lens openings. Good for limited distance range of sharp focus. Good for obtaining proper exposure when lighting conditions are less than optimum, such as on cloudy days or in the shade.	f/4 and f/5
Two stops larger than minimum lens opening	Moderate depth of field. Good all around lens opening to use for outdoor daylight pictures. Excellent image quality.	f/8
One stop larger than minimum lens opening	Great depth of field. Good all around lens opening to use for outdoor daylight conditions. Excellent image quality.	f/11
Minimum for lens	Maximum depth of field. Very slight loss of sharpness due to optical effects. When maximum depth of field is important, the benefits from increased depth of field with this lens opening outweigh the disadvantages from an almost imperceptible loss in sharpness.	f/16

GUIDELINES FOR SELECTING THE SHUTTER SPEED

Shutter Speed	Guidelines
B (Bulb)	Use camera support, such as tripod. Shutter remains open as long as shutter release is depressed. Good for obtaining great depth of field with small lens openings in outdoor night scenes, for photographing fireworks and lightning, and for recording streak patterns from moving lights at night, such as automobile traffic. Long exposures can cause an over color cast with color films.
1 second and 1/2 second	Use camera support, such as a tripod. Good for obtaining great depth of field with small lens openings and enough exposure under dim lighting conditions, such as existing light or photolamps. Good for photographing inanimate objects and stationary subjects. These shutter speeds can cause a very slight color cast with some color films.
1/4 second	Use camera support. Slowest recommended shutter speed for portraits of adults. Good for great depth of field with small lens openings and enough exposures under dim lighting. Good for stationary subjects.
1/8 second	Use camera support. Better shutter speed than 1/4-second for photographing adults at close range. Good for obtaining great depth of field with small lens openings and enough exposure under dim lighting conditions. Good for stationary subjects.
1/15 second	Use camera support. Some people can handhold their camera using this shutter speed with a normal or wide-angle lens on the camera. This is possible if the camera is held very steady during the exposure. Good for obtaining increased depth of field with small lens openings and enough exposure under dim lighting conditions, such as existing light.
1/30 second	Slowest recommended shutter speed for handholding your camera with a normal or wide-angle lens. Camera must be held very steady for sharp pictures. Good all around shutter speed for existing-light photography. Good for obtaining increased depth of field with small lends openings on cloudy days or in the shade. Recommended shutter speed for flashbulbs with most cameras and for electronic flash with rangefinder cameras.
1/60 second	Good shutter speed to use for daylight pictures outdoors when the lighting conditions are less than ideal, such as on cloudy days, in the shade, or for backlighted subjects. Useful shutter speed for increasing depth of field with a smaller lens opening. Also, good shutter speed to use for brighter existing-light scenes. Less chance of camera motion spoiling the picture than with 1/30 second. Recommended shutter speed for electronic flash with many SLR cameras.
1/125 second	Best all around shutter speed to use for outdoor daylight pictures. Produces good depth of field with medium to small lens openings under bright lighting conditions, minimizes the effects from *slight* camera motion, and stops some moderate kinds of action, such as people walking, children playing, or babies not holding still. This is the minimum safe shutter speed for handholding your camera with a short telephoto lens, such as those shorter in focal length than 105 mm. Recommended shutter speed for electronic flash with some SLR cameras.
1/250 second	Good for stopping moderate fast action like runners, swimmers, bicyclists at a medium speed, running horses at a distance, parades, running children, sailboats, or baseball and football players moving at a medium pace. Good all around shutter speed for outdoor daylight pictures when you don't require great depth of field and you want to stop some action. Helps minimize the effects of camera motion. Good shutter speed to use for handholding your camera with a telephoto lens up to 250 mm in focal length.
1/500 second	Good for stopping fast action like fast moving runners, running horses at a medium distance, divers, fast moving bicyclists, moving cars in traffic, or basketball players. A good shutter speed to use for stopping all but the fastest kinds of action. Gives better depth of field with the appropriate lens opening than 1/1000 second. Excellent shutter speed to use with telephoto lenses. Good for lenses up to 400 mm in focal length with a handheld camera.
1/1000 second	Best shutter speed for stopping fast action like race cars, motorcycles, airplanes, speedboats, field and track events, tennis players, skiers and golfers, for example. This shutter speed gives the least depth of field because it requires a larger lens opening than the other shutter speeds. Excellent shutter speed to use with long telephoto lenses up to 400 mm in focal length with a handheld camera.

BIBLIOGRAPHY

Abrams, Bernard S. Personal communication: technical report on reaction time and visibility, November 1, 1993.

Asimov, Isaac. *Understanding Physics: Motion, Sound and Heat*. Allen & Unwin, London, U.K., 1967.

Baker, J. Stannard and Fricke, Lynn B. *The Traffic Accident Investigation Manual* (9th ed.). Traffic Institute, Northwestern University, Evanston, Illinois, 1986.

Baxter, Albert T. *Motorcycle Accident Investigation*. Institute of Police Technology and Management, University of North Florida, Jacksonville, Florida, 1993.

Brown, John Fiske and Obenski, Kenneth S. *Forensic Engineering Reconstruction of Accidents*. Charles C. Thomas, Publisher, Springfield, Illinois, 1990.

Craig, Victor, ed. *Accident Investigation Quarterly*. Published by the Accident Reconstruction Journal, Waldorf, Maryland, 1994 - 1995 issues.

Craig, Victor, ed. *Accident Reconstruction Journal*. Published by the Accident Reconstruction Journal, Waldorf, Maryland, 1989 - 1995 issues.

Daily, John. *Fundamentals of Traffic Accident Reconstruction*. Institute of Police Technology and Management, University of North Florida, Jacksonville, Florida, 1988.

Fogiel, M., ed. *The Physics Problem Solver*. Research and Education Association, New York, N.Y., 1983.

Freeman, Ira M. *Physics Made Simple*. Doubleday, New York, N.Y., 1990.

Fricke, Lynn B. *Traffic Accident Reconstruction* (Vol.2). Traffic Institute, Northwestern University, Evanston, Illinois, 1990.

Grogan, R.J. *An Investigator's Guide to Tire Failures*. Institute of Police Technology and Management, University of North Florida, Jacksonville, Florida, 1986.

Holburger, Wolfgang S. and Kell, James H. *Fundamentals of Traffic Engineering* (11th ed.). Institute of Transportation Studies, University of California, Berkeley, California, 1984.

Howell, Wiley L. *Derivations Manual for Formulas Used in Traffic Accident Investigation and Reconstruction*. Institute of Police Technology and Management, University of North Florida, Jacksonville, Florida, 1994.

James, L., ed. *Traffic Engineering Handbook* (4th ed.). Institute of Transportation Engineers, Prentice-Hall, Inc., Englewood Cliffs, New Jersey, 1992.

Kennedy, Walter A. *Impact Velocity from Conservation of Linear Momentum for the Traffic Accident Investigator and Reconstructionist*. Institute of Police Technology and Management, University of North Florida, Jacksonville, Florida, 1993.

Limpert, Rudolph. *Motor Vehicle Accident Reconstruction and Cause Analysis* (4th ed.). The Mitchie Company, Charlottesville, Virginia, 1994.

Lofgren, M.J. *Handbook for the Reconstructionist* (3rd ed.). Institute of Police Technology and Management, University of North Florida, Jacksonville, Florida, 1983.

Martindale, David G., Heath, Robert W. and Eastman, Philip C. *Fundamentals of Physics; A Senior Course*. D. C. Heath Canada Limited, Toronto, Ontario, 1986.

Navin, Francis, P.D. *The Coefficient of Friction Definition and Models*. Paper prepared by CATAIR/TAARS/WAIT/SOAR Joint Meeting and published by the Canadian Association of Traffic Accident Investigators and Reconstructionists, Kelowna, B.C., Canada, 1992.

Navin, Francis P.D. *Truck Braking Distance and Speed Estimates*. Canadian Journal of Civil Engineering, Ottawa, Ontario, 1986.

Navin, Francis P.D. *Hydroplaning*. Personal communication (technical report), Department of Civil Engineering, University of British Columbia, Vancouver, Canada, 1983.

Navin, Francis P.D. *Estimating Truck's Critical Cornering Speed and Factor of Safety.* Department of Civil Engineering, University of British Columbia, Vancouver, Canada, 1990.

Rivers, R.W. *Speed Analysis for Traffic Accident Investigation.* Institute of Police Technology and Management, University of North Florida, Jacksonville, Florida, 1995.

Rivers, R.W. *Traffic Accident Investigation Manual* (A Levels 1 and 2 Reference, Training and Investigation Manual). Charles C. Thomas, Publisher, Springfield, Illinois, 1995.

Rivers, R.W. *Technical Traffic Accident Investigation Manual* (A Level 3 Reference, Training and Investigation Manual). Charles C. Thomas, Publisher, Springfield, Illinois, 1995.

Rivers, R.W. *Traffic Accident Field Measurements and Scale Diagrams Manual.* Charles C. Thomas, Publisher, Springfield, Illinois, 1983.

Rivers, R.W. *Traffic Accident Investigators' Book of Formulae and Tables.* Charles C. Thomas, Publisher, Springfield, Illinois, 1981.

Ruller, R.J. Personal communication: accident reconstruction technical papers. Queensland Police Service, Queensland, Australia, 1994.

Society of Automotive Engineers. Technical Papers, Warrendale, Pennsylvania, 1990 - 1995.

Williams, Dudley and Spangler, John. *Physics for Science and Engineering.* D. Van Nostrand Company, New York, N.Y., 1981.

INDEX

552

THE DEFINITIVE SERIES OF BOOKS
FOR TRAFFIC ACCIDENT INVESTIGATORS
by R. W. Rivers

Inspector Rivers, Royal Canadian Mounted Police, retired in 1985 as Officer-in-Charge of the Traffic Branch in the Province of British Columbia. During his service, he was employed extensively in general police work, highway patrol, accident investigation, planning and research, and training and development. He developed the RCMP's Traffic Accident Investigation and Traffic Law Enforcement programs and is the author of several internationally acclaimed textbooks, including those listed below.

☐ **TRAFFIC ACCIDENT INVESTIGATORS' BOOK OF FORMULAE AND TABLES**

After an introductory discussion of basic definitions and procedures, this book offers formulae relating to acceleration, center of mass, curves and circles, coefficient of friction, distance, speed, field measurements, and momentum. Each formula is illustrated with examples of accidents that are worked out in detail to clarify the equations and their applications. Appendices provide U.S. and metric conversions, mathematical tables, velocity tables, and a speedometer accuracy checklist. Throughout the book, formulae and tables are independently presented in both United States and metric systems of measurement.
'81, 160 pp., 23 il., 31 tables, $38.95, spiral (paper)

☐ **TRAFFIC ACCIDENT FIELD MEASUREMENTS AND SCALE DIAGRAMS MANUAL**

Detailed and authoritative, this manual shows the reader how to measure the scene of an accident in an orderly, professional manner and how later to prepare diagrams and maps. The author explains analysis of events preceding collision, methods of measurement, and equipment. He conveys an understanding of triangulation, coordinate and grid measurements, angles, curves and circles, and horizontal and vertical measurements. The text is amplified by numerous definitions, illustrations, examples, typically encountered situations and problems, and mathematical tables.
'83, 154 pp., 97 il., 4 tables, $31.95, spiral (paper)

☐ **TECHNICAL TRAFFIC ACCIDENT INVESTIGATORS' HANDBOOK**
(A Level 3 Reference, Training and Investigation Manual)

If the accident investigator could have only one manual, this should be it, covering as it does the range of essential areas in a clear and thorough manner. Inspector Rivers introduces the fundamentals of traffic accident investigation, from establishing the series of events to investigative procedures. The individual chapters that follow focus on vehicle behavior, vehicle placement on the roadway, speed estimates (including momentum), failure to remain at the scene of an accident, photography, and field measurements and scale diagrams. Abundant illustrations, drawings, diagrams and photographs found throughout the book help the reader visualize the circumstances under discussion and thus better understand the principles, procedures and techniques of traffic accident investigation.
Replaces Traffic Accident Investigators' Handbook.
'97, 504 pp., 250 il, 8 tables
$86.95 (cloth), $66.95 (paper)

☐ **TRAFFIC ACCIDENT INVESTIGATORS'** *NEW!* **MANUAL**
(A Levels 1 and 2 Reference, Training and Investigation Manual)

This new 1995 edition has been thoroughly updated and revised to meet the needs of all individuals involved in traffic accident investigation, especially police officers, insurance adjusters and investigators, private investigators, attorneys, judges, and instructors and students in at-scene or advanced traffic investigation programs. Chapters are titled as follows: Introduction to Traffic Accident Investigation, Series of Events, Investigation Procedures, the Human Element, Questioning Drivers and Witnesses, Environmental Factors, Highway and Vehicles Marks and Damages, Vehicle Mechanical Inspection, Photography, Failure to Remain at Scene of Accident, Field Sketches and Diagrams, and Speed Estimates.

Former edition published under the title On-Scene Traffic Accident Investigators' Manual.
'96, 240 pp., 135 il., 7 tables
$59.95 (cloth), $34.95 (paper)

NOTE: In each book *both* the U.S. and the metric systems of measurement are used.
Please check the box next to each book that you want to order, legibly fill in the form and mail entire sheet to address below. Visa/MasterCard holders may call orders to (800) 258-8980. A minimum of $5.50 is charged for shipping/handling. Please include when sending remittance with order. Illinois residents add 7¼% sales tax. FOREIGN: Unless you have an open account with us, please include U.S. currency with order and a minimum of $6.50 for the cost of Surface Mail shipping/handling. Air Mail charges are extra. Please include when ordering.

☐ Bill me   ☐ MasterCard   ☐ Visa   ☐ FAX (217) 789-9130

☐ Payment enclosed   Card No._____   Exp. date_____

Name_____   Confirming signature_____

Address_____   City_____   State_____

Zip_____

CHARLES C THOMAS • PUBLISHER
2600 South First Street • Springfield • IL • 62794-9265